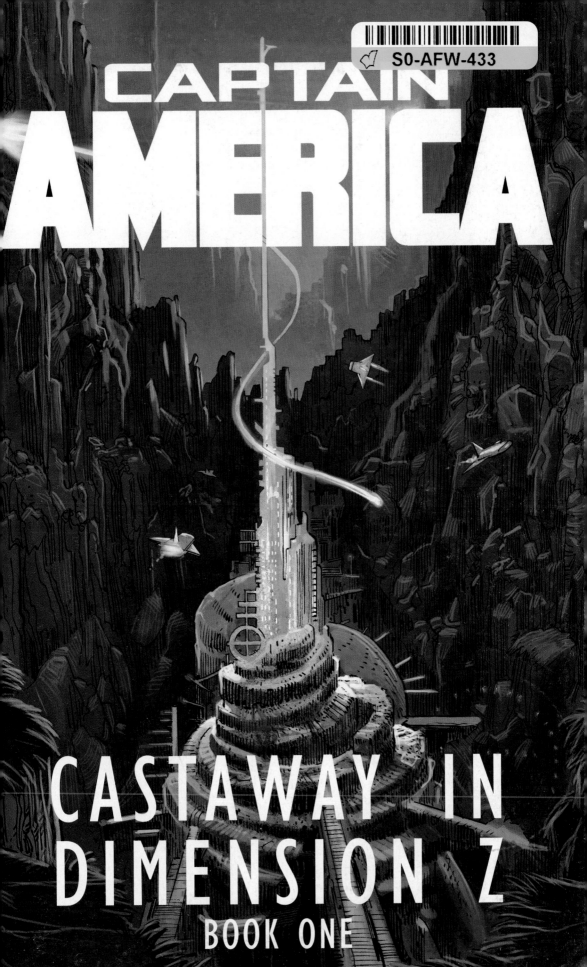

CAPTAIN AMERICA

CASTAWAY IN DIMENSION Z

BOOK ONE

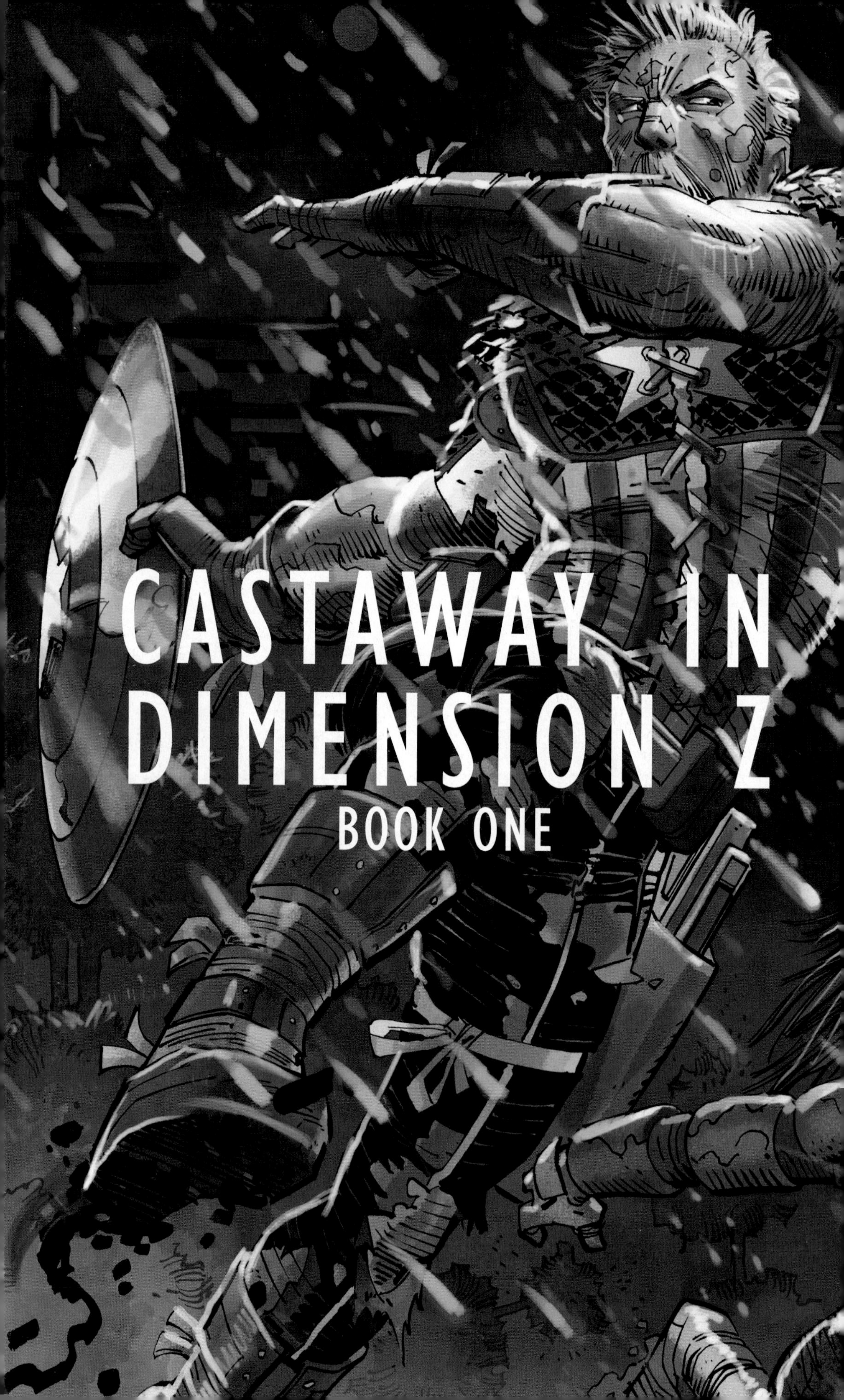
CASTAWAY IN
DIMENSION Z
BOOK ONE

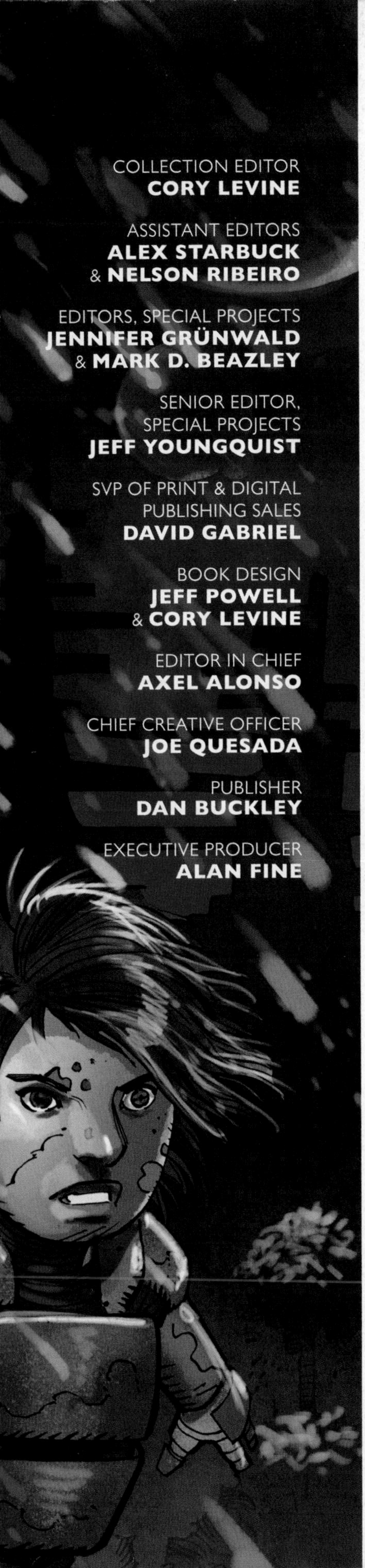

COLLECTION EDITOR
CORY LEVINE

ASSISTANT EDITORS
ALEX STARBUCK
& **NELSON RIBEIRO**

EDITORS, SPECIAL PROJECTS
JENNIFER GRÜNWALD
& **MARK D. BEAZLEY**

SENIOR EDITOR,
SPECIAL PROJECTS
JEFF YOUNGQUIST

SVP OF PRINT & DIGITAL
PUBLISHING SALES
DAVID GABRIEL

BOOK DESIGN
JEFF POWELL
& **CORY LEVINE**

EDITOR IN CHIEF
AXEL ALONSO

CHIEF CREATIVE OFFICER
JOE QUESADA

PUBLISHER
DAN BUCKLEY

EXECUTIVE PRODUCER
ALAN FINE

WRITER
RICK REMENDER

PENCILER
JOHN ROMITA JR.

INKERS
KLAUS JANSON (#1-4),
TOM PALMER (#5)
& **SCOTT HANNA** (#5)

COLORISTS
DEAN WHITE (#1-5)
& **LEE LOUGHRIDGE** (#2-5)
WITH **DAN BROWN** (#2)

LETTERER
VC'S JOE CARAMAGNA

COVER ARTISTS
JOHN ROMITA JR., KLAUS JANSON,
DEAN WHITE & **MORRY HOLLOWELL**

ASSISTANT EDITOR
JAKE THOMAS

EDITORS
TOM BREVOORT
WITH **LAUREN SANKOVITCH**

CAPTAIN AMERICA CREATED BY
JOE SIMON & **JACK KIRBY**

CAPTAIN AMERICA VOL. 1: CASTAWAY IN DIMENSION Z BOOK 1. Contains material originally published in magazine form as CAPTAIN AMERICA #1-5. First printing 2014. ISBN# 978-0-7851-6655-9. Published by MARVEL WORLDWIDE, INC., a subsidiary of MARVEL ENTERTAINMENT, LLC. OFFICE OF PUBLICATION: 135 West 50th Street, New York, NY 10020. **Printed in the U.S.A.** ALAN FINE, EVP - Office of the President, Marvel Worldwide, Inc. and EVP & CMO Marvel Characters B.V.; DAN BUCKLEY, Publisher & President - Print, Animation & Digital Divisions; JOE QUESADA, Chief Creative Officer; TOM BREVOORT, SVP of Publishing; DAVID BOGART, SVP of Operations & Procurement, Publishing; C.B. CEBULSKI, SVP of Creator & Content Development; DAVID GABRIEL, SVP of Print & Digital Publishing Sales; JIM O'KEEFE, VP of Operations & Logistics; DAN CARR, Executive Director of Publishing Technology; SUSAN CRESPI, Editorial Operations Manager; ALEX MORALES, Publishing Operations Manager; STAN LEE, Chairman Emeritus. For information regarding advertising in Marvel Comics or on Marvel.com, please contact Niza Disla, Director of Marvel Partnerships, at ndisla@marvel.com. For Marvel subscription inquiries, please call 800-217-9158. **Manufactured between 12/20/2013 and 1/27/2014 by R.R. DONNELLEY, INC., SALEM, VA, USA.**

10 9 8 7 6 5 4 3 2 1

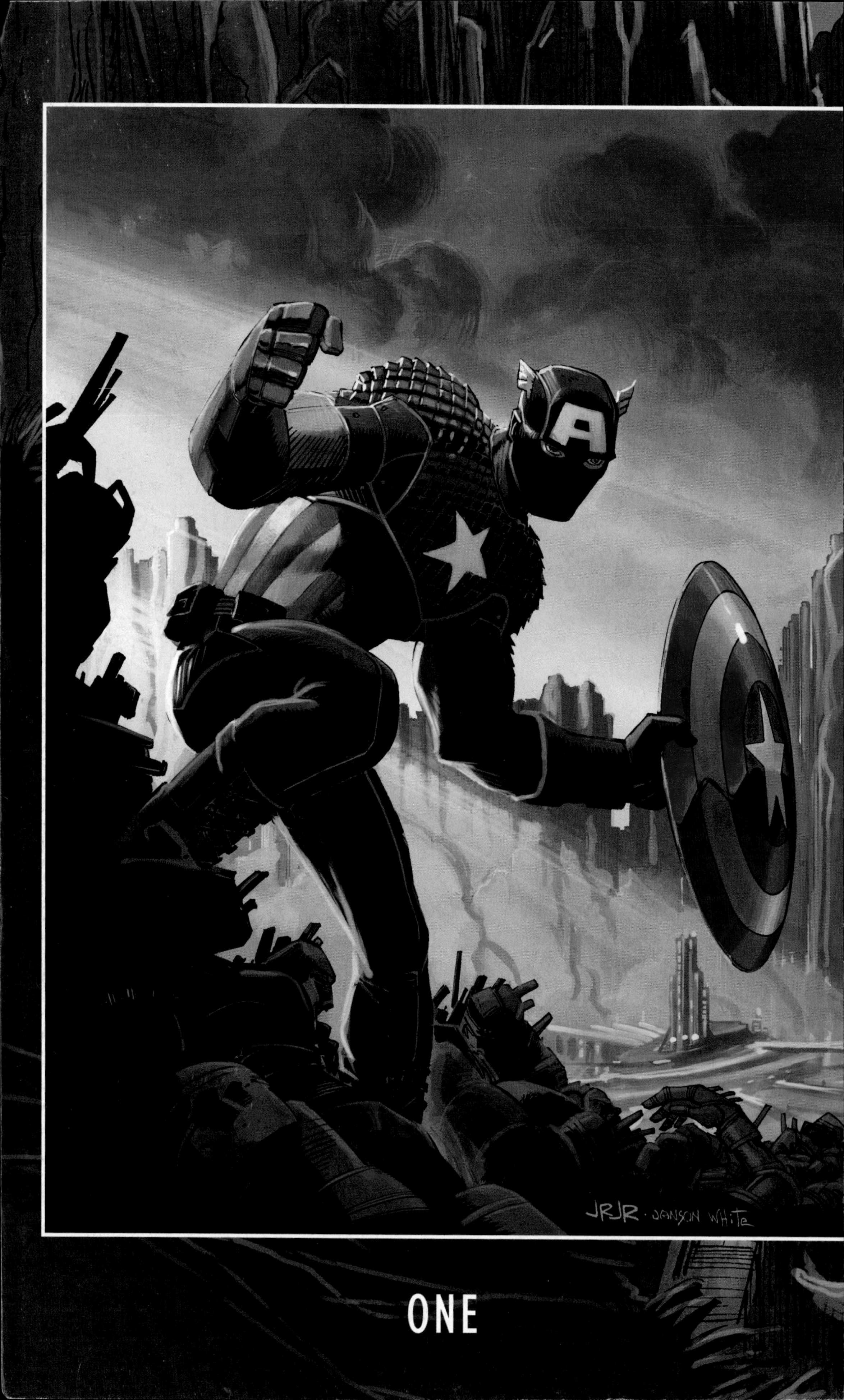
JRJR · JANSON WHITE

ONE

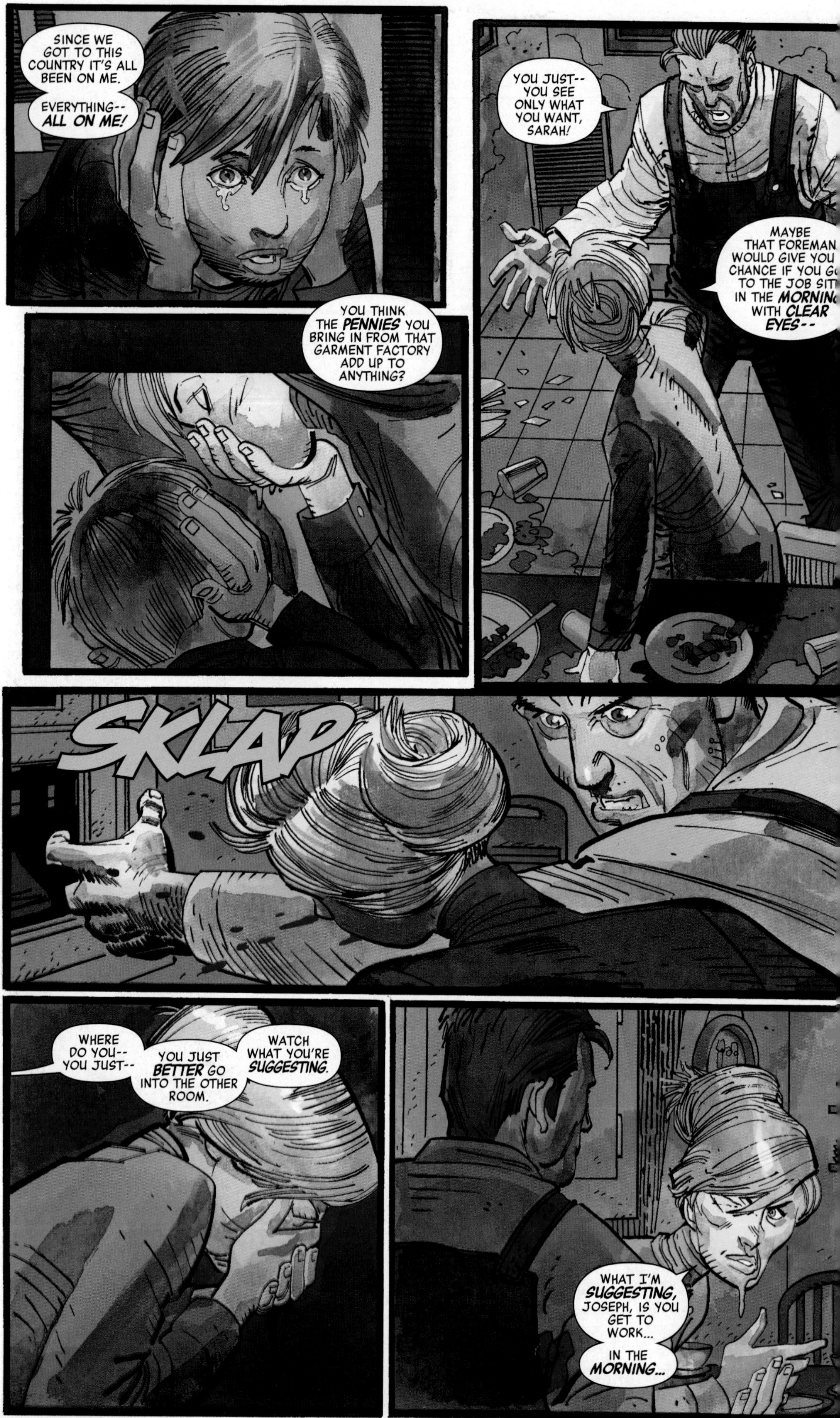
SINCE WE GOT TO THIS COUNTRY IT'S ALL BEEN ON ME.
EVERYTHING-- ALL ON ME!
YOU JUST-- YOU SEE ONLY WHAT YOU WANT, SARAH!
YOU THINK THE PENNIES YOU BRING IN FROM THAT GARMENT FACTORY ADD UP TO ANYTHING?
MAYBE THAT FOREMAN WOULD GIVE YOU CHANCE IF YOU G TO THE JOB SIT IN THE MORNIN WITH CLEAR EYES--
SKLAP
WHERE DO YOU-- YOU JUST--
YOU JUST BETTER GO INTO THE OTHER ROOM.
WATCH WHAT YOU'RE SUGGESTING.
WHAT I'M SUGGESTING, JOSEPH, IS YOU GET TO WORK...
IN THE MORNING...

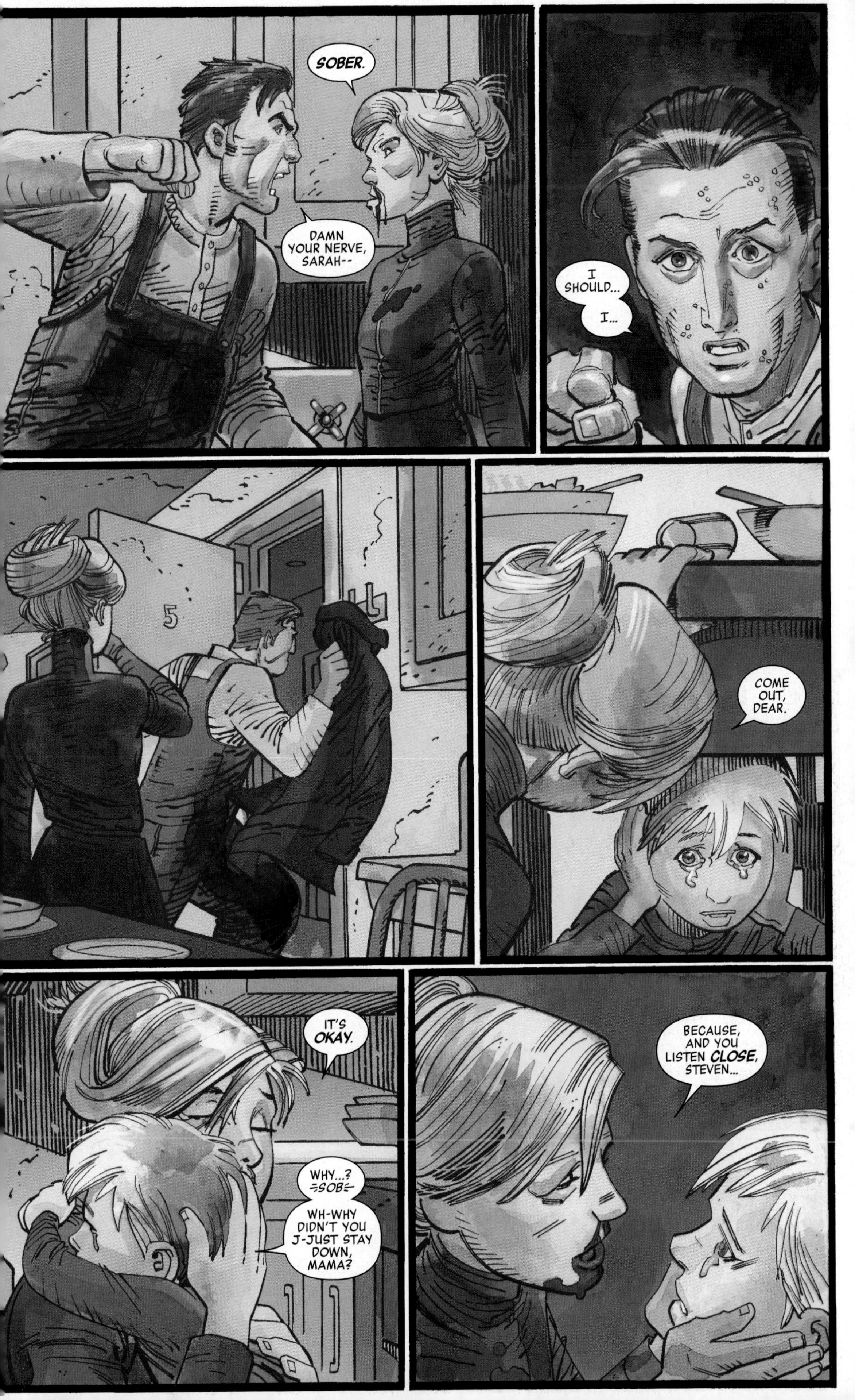
SOBER.
DAMN YOUR NERVE, SARAH--
I SHOULD...
I...
COME OUT, DEAR.
IT'S *OKAY*.
WHY...?
=SOB=
WH-WHY DIDN'T YOU J-JUST STAY DOWN, MAMA?
BECAUSE, AND YOU LISTEN *CLOSE*, STEVEN...

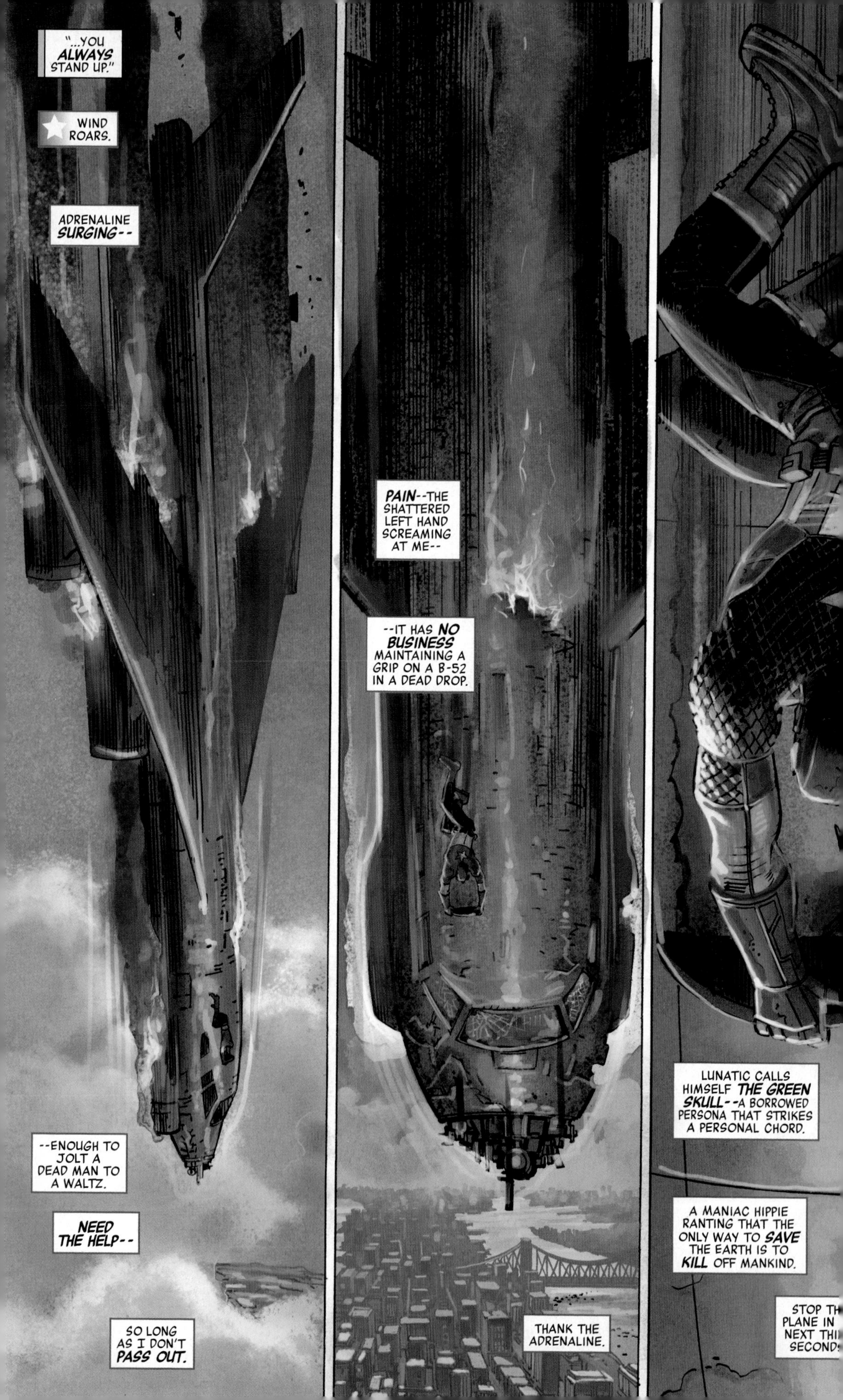
"...YOU ALWAYS STAND UP."
WIND ROARS.
ADRENALINE SURGING--
--ENOUGH TO JOLT A DEAD MAN TO A WALTZ.
NEED THE HELP--
SO LONG AS I DON'T PASS OUT.
PAIN--THE SHATTERED LEFT HAND SCREAMING AT ME--
--IT HAS NO BUSINESS MAINTAINING A GRIP ON A B-52 IN A DEAD DROP.
THANK THE ADRENALINE.
LUNATIC CALLS HIMSELF THE GREEN SKULL--A BORROWED PERSONA THAT STRIKES A PERSONAL CHORD.
A MANIAC HIPPIE RANTING THAT THE ONLY WAY TO SAVE THE EARTH IS TO KILL OFF MANKIND.
STOP TH PLANE IN NEXT THI SECOND

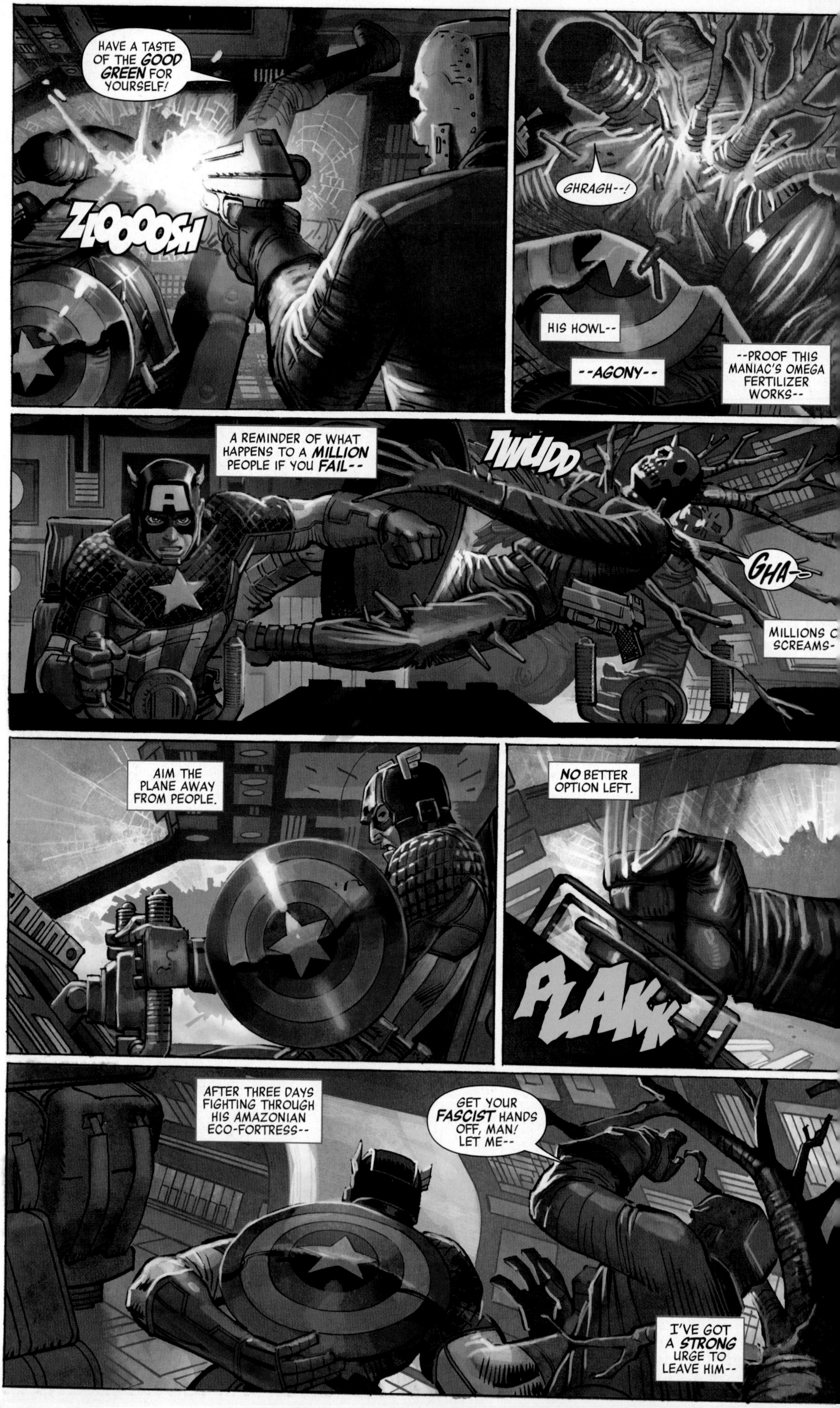

HAVE A TASTE OF THE GOOD GREEN FOR YOURSELF!
ZLOOOOSH
GHRAGH--!
HIS HOWL--
--AGONY--
--PROOF THIS MANIAC'S OMEGA FERTILIZER WORKS--
A REMINDER OF WHAT HAPPENS TO A MILLION PEOPLE IF YOU FAIL--
TWUDD
GHA-
MILLIONS O
SCREAMS-
AIM THE PLANE AWAY FROM PEOPLE.
NO BETTER OPTION LEFT.
PLAKK
AFTER THREE DAYS FIGHTING THROUGH HIS AMAZONIAN ECO-FORTRESS--
GET YOUR FASCIST HANDS OFF, MAN! LET ME--
I'VE GOT A STRONG URGE TO LEAVE HIM--

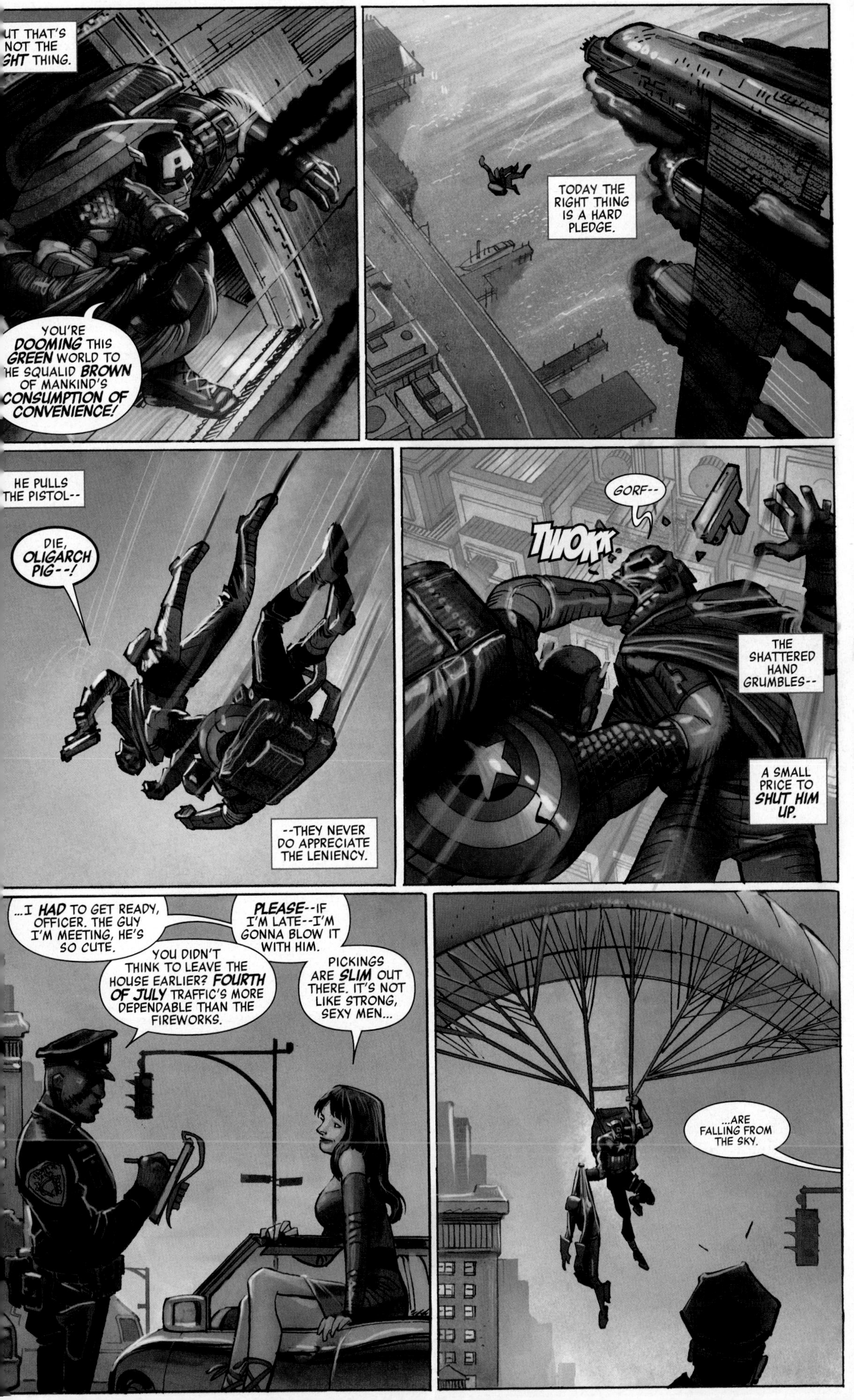
UT THAT'S NOT THE GHT THING.
YOU'RE DOOMING THIS GREEN WORLD TO HE SQUALID BROWN OF MANKIND'S CONSUMPTION OF CONVENIENCE!
TODAY THE RIGHT THING IS A HARD PLEDGE.
HE PULLS THE PISTOL--
DIE, OLIGARCH PIG--!
--THEY NEVER DO APPRECIATE THE LENIENCY.
GORF--
TWOKK
THE SHATTERED HAND GRUMBLES--
A SMALL PRICE TO SHUT HIM UP.
...I HAD TO GET READY, OFFICER. THE GUY I'M MEETING, HE'S SO CUTE.
PLEASE--IF I'M LATE--I'M GONNA BLOW IT WITH HIM.
YOU DIDN'T THINK TO LEAVE THE HOUSE EARLIER? FOURTH OF JULY TRAFFIC'S MORE DEPENDABLE THAN THE FIREWORKS.
PICKINGS ARE SLIM OUT THERE. IT'S NOT LIKE STRONG, SEXY MEN...
...ARE FALLING FROM THE SKY.

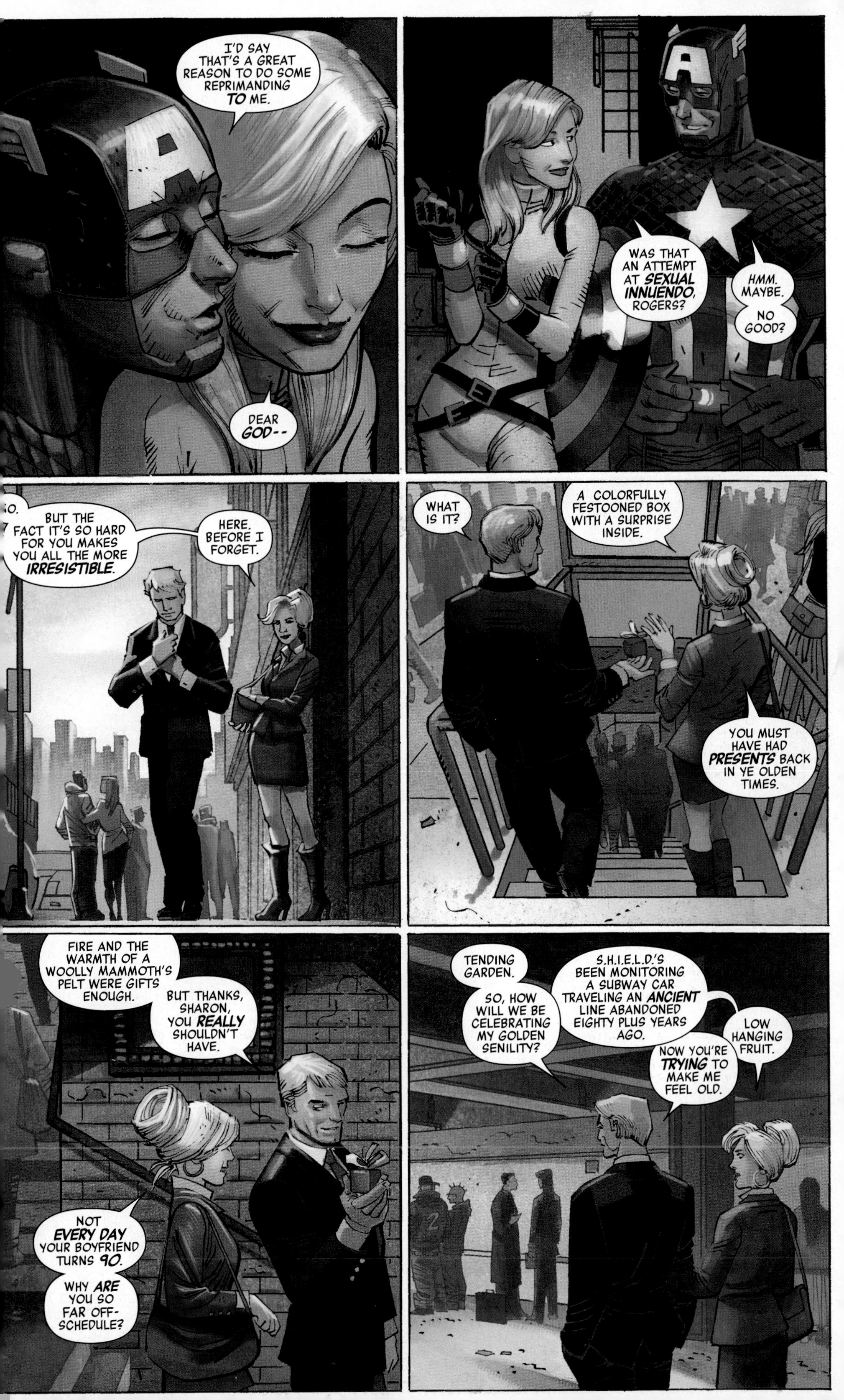
I'D SAY THAT'S A GREAT REASON TO DO SOME REPRIMANDING **TO** ME.
DEAR **GOD--**
WAS THAT AN ATTEMPT AT **SEXUAL INNUENDO**, ROGERS?
HMM. MAYBE.
NO GOOD?
BUT THE FACT IT'S SO HARD FOR YOU MAKES YOU ALL THE MORE **IRRESISTIBLE**.
HERE. BEFORE I FORGET.
WHAT IS IT?
A COLORFULLY FESTOONED BOX WITH A SURPRISE INSIDE.
YOU MUST HAVE HAD **PRESENTS** BACK IN YE OLDEN TIMES.
FIRE AND THE WARMTH OF A WOOLLY MAMMOTH'S PELT WERE GIFTS ENOUGH.
BUT THANKS, SHARON, YOU **REALLY** SHOULDN'T HAVE.
NOT **EVERY DAY** YOUR BOYFRIEND TURNS **90**.
WHY **ARE** YOU SO FAR OFF-SCHEDULE?
TENDING GARDEN.
SO, HOW WILL WE BE CELEBRATING MY GOLDEN SENILITY?
S.H.I.E.L.D.'S BEEN MONITORING A SUBWAY CAR TRAVELING AN **ANCIENT** LINE ABANDONED EIGHTY PLUS YEARS AGO.
LOW HANGING FRUIT.
NOW YOU'RE **TRYING** TO MAKE ME FEEL OLD.

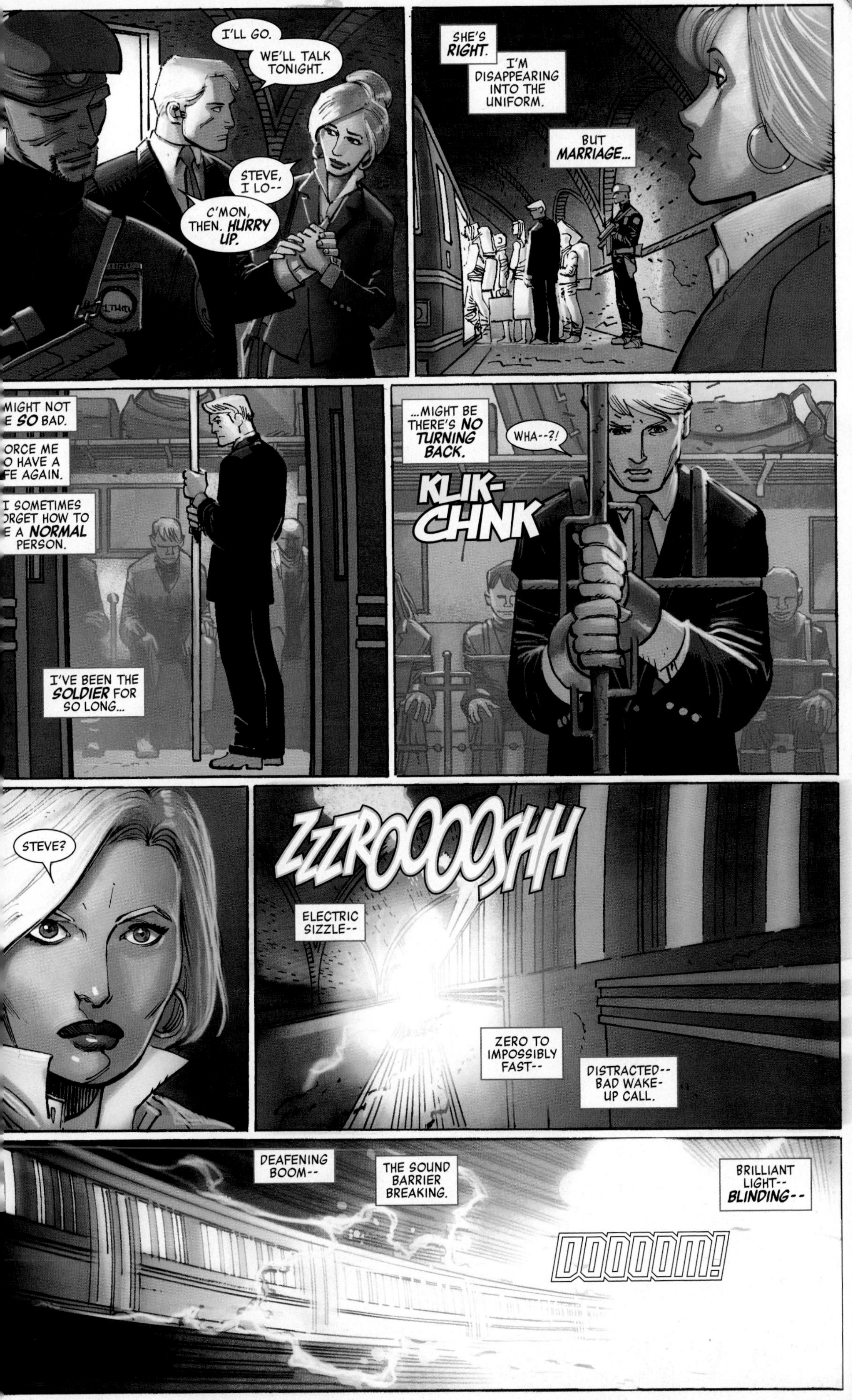

I'LL GO.
WE'LL TALK TONIGHT.
STEVE, I LO--
C'MON, THEN. HURRY UP.
SHE'S RIGHT.
I'M DISAPPEARING INTO THE UNIFORM.
BUT MARRIAGE...
MIGHT NOT E SO BAD.
ORCE ME O HAVE A FE AGAIN.
I SOMETIMES ORGET HOW TO E A NORMAL PERSON.
I'VE BEEN THE SOLDIER FOR SO LONG...
...MIGHT BE THERE'S NO TURNING BACK.
WHA--?!
KLIK-CHNK
STEVE?
ZZZROOOOOSHH
ELECTRIC SIZZLE--
ZERO TO IMPOSSIBLY FAST--
DISTRACTED-- BAD WAKE-UP CALL.
DEAFENING BOOM--
THE SOUND BARRIER BREAKING.
BRILLIANT LIGHT-- BLINDING--
DOOOOOM!

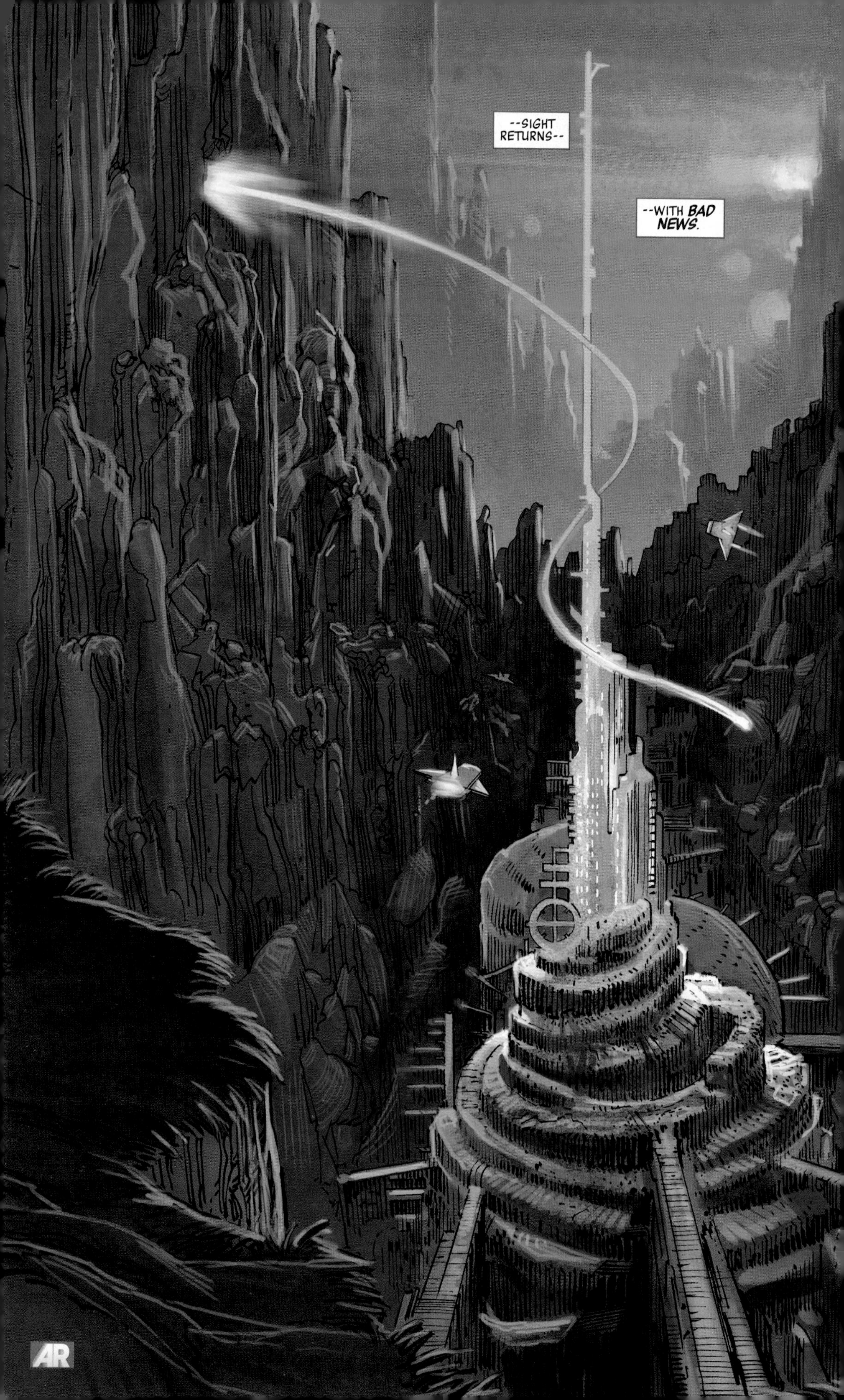
--SIGHT RETURNS--
--WITH BAD NEWS.

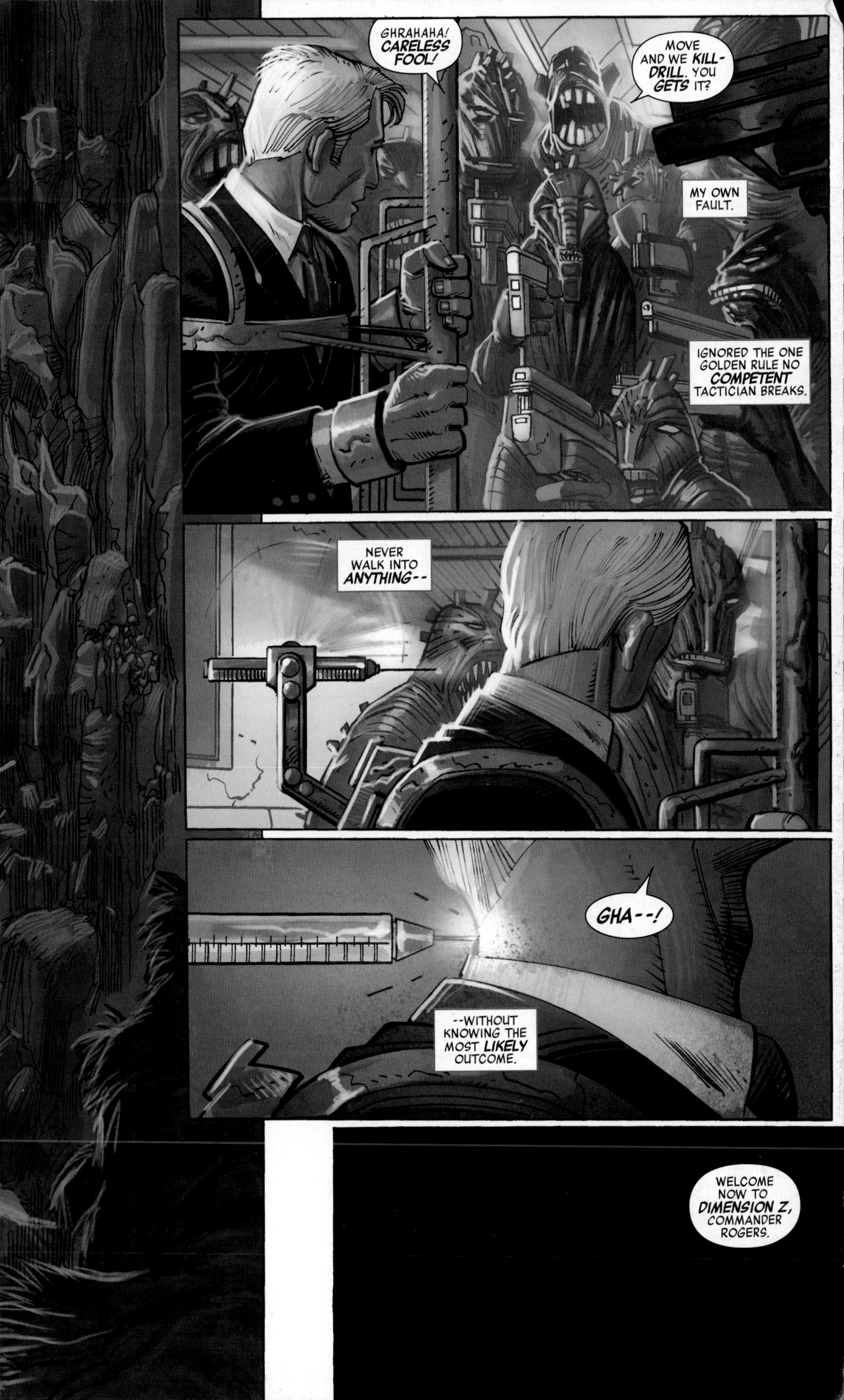
GHRAHAHA! CARELESS FOOL!
MOVE AND WE KILL-DRILL. YOU GETS IT?
MY OWN FAULT.
IGNORED THE ONE GOLDEN RULE NO COMPETENT TACTICIAN BREAKS.
NEVER WALK INTO ANYTHING--
GHA--!
--WITHOUT KNOWING THE MOST LIKELY OUTCOME.
WELCOME NOW TO DIMENSION Z, COMMANDER ROGERS.

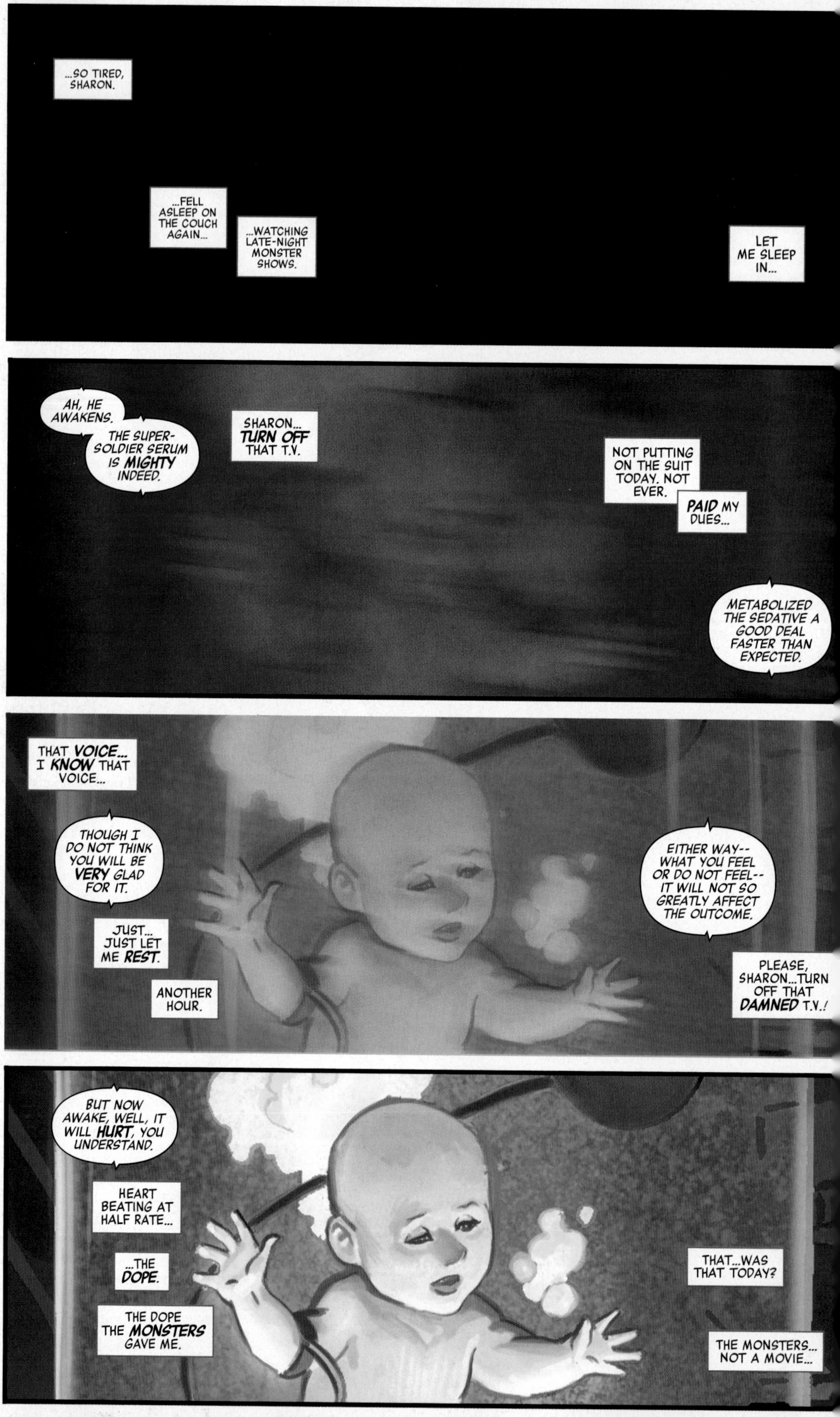

...SO TIRED, SHARON.
...FELL ASLEEP ON THE COUCH AGAIN...
...WATCHING LATE-NIGHT MONSTER SHOWS.
LET ME SLEEP IN...
AH, HE AWAKENS.
THE SUPER-SOLDIER SERUM IS MIGHTY INDEED.
SHARON... TURN OFF THAT T.V.
NOT PUTTING ON THE SUIT TODAY. NOT EVER.
PAID MY DUES...
METABOLIZED THE SEDATIVE A GOOD DEAL FASTER THAN EXPECTED.
THAT VOICE... I KNOW THAT VOICE...
THOUGH I DO NOT THINK YOU WILL BE VERY GLAD FOR IT.
JUST... JUST LET ME REST.
ANOTHER HOUR.
EITHER WAY-- WHAT YOU FEEL OR DO NOT FEEL-- IT WILL NOT SO GREATLY AFFECT THE OUTCOME.
PLEASE, SHARON...TURN OFF THAT DAMNED T.V.!
BUT NOW AWAKE, WELL, IT WILL HURT, YOU UNDERSTAND.
HEART BEATING AT HALF RATE...
...THE DOPE.
THE DOPE THE MONSTERS GAVE ME.
THAT...WAS THAT TODAY?
THE MONSTERS... NOT A MOVIE...

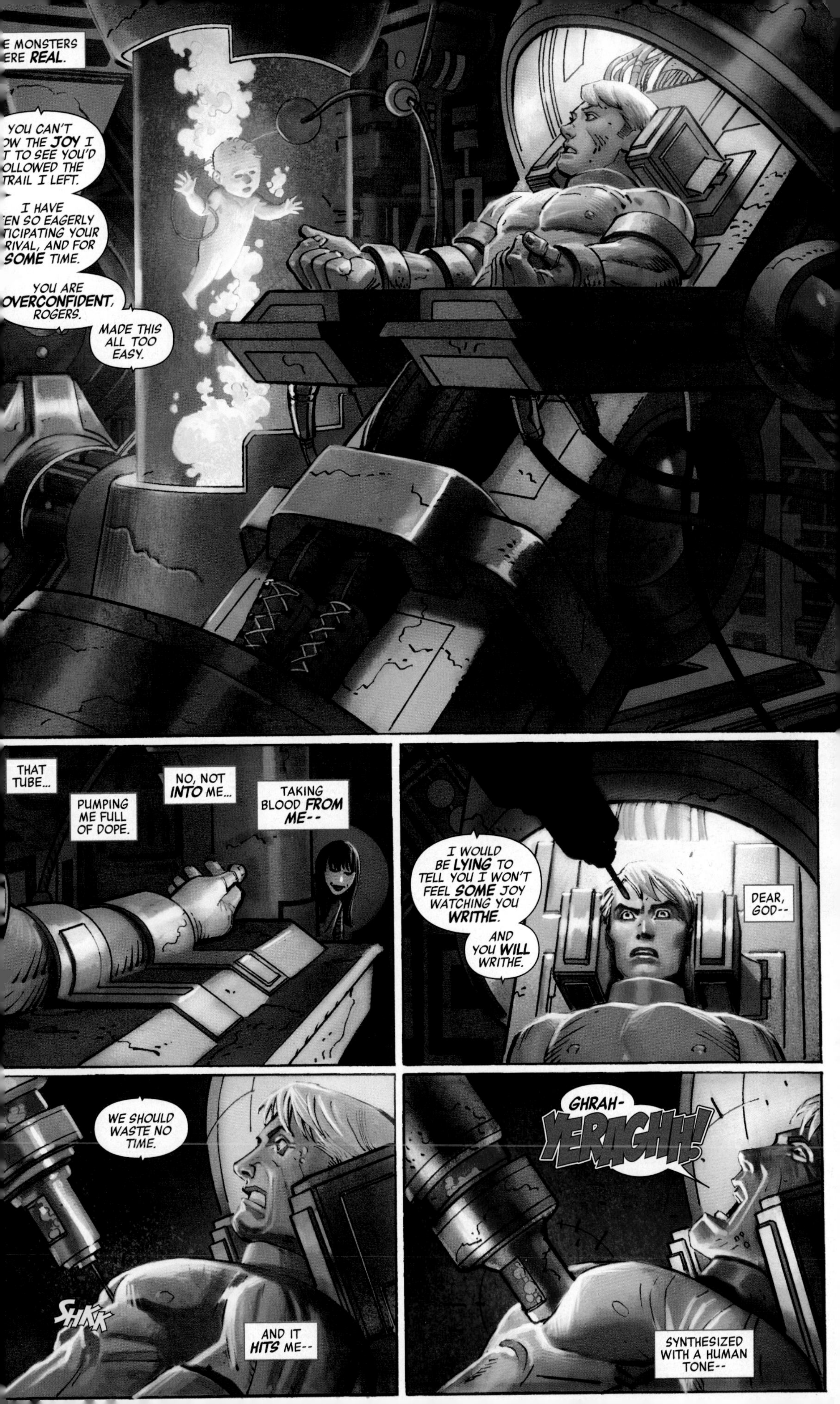

E MONSTERS ERE REAL.
YOU CAN'T OW THE JOY I T TO SEE YOU'D OLLOWED THE TRAIL I LEFT.
I HAVE EN SO EAGERLY TICIPATING YOUR RIVAL, AND FOR SOME TIME.
YOU ARE OVERCONFIDENT, ROGERS.
MADE THIS ALL TOO EASY.
THAT TUBE...
PUMPING ME FULL OF DOPE.
NO, NOT INTO ME...
TAKING BLOOD FROM ME--
I WOULD BE LYING TO TELL YOU I WON'T FEEL SOME JOY WATCHING YOU WRITHE.
AND YOU WILL WRITHE.
DEAR, GOD--
WE SHOULD WASTE NO TIME.
SHKK
AND IT HITS ME--
GHRAH-
YERAGHH!
SYNTHESIZED WITH A HUMAN TONE--

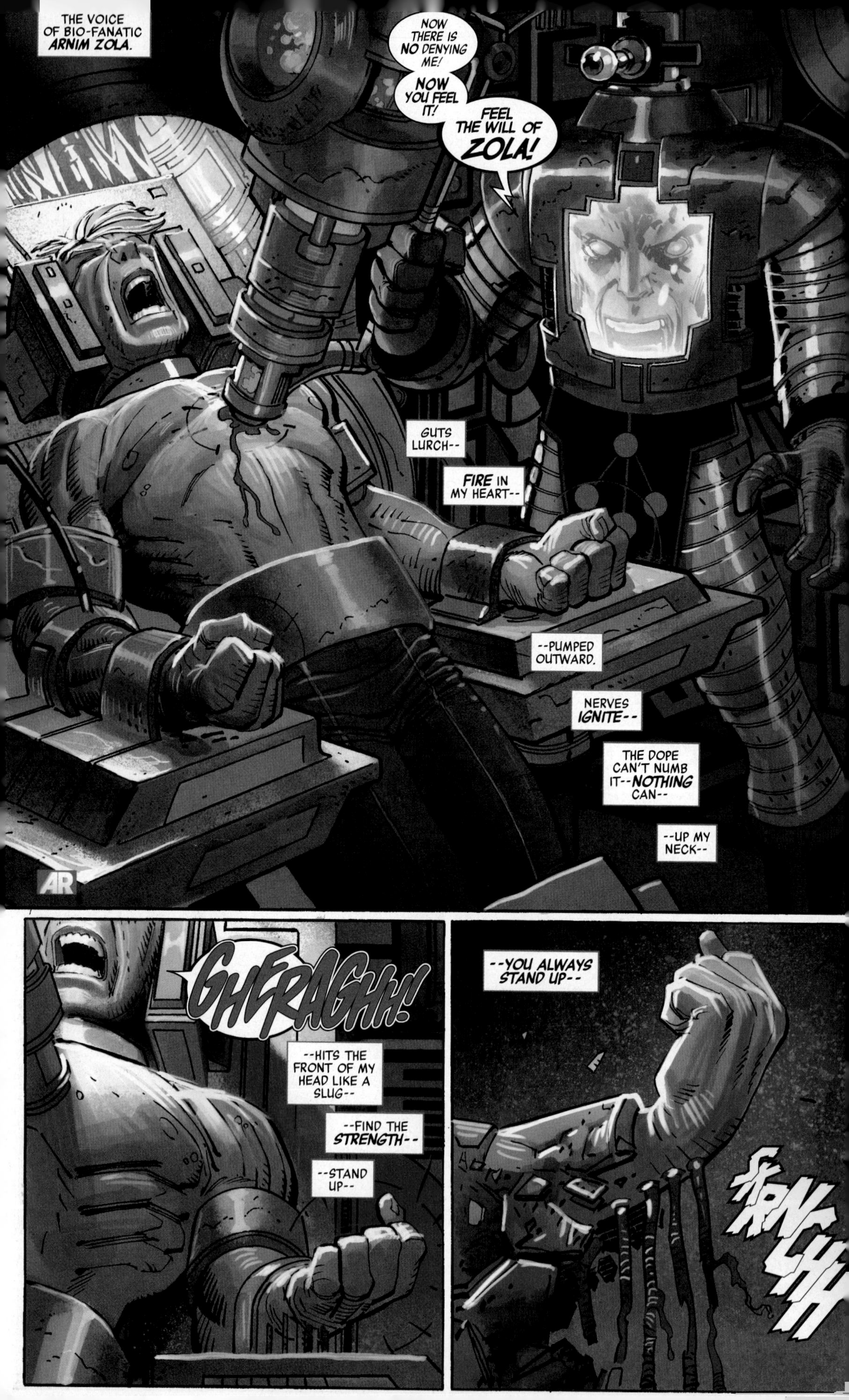
THE VOICE OF BIO-FANATIC ARNIM ZOLA.
NOW THERE IS NO DENYING ME!
NOW YOU FEEL IT!
FEEL THE WILL OF ZOLA!
GUTS LURCH--
FIRE IN MY HEART--
--PUMPED OUTWARD.
NERVES IGNITE--
THE DOPE CAN'T NUMB IT--NOTHING CAN--
--UP MY NECK--
GHERAGHH!
--HITS THE FRONT OF MY HEAD LIKE A SLUG--
--FIND THE STRENGTH--
--STAND UP--
--YOU ALWAYS STAND UP--
SKRNCHH

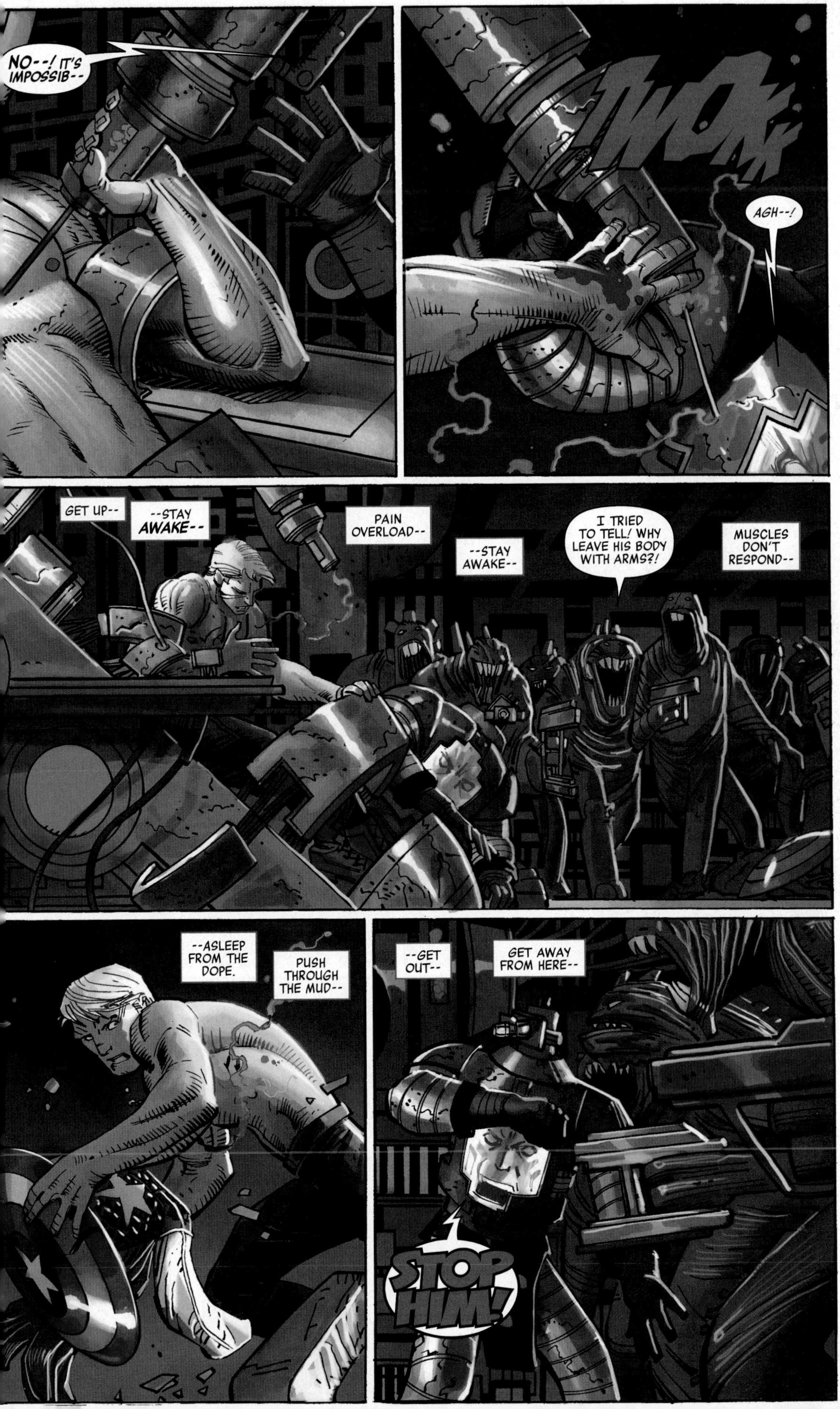
NO--! IT'S IMPOSSIB--
THWOK
AGH--!
GET UP--
--STAY AWAKE--
PAIN OVERLOAD--
--STAY AWAKE--
I TRIED TO TELL! WHY LEAVE HIS BODY WITH ARMS?!
MUSCLES DON'T RESPOND--
--ASLEEP FROM THE DOPE.
PUSH THROUGH THE MUD--
--GET OUT--
GET AWAY FROM HERE--
STOP HIM!

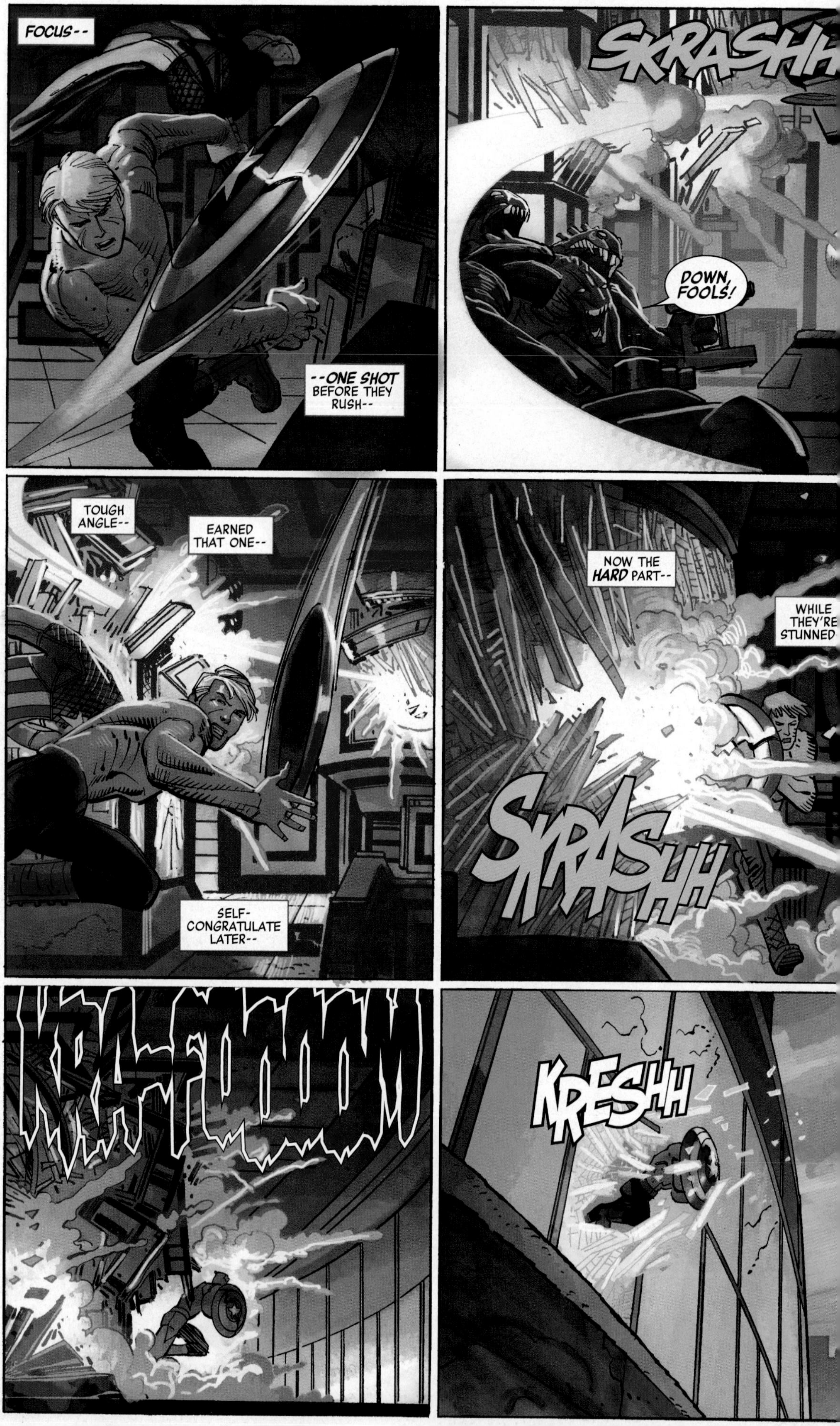

FOCUS--
--ONE SHOT BEFORE THEY RUSH--
SKRASHH
DOWN, FOOLS!
TOUGH ANGLE--
EARNED THAT ONE--
SELF-CONGRATULATE LATER--
NOW THE HARD PART--
WHILE THEY'RE STUNNED
SKRASHH
KRESHH

I'VE HAD SOME PRACTICE--

--BUT IT'S A *LUCKY* FALL.

OOF--!

FAPP

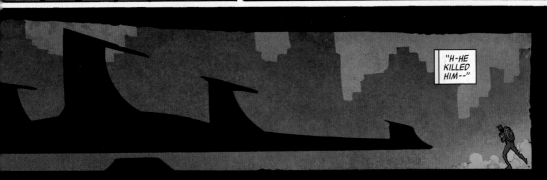

"H-HE KILLED HIM--"

--KILLED MY BOY.

DECADES DESIGNING HIM--

--GONE.

MY PERFECT SON...

...HE KILLED YOUR BABY BROTHER, DEAR JET.

PAPA...?

I ONLY WANTED THE SUPER-SOLDIER SERUM FOR YOU BOTH...

...AND NOW MY BOY IS DEAD.

LISTEN TO ME, MUTATES OF ZOLANDIA--

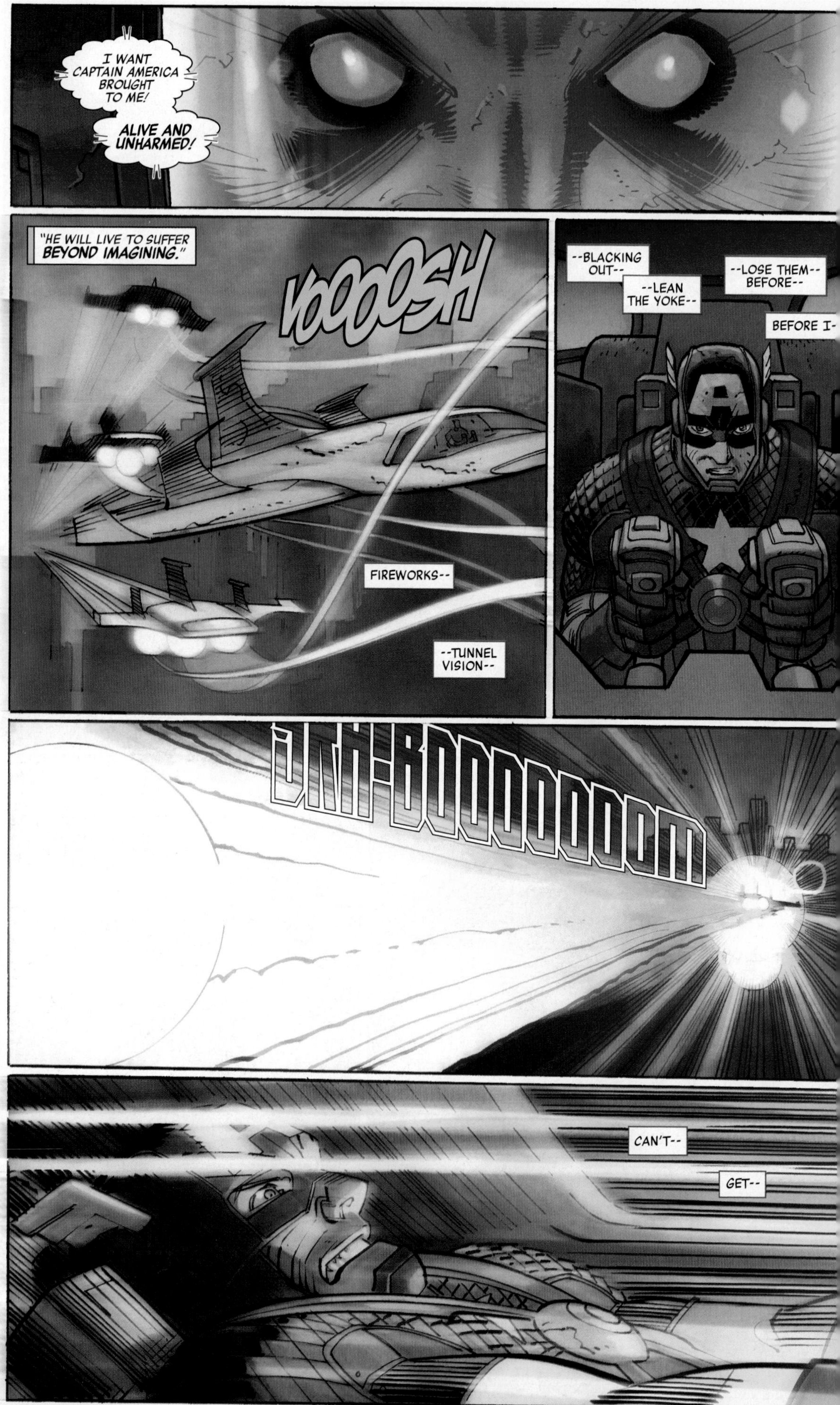
I WANT CAPTAIN AMERICA BROUGHT TO ME!
ALIVE AND UNHARMED!
"HE WILL LIVE TO SUFFER BEYOND IMAGINING."
VOOOOSH
FIREWORKS--
--TUNNEL VISION--
--BLACKING OUT--
--LEAN THE YOKE--
--LOSE THEM--BEFORE--
BEFORE I-
KA-BOOOOOOOOM
CAN'T--
GET--

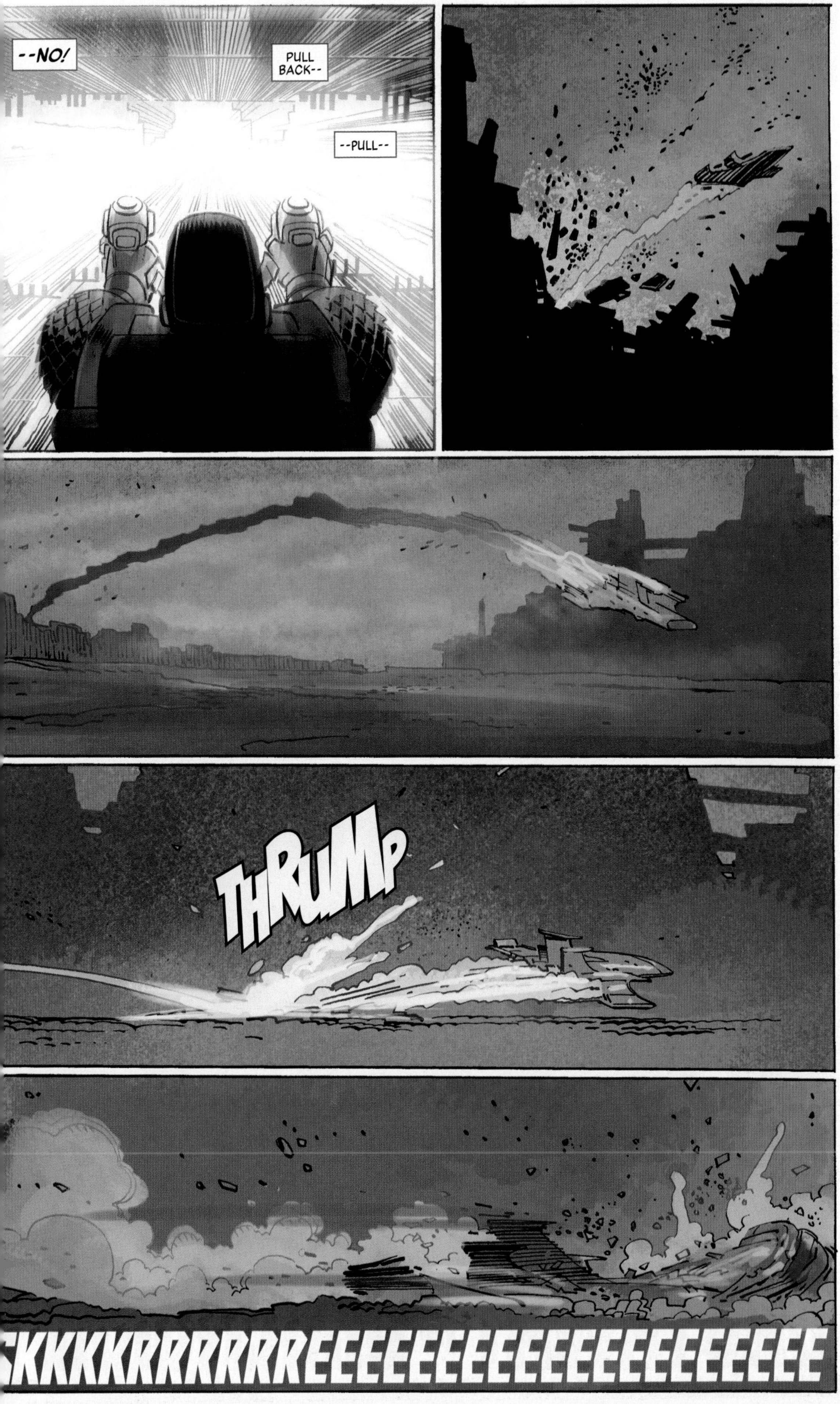
--NO!
PULL BACK--
--PULL--
THRUMP
SKKKKRRRRRREEEEEEEEEEEEEEEEEEEEEE

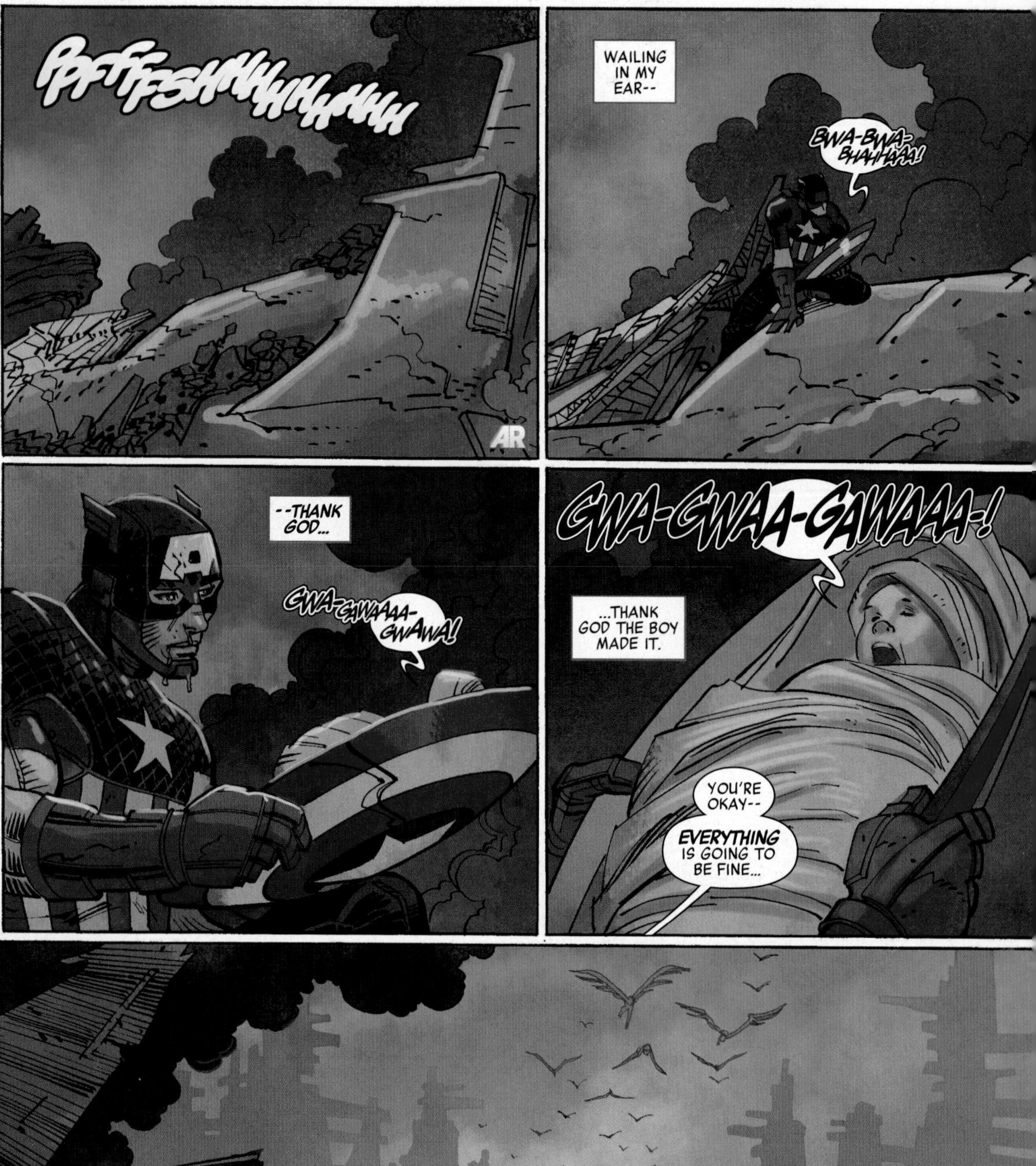

PPFFFSHHHHHHHHH
WAILING IN MY EAR--
BWA-BWA-BHAHHAAA!
--THANK GOD...
GWA-GAWAAAA-GWAWA!
GWA-GWAA-GAWAAA-!
...THANK GOD THE BOY MADE IT.
YOU'RE OKAY--
EVERYTHING IS GOING TO BE FINE...
...JUST FINE.

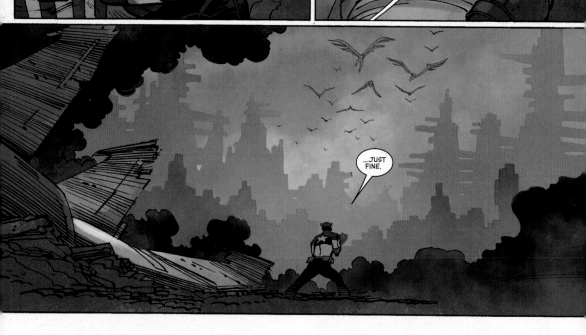

CASTAWAY IN DIMENSION

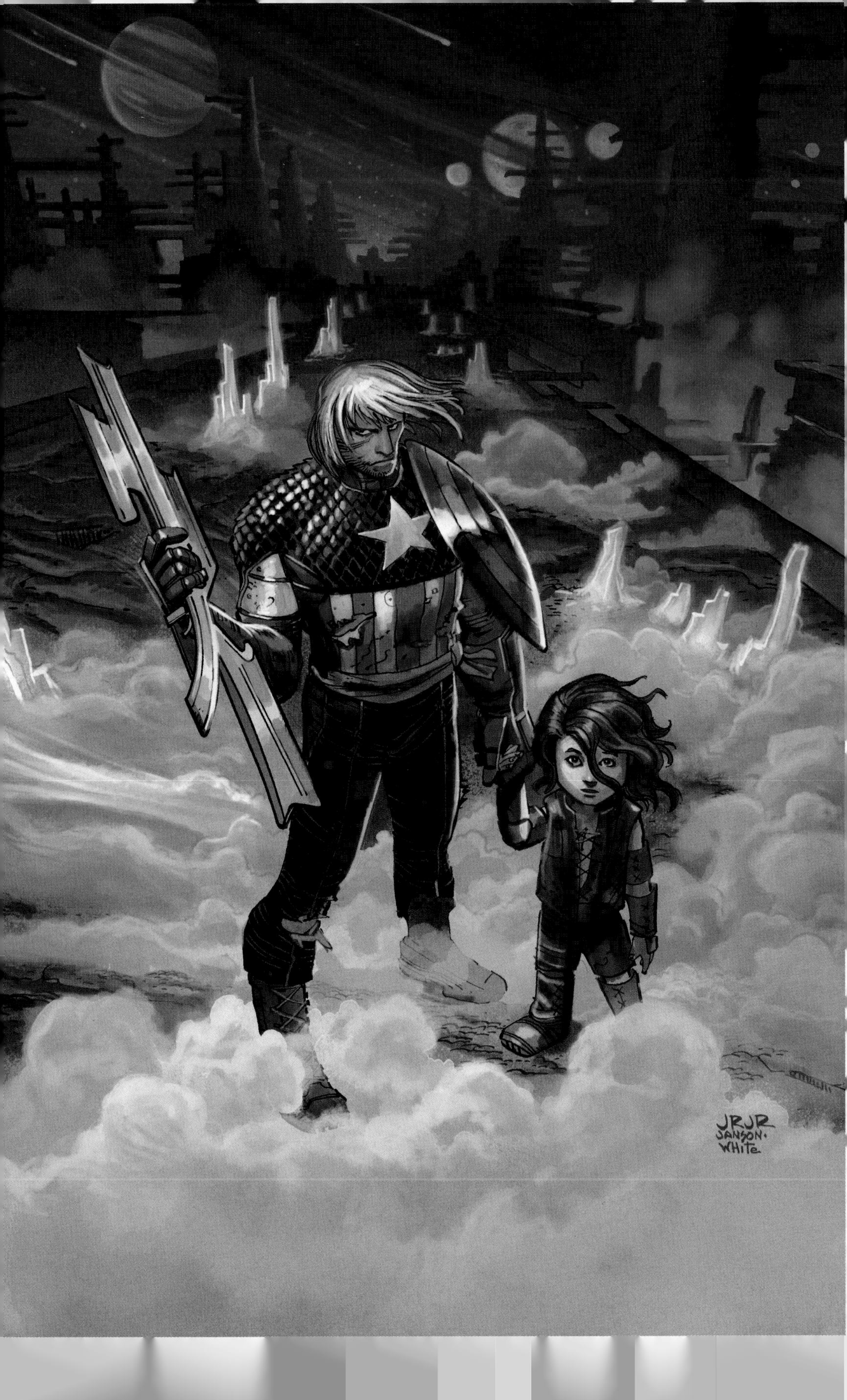
JRJR
JANSON.
WHITE

ONE YEAR LATER.

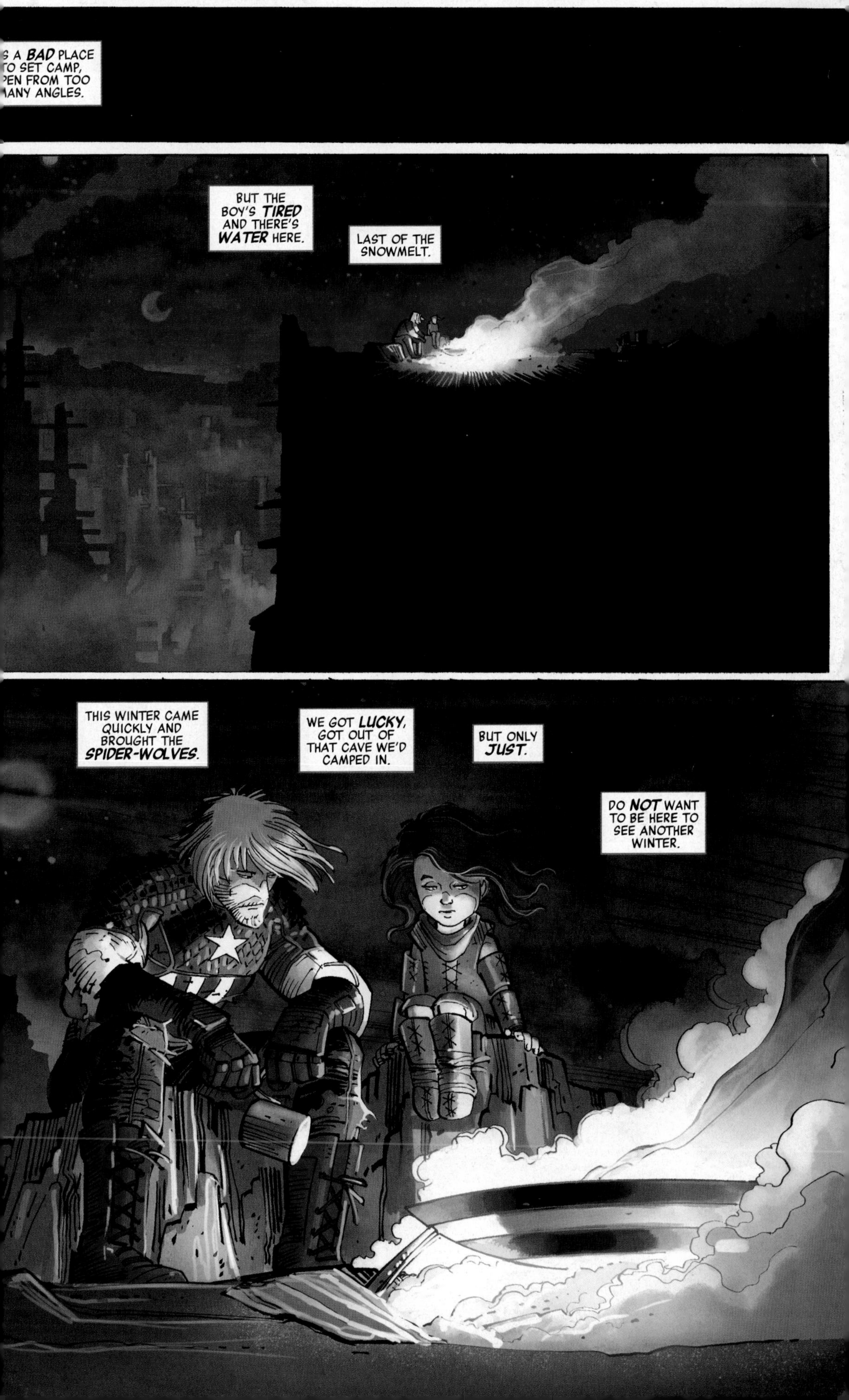
S A BAD PLACE TO SET CAMP, PEN FROM TOO ANY ANGLES.
BUT THE BOY'S TIRED AND THERE'S WATER HERE.
LAST OF THE SNOWMELT.
THIS WINTER CAME QUICKLY AND BROUGHT THE SPIDER-WOLVES.
WE GOT LUCKY, GOT OUT OF THAT CAVE WE'D CAMPED IN.
BUT ONLY JUST.
DO NOT WANT TO BE HERE TO SEE ANOTHER WINTER.

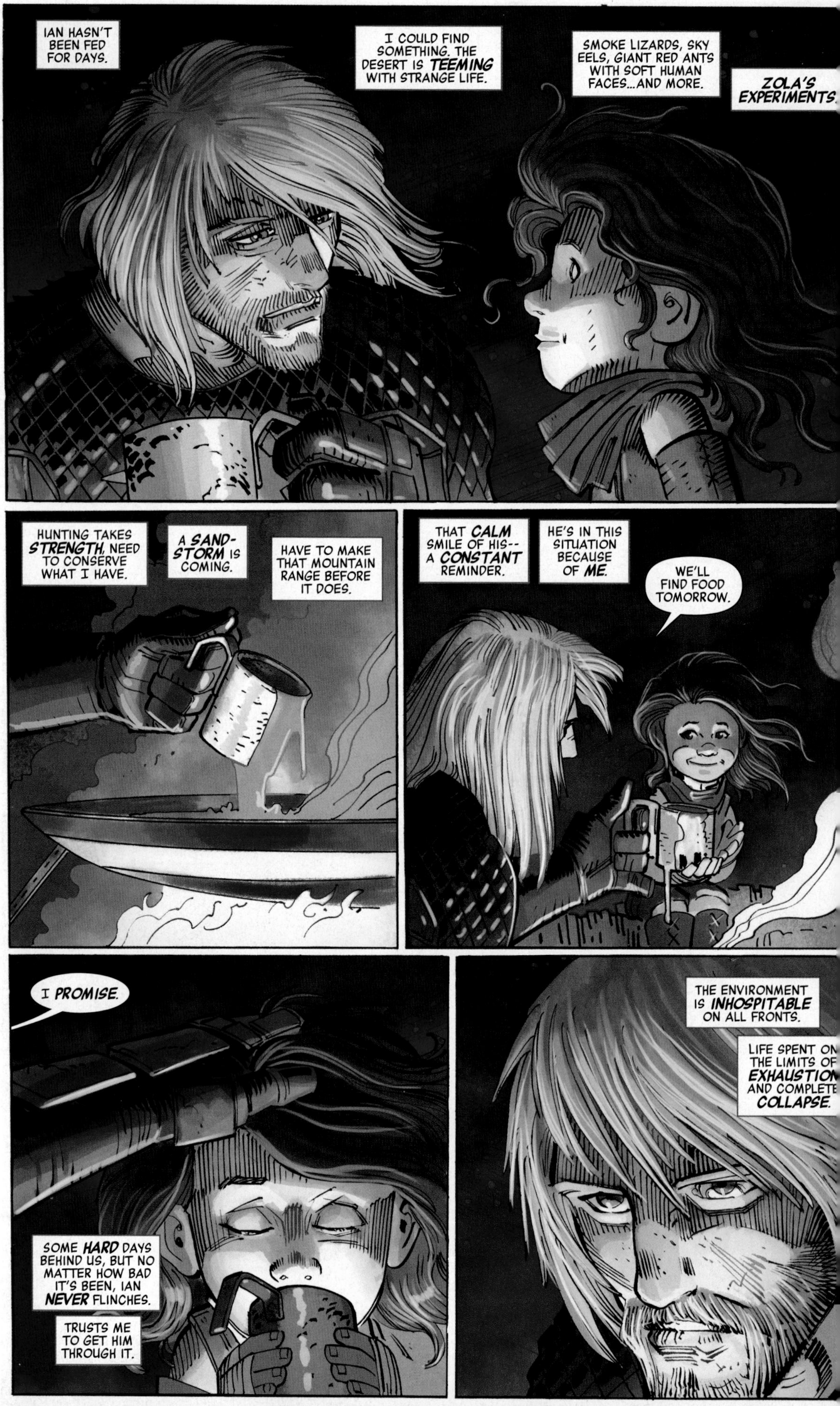
IAN HASN'T BEEN FED FOR DAYS.
I COULD FIND SOMETHING. THE DESERT IS TEEMING WITH STRANGE LIFE.
SMOKE LIZARDS, SKY EELS, GIANT RED ANTS WITH SOFT HUMAN FACES...AND MORE.
ZOLA'S EXPERIMENTS.
HUNTING TAKES STRENGTH, NEED TO CONSERVE WHAT I HAVE.
A SANDSTORM IS COMING.
HAVE TO MAKE THAT MOUNTAIN RANGE BEFORE IT DOES.
THAT CALM SMILE OF HIS-- A CONSTANT REMINDER.
HE'S IN THIS SITUATION BECAUSE OF ME.
WE'LL FIND FOOD TOMORROW.
I PROMISE.
SOME HARD DAYS BEHIND US, BUT NO MATTER HOW BAD IT'S BEEN, IAN NEVER FLINCHES.
TRUSTS ME TO GET HIM THROUGH IT.
THE ENVIRONMENT IS INHOSPITABLE ON ALL FRONTS.
LIFE SPENT ON THE LIMITS OF EXHAUSTION AND COMPLETE COLLAPSE.

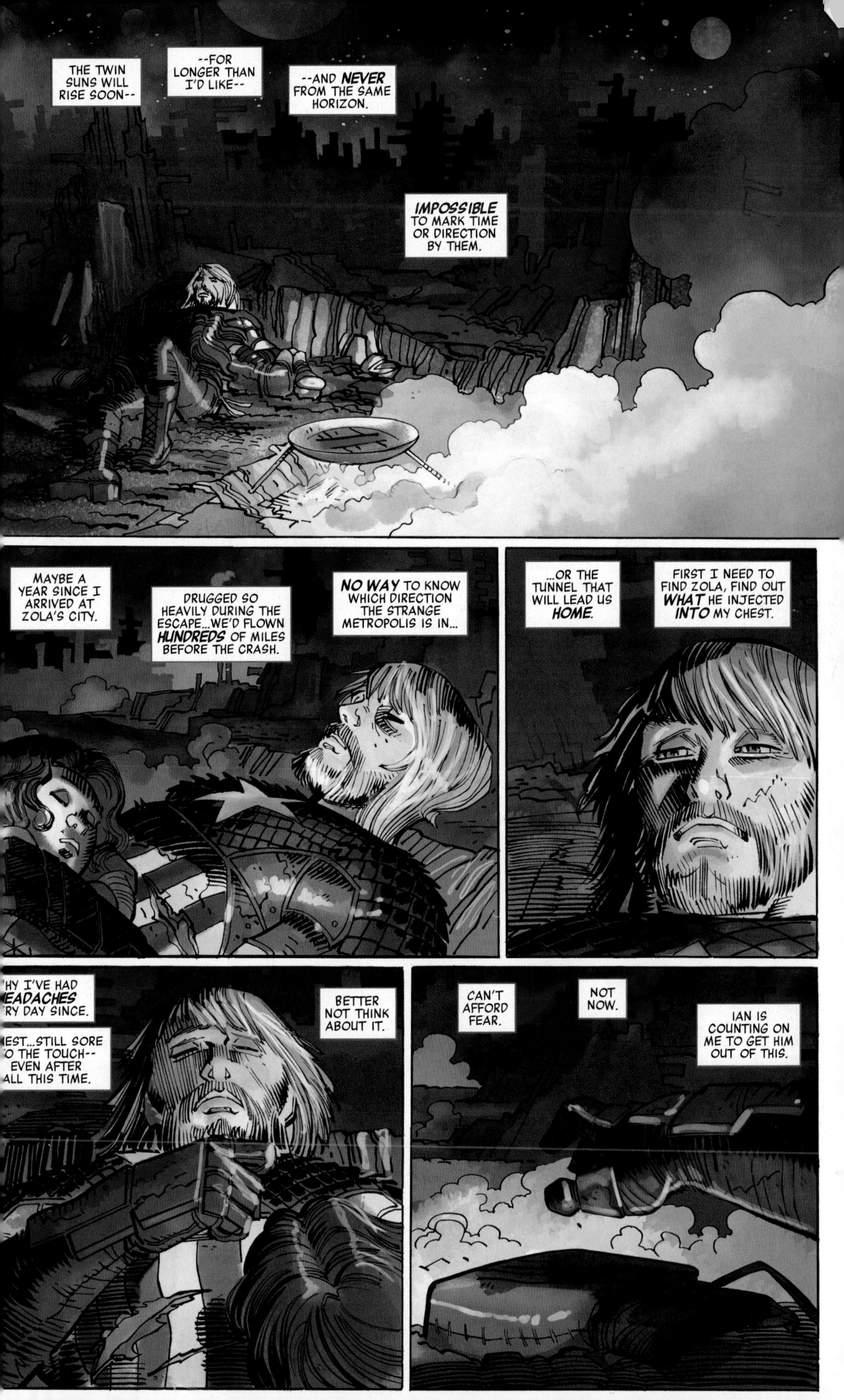
THE TWIN SUNS WILL RISE SOON--
--FOR LONGER THAN I'D LIKE--
--AND NEVER FROM THE SAME HORIZON.
IMPOSSIBLE TO MARK TIME OR DIRECTION BY THEM.
MAYBE A YEAR SINCE I ARRIVED AT ZOLA'S CITY.
DRUGGED SO HEAVILY DURING THE ESCAPE...WE'D FLOWN HUNDREDS OF MILES BEFORE THE CRASH.
NO WAY TO KNOW WHICH DIRECTION THE STRANGE METROPOLIS IS IN...
...OR THE TUNNEL THAT WILL LEAD US HOME.
FIRST I NEED TO FIND ZOLA, FIND OUT WHAT HE INJECTED INTO MY CHEST.
HY I'VE HAD EADACHES RY DAY SINCE.
EST...STILL SORE O THE TOUCH-- EVEN AFTER ALL THIS TIME.
BETTER NOT THINK ABOUT IT.
CAN'T AFFORD FEAR.
NOT NOW.
IAN IS COUNTING ON ME TO GET HIM OUT OF THIS.

NIGHTS ARE THE *WORST*.

WHEN IAN'S SLEEPING, AND NO LONGER IN NEED OF CONSTANT ATTENTION.

LEAVING ME TO PONDER *HARSH REALITIES*.

WHAT HAPPENS IF I *CAN'T* FIND THE WAY HOME?

HOW LONG CAN WE KEEP DOING THIS?

STRANDED HERE, FIGHTING *FOREVER*--

WHERE'S OUR BREAKING POINT?

HOW MANY *YEARS* WILL PASS BEFORE WE FIND *SOME* SIGN OF HOPE?

WHEN WILL IT BECOME TOO *MUCH*?

THE OTHER WAY OUT...

KLPP

THE OTHER WAY OUT *ISN'T* ONE YOU CONSIDER.

ESSEX STREET.
THE LOWER
EAST SIDE OF
MANHATTAN,
1926.

NEWS! HOT OFF THE PRESS--*GET YER PAPER!*

TWO CENTS!

THANK YOU, SIR.

YGAA--

POKK

HEARD YER OL' MAN FINALLY UP AN' *DRANK* HIMSELF TA *DEATH.*

INTRODUCE ME TO YER MA. I'LL KEEP 'ER *WARM* FER YA.

HITTIN' TOO LOW, HUTCH.

MAS ARE OFF LIMITS. *STREET CODE.*

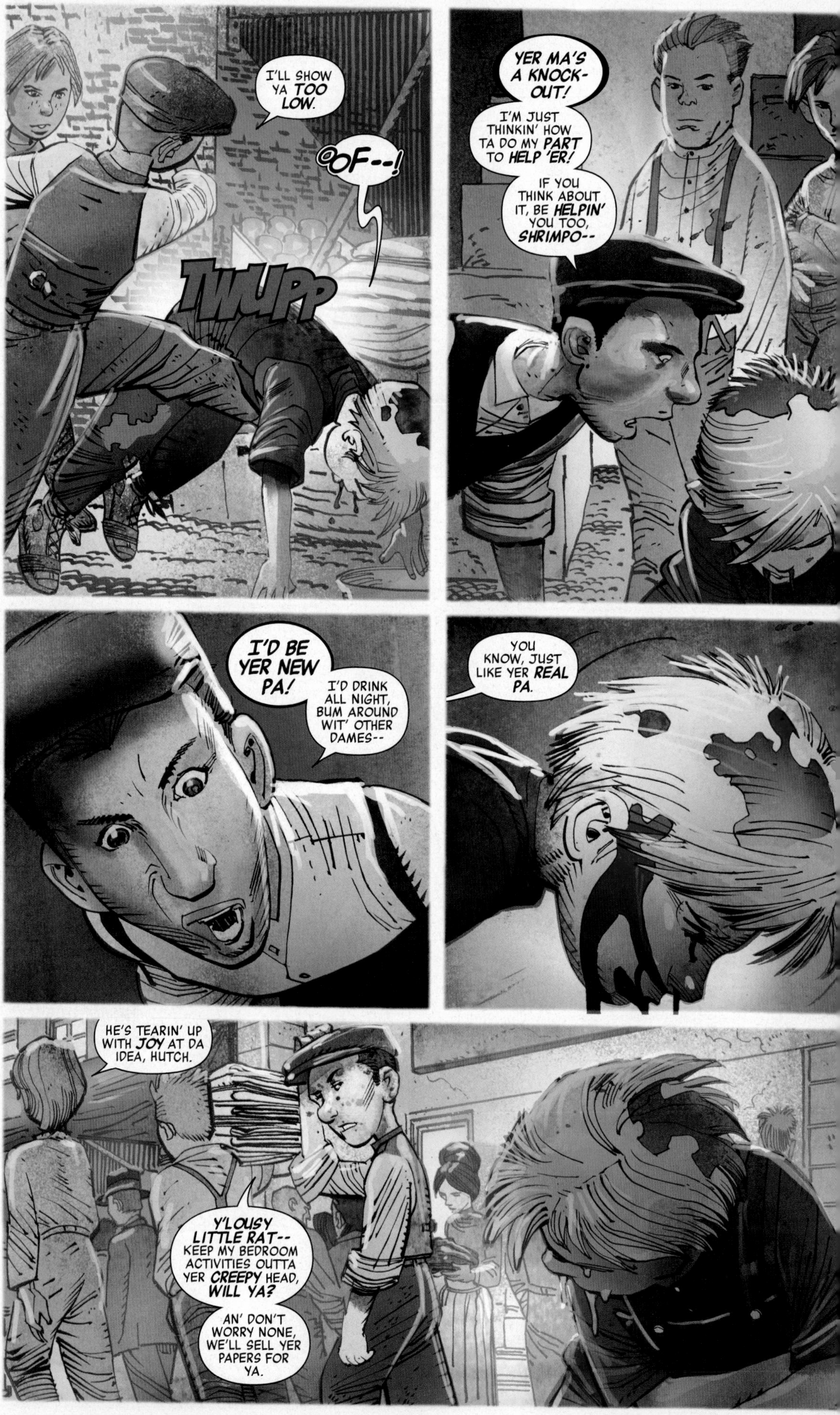
I'LL SHOW YA TOO LOW.
OOF--!
TWUPP
YER MA'S A KNOCK-OUT!
I'M JUST THINKIN' HOW TA DO MY PART TO HELP 'ER!
IF YOU THINK ABOUT IT, BE HELPIN' YOU TOO, SHRIMPO--
I'D BE YER NEW PA!
I'D DRINK ALL NIGHT, BUM AROUND WIT' OTHER DAMES--
YOU KNOW, JUST LIKE YER REAL PA.
HE'S TEARIN' UP WITH JOY AT DA IDEA, HUTCH.
Y'LOUSY LITTLE RAT-- KEEP MY BEDROOM ACTIVITIES OUTTA YER CREEPY HEAD, WILL YA?
AN' DON'T WORRY NONE, WE'LL SELL YER PAPERS FOR YA.

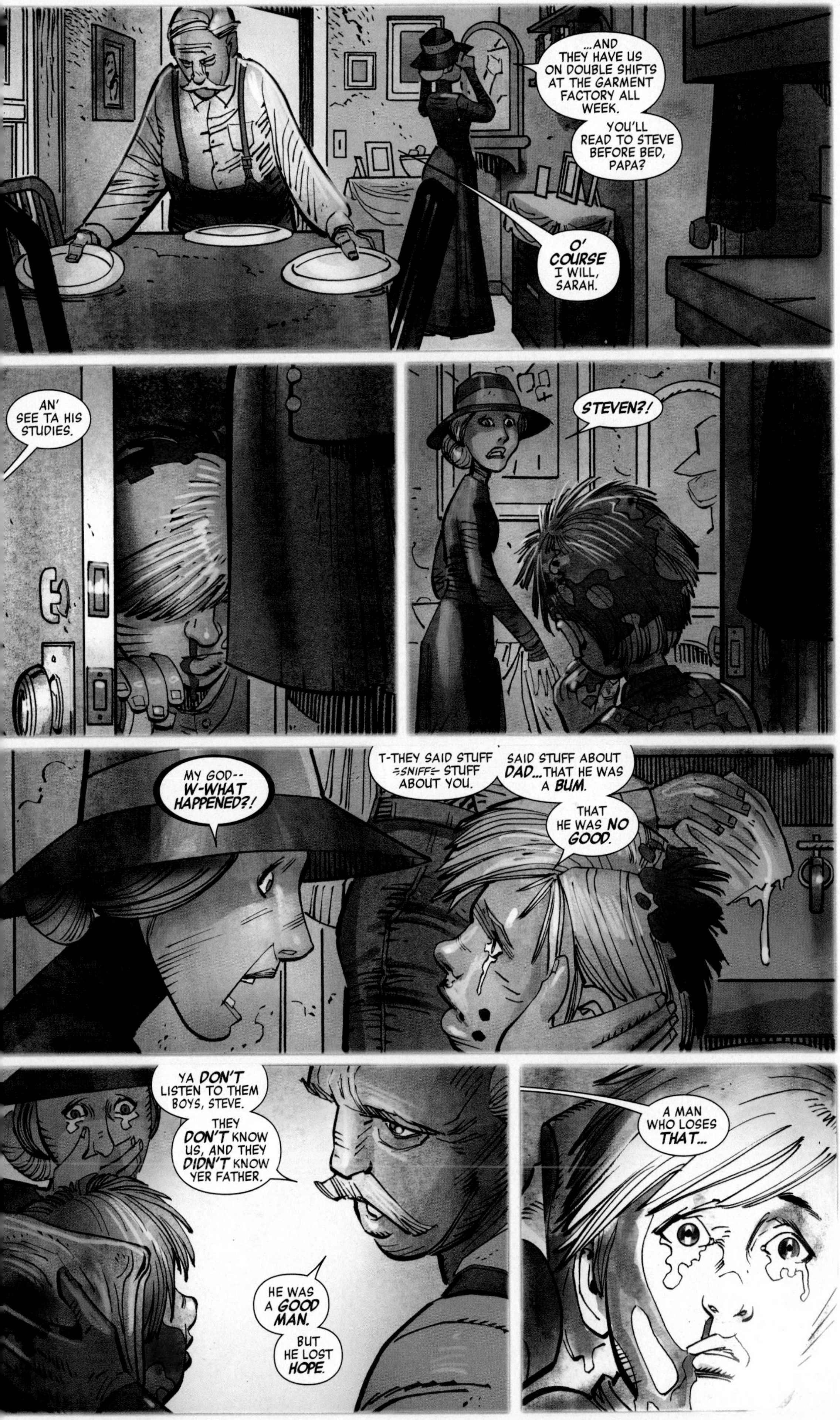
...AND THEY HAVE US ON DOUBLE SHIFTS AT THE GARMENT FACTORY ALL WEEK.
YOU'LL READ TO STEVE BEFORE BED, PAPA?
O' COURSE I WILL, SARAH.
AN' SEE TA HIS STUDIES.
STEVEN?!
MY GOD-- W-WHAT HAPPENED?!
T-THEY SAID STUFF *SNIFF* STUFF ABOUT YOU.
SAID STUFF ABOUT DAD... THAT HE WAS A BUM.
THAT HE WAS NO GOOD.
YA DON'T LISTEN TO THEM BOYS, STEVE.
THEY DON'T KNOW US, AND THEY DIDN'T KNOW YER FATHER.
HE WAS A GOOD MAN.
BUT HE LOST HOPE.
A MAN WHO LOSES THAT...

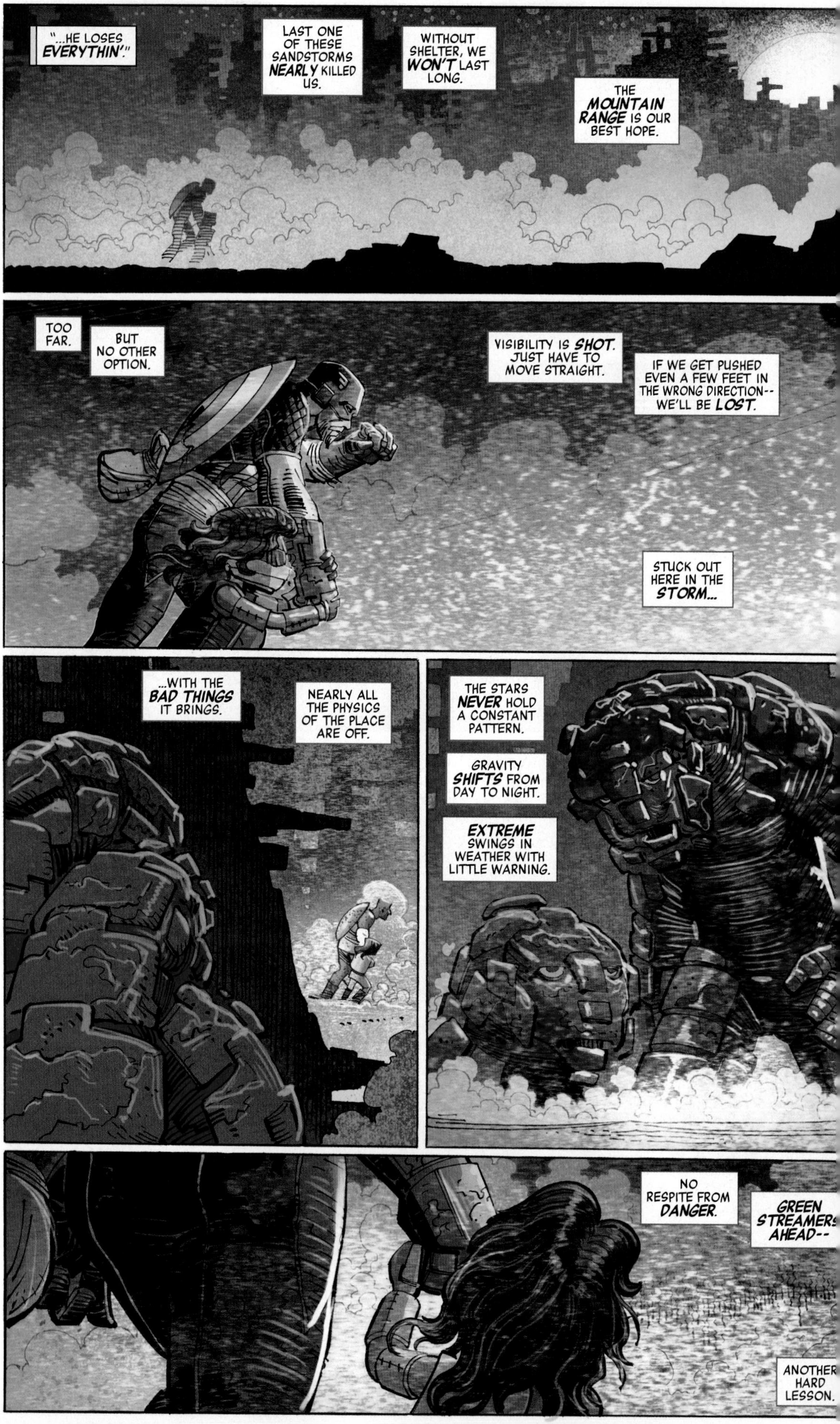
"...HE LOSES EVERYTHIN'."
LAST ONE OF THESE SANDSTORMS NEARLY KILLED US.
WITHOUT SHELTER, WE WON'T LAST LONG.
THE MOUNTAIN RANGE IS OUR BEST HOPE.
TOO FAR.
BUT NO OTHER OPTION.
VISIBILITY IS SHOT. JUST HAVE TO MOVE STRAIGHT.
IF WE GET PUSHED EVEN A FEW FEET IN THE WRONG DIRECTION-- WE'LL BE LOST.
STUCK OUT HERE IN THE STORM...
...WITH THE BAD THINGS IT BRINGS.
NEARLY ALL THE PHYSICS OF THE PLACE ARE OFF.
THE STARS NEVER HOLD A CONSTANT PATTERN.
GRAVITY SHIFTS FROM DAY TO NIGHT.
EXTREME SWINGS IN WEATHER WITH LITTLE WARNING.
NO RESPITE FROM DANGER.
GREEN STREAMERS AHEAD--
ANOTHER HARD LESSON.

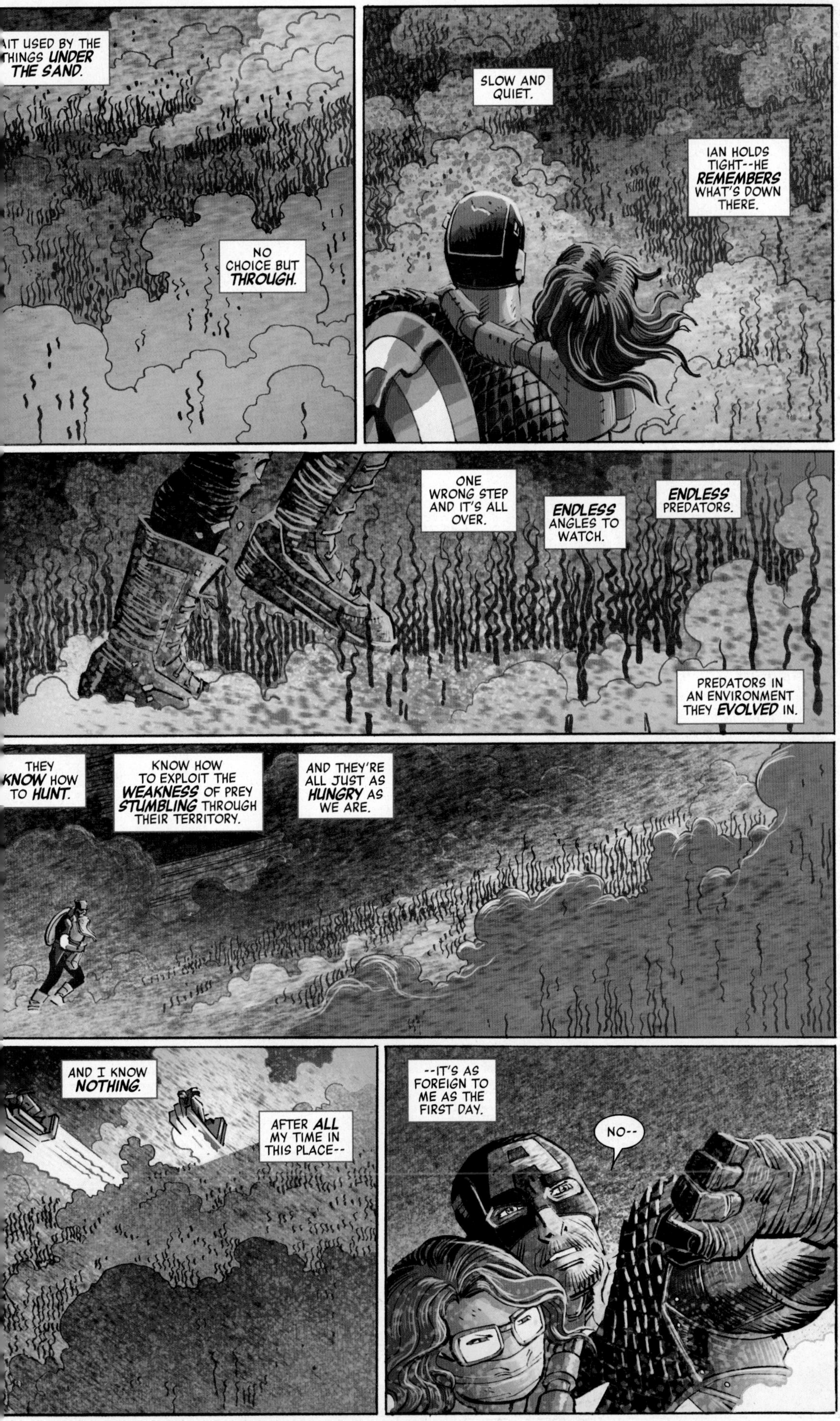

AIT USED BY THE THINGS UNDER THE SAND.
NO CHOICE BUT THROUGH.
SLOW AND QUIET.
IAN HOLDS TIGHT--HE REMEMBERS WHAT'S DOWN THERE.
ONE WRONG STEP AND IT'S ALL OVER.
ENDLESS ANGLES TO WATCH.
ENDLESS PREDATORS.
PREDATORS IN AN ENVIRONMENT THEY EVOLVED IN.
THEY KNOW HOW TO HUNT.
KNOW HOW TO EXPLOIT THE WEAKNESS OF PREY STUMBLING THROUGH THEIR TERRITORY.
AND THEY'RE ALL JUST AS HUNGRY AS WE ARE.
AND I KNOW NOTHING.
AFTER ALL MY TIME IN THIS PLACE--
--IT'S AS FOREIGN TO ME AS THE FIRST DAY.
NO--

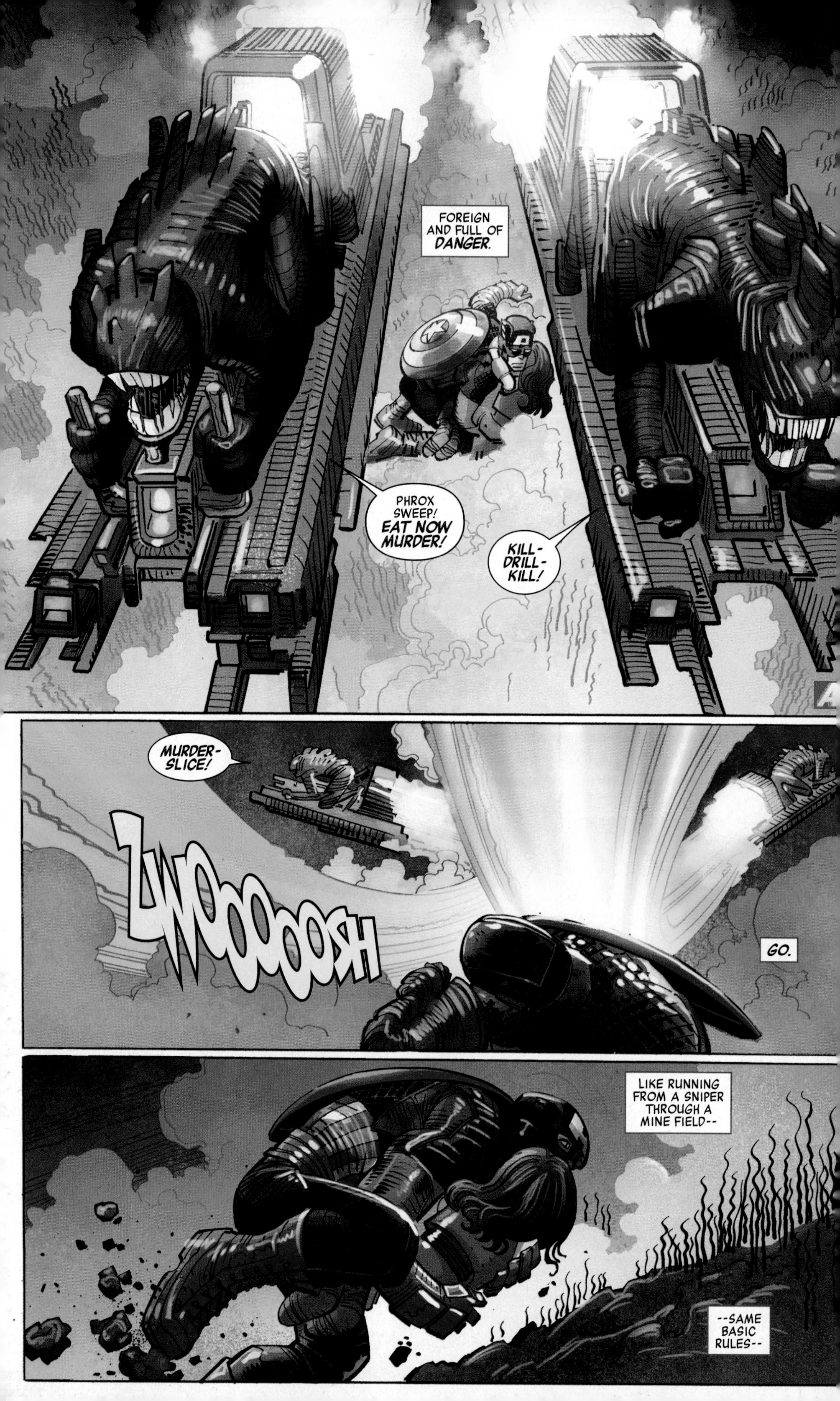
FOREIGN AND FULL OF DANGER.
PHROX SWEEP! EAT NOW MURDER!
KILL-DRILL-KILL!
MURDER-SLICE!
ZWOOOOOSH
GO.
LIKE RUNNING FROM A SNIPER THROUGH A MINE FIELD--
--SAME BASIC RULES--

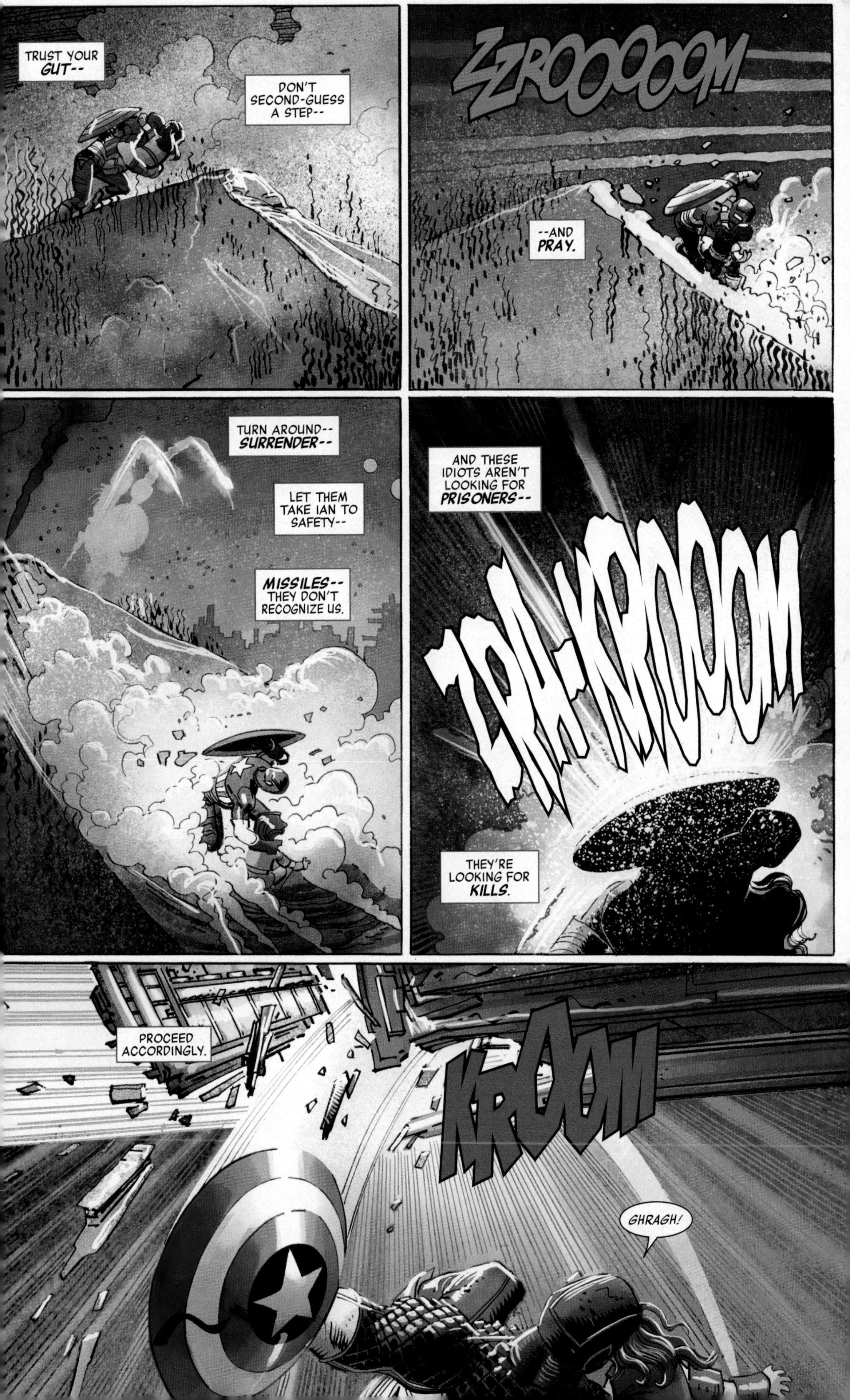
TRUST YOUR GUT--
DON'T SECOND-GUESS A STEP--
ZZROOOOOM
--AND PRAY.
TURN AROUND-- SURRENDER--
LET THEM TAKE IAN TO SAFETY--
MISSILES-- THEY DON'T RECOGNIZE US.
AND THESE IDIOTS AREN'T LOOKING FOR PRISONERS--
ZDAH-KRROOOM
THEY'RE LOOKING FOR KILLS.
PROCEED ACCORDINGLY.
KRROOM
GHRAGH!

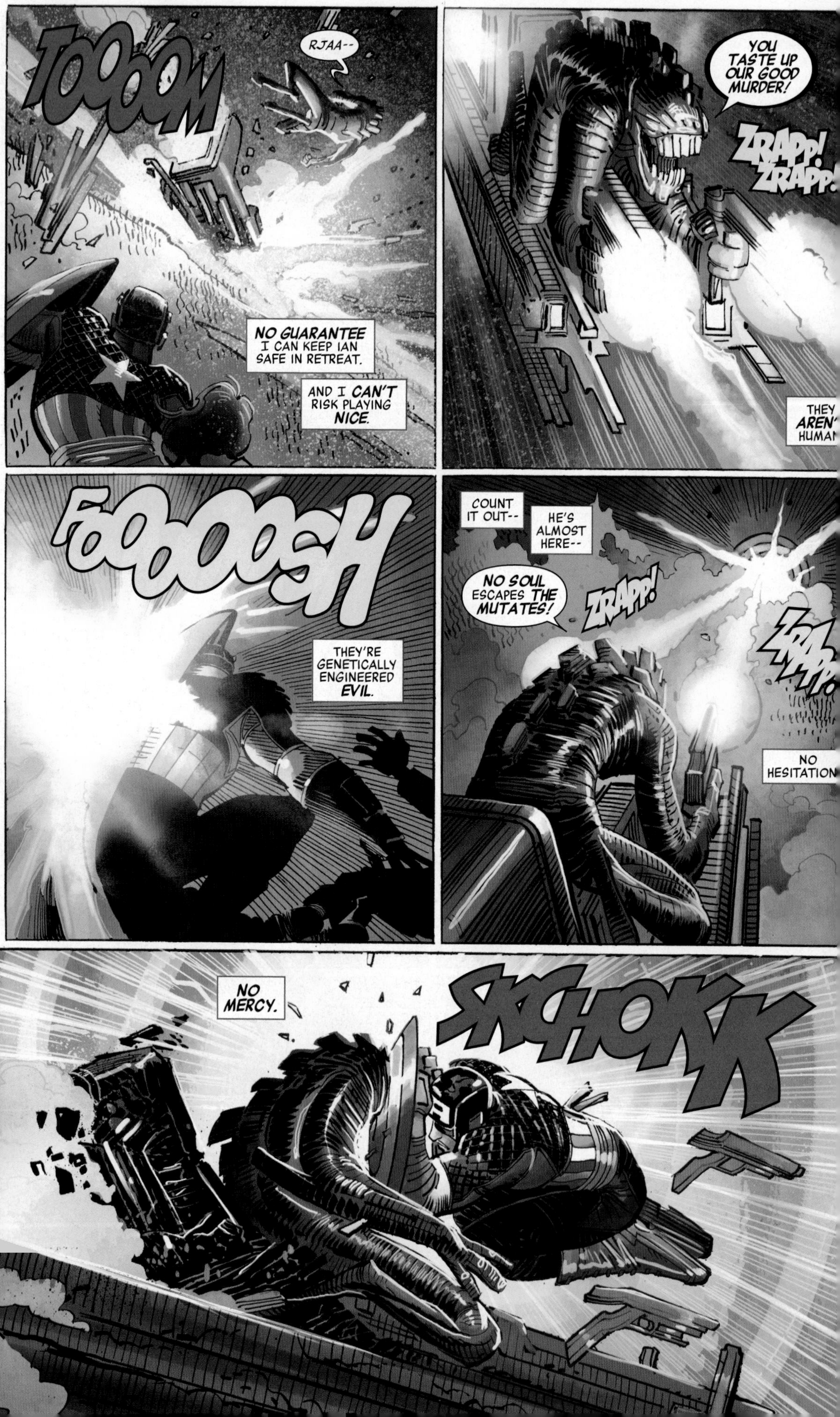
TOOOOM
RJAA--
NO GUARANTEE I CAN KEEP IAN SAFE IN RETREAT.
AND I CAN'T RISK PLAYING NICE.
YOU TASTE UP OUR GOOD MURDER!
ZRAPP! ZRAPP!
THEY AREN' HUMAN
FOOOOOSH
THEY'RE GENETICALLY ENGINEERED EVIL.
COUNT IT OUT--
HE'S ALMOST HERE--
NO SOUL ESCAPES THE MUTATES!
ZRAPP!
NO HESITATION
NO MERCY.
SKCHOKK

HIS FACE CRUMPLED.

GRISLY BEASTS, BUT THEIR BONES *DO* BREAK.

GIVES ME STEAM TO FACE THE THING *HISSING* SLURS BEHIND ME...

...AND THE FIRE UNRAVELING IN HIS FISTS.

WE *EAT* WHEN WE *PLEASE*. COOK IT AND EAT.

WE *KNOWS* YOU *WILL* FEEL--

NOW TO BURN!

RHOOOOOOOM

NAPALM HEAT--

CHAINMAIL *SEARING* MY SKIN--

IAN *SCREAMS*--

CAN'T OUTRUN IT--

ONE MORE SHOT AND WE'RE *DEAD*--

SO DO THE *LAST THING* I SHOULD--

RAAKKA--

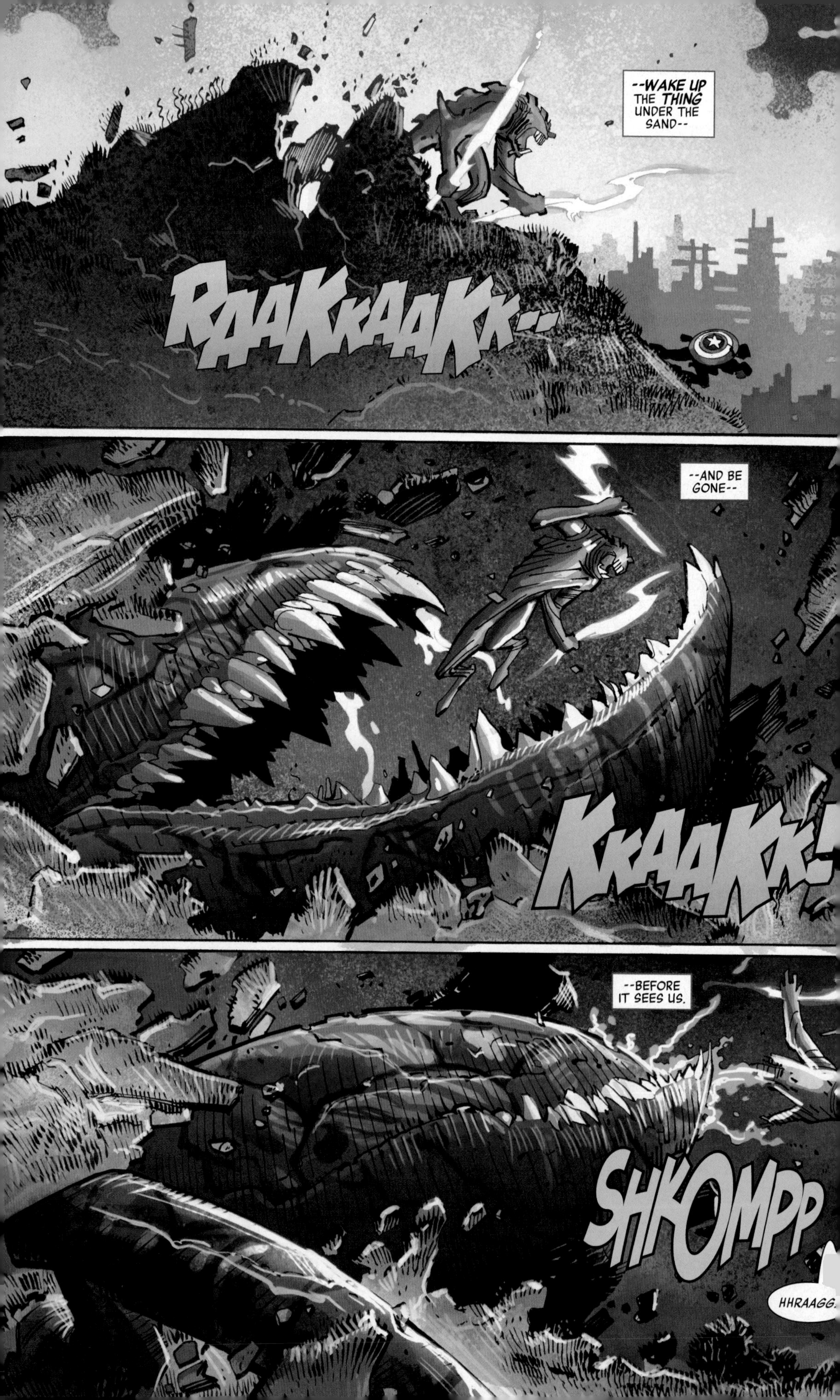
--WAKE UP THE THING UNDER THE SAND--
RAAKKAAKK--
--AND BE GONE--
KRAAKK!
--BEFORE IT SEES US.
SHKOMPP
HHRAAGG

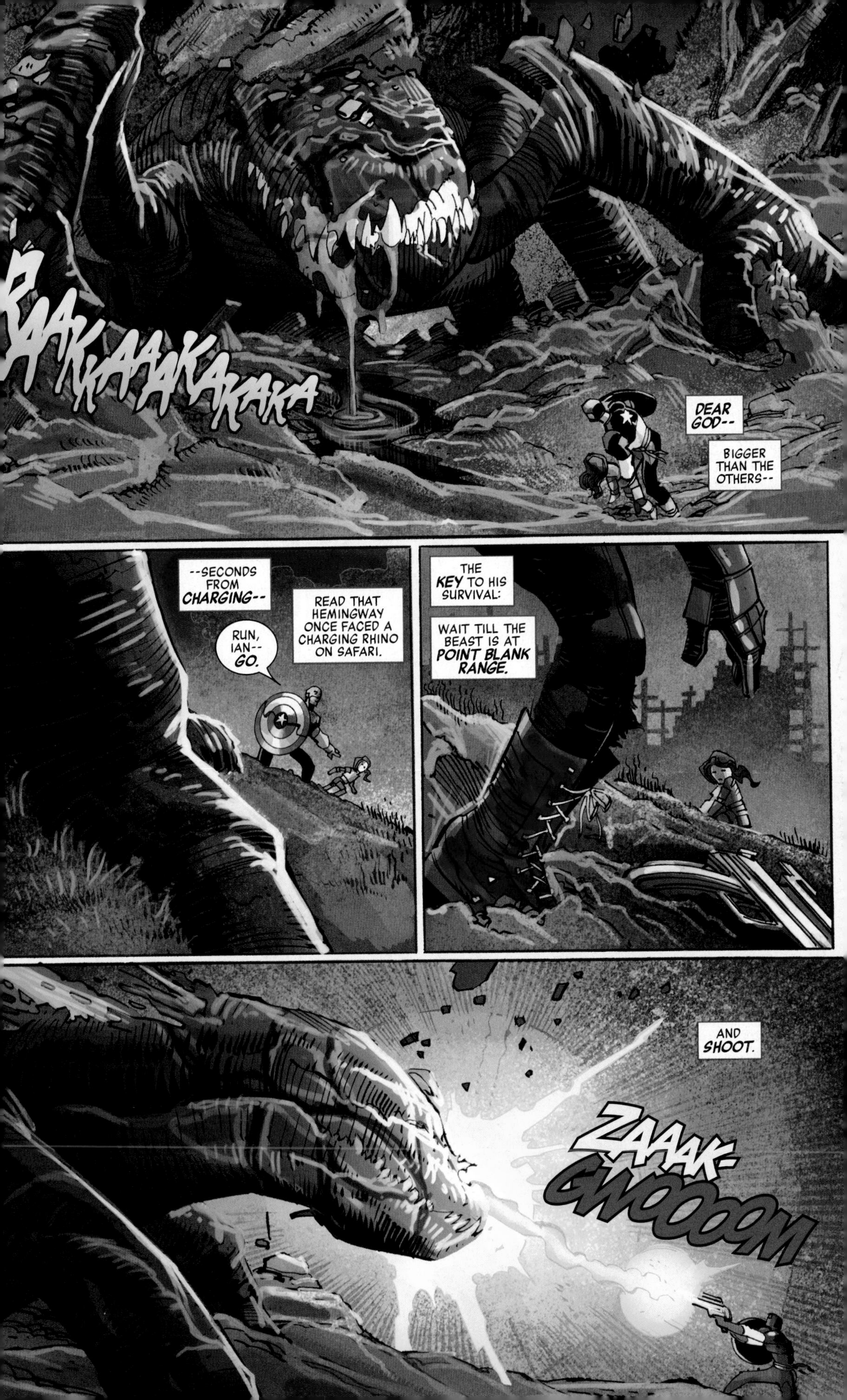
RAAKKAAAKAKAKA
DEAR GOD--
BIGGER THAN THE OTHERS--
--SECONDS FROM CHARGING--
READ THAT HEMINGWAY ONCE FACED A CHARGING RHINO ON SAFARI.
RUN, IAN-- GO.
THE KEY TO HIS SURVIVAL:
WAIT TILL THE BEAST IS AT POINT BLANK RANGE.
AND SHOOT.
ZAAAK-GWOOOOOM

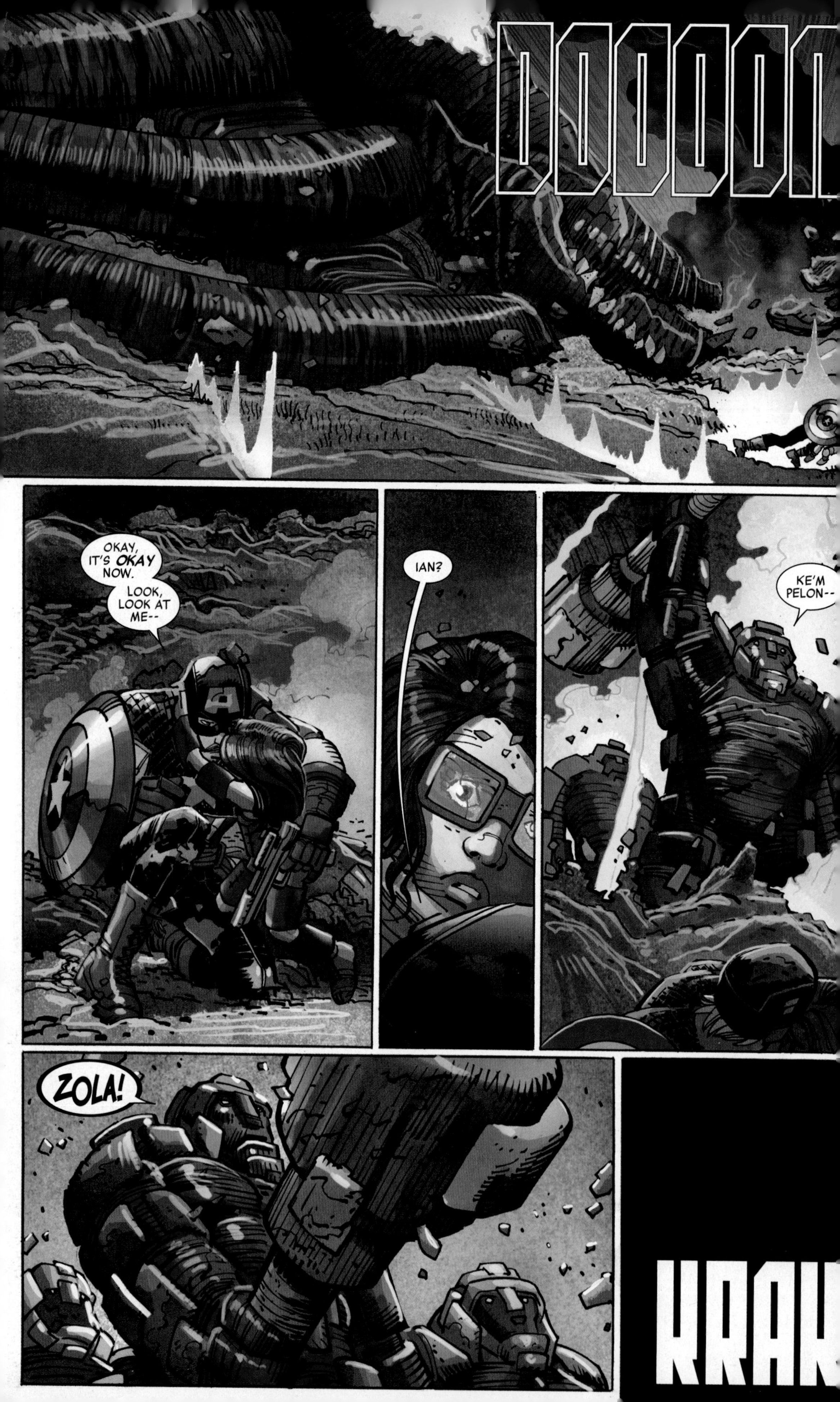
DOOOOM
OKAY, IT'S OKAY NOW.
LOOK, LOOK AT ME--
IAN?
KE'M PELON--
ZOLA!
KRAK

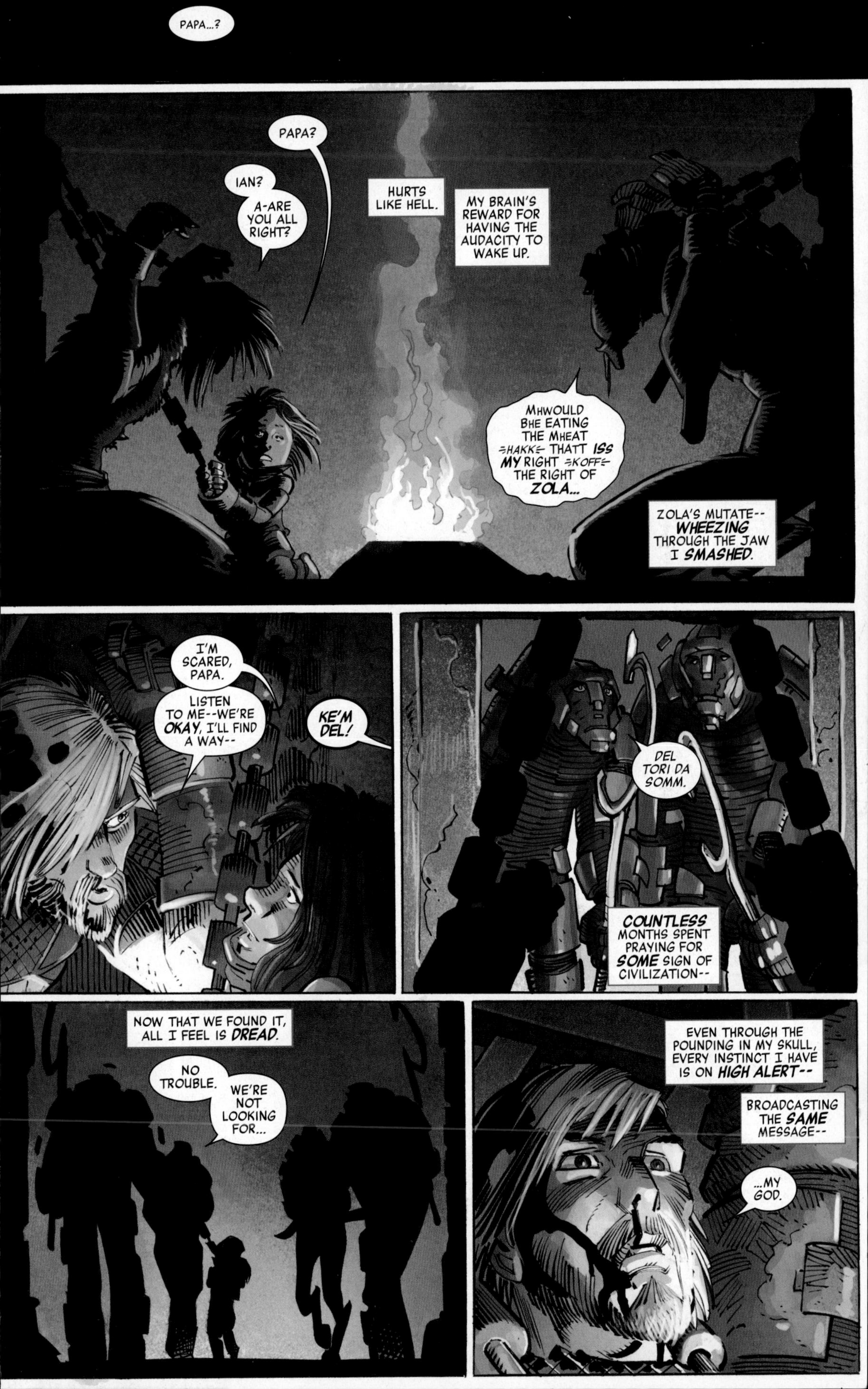
PAPA...?
PAPA?
IAN?
A-ARE YOU ALL RIGHT?
HURTS LIKE HELL.
MY BRAIN'S REWARD FOR HAVING THE AUDACITY TO WAKE UP.
MHWOULD BHE EATING THE MHEAT =HAKK= THATT ISS MY RIGHT =KOFF= THE RIGHT OF ZOLA...
ZOLA'S MUTATE-- WHEEZING THROUGH THE JAW I SMASHED.
I'M SCARED, PAPA.
LISTEN TO ME--WE'RE OKAY, I'LL FIND A WAY--
KE'M DEL!
DEL TORI DA SOMM.
COUNTLESS MONTHS SPENT PRAYING FOR SOME SIGN OF CIVILIZATION--
NOW THAT WE FOUND IT, ALL I FEEL IS DREAD.
NO TROUBLE.
WE'RE NOT LOOKING FOR...
EVEN THROUGH THE POUNDING IN MY SKULL, EVERY INSTINCT I HAVE IS ON HIGH ALERT--
BROADCASTING THE SAME MESSAGE--
...MY GOD.

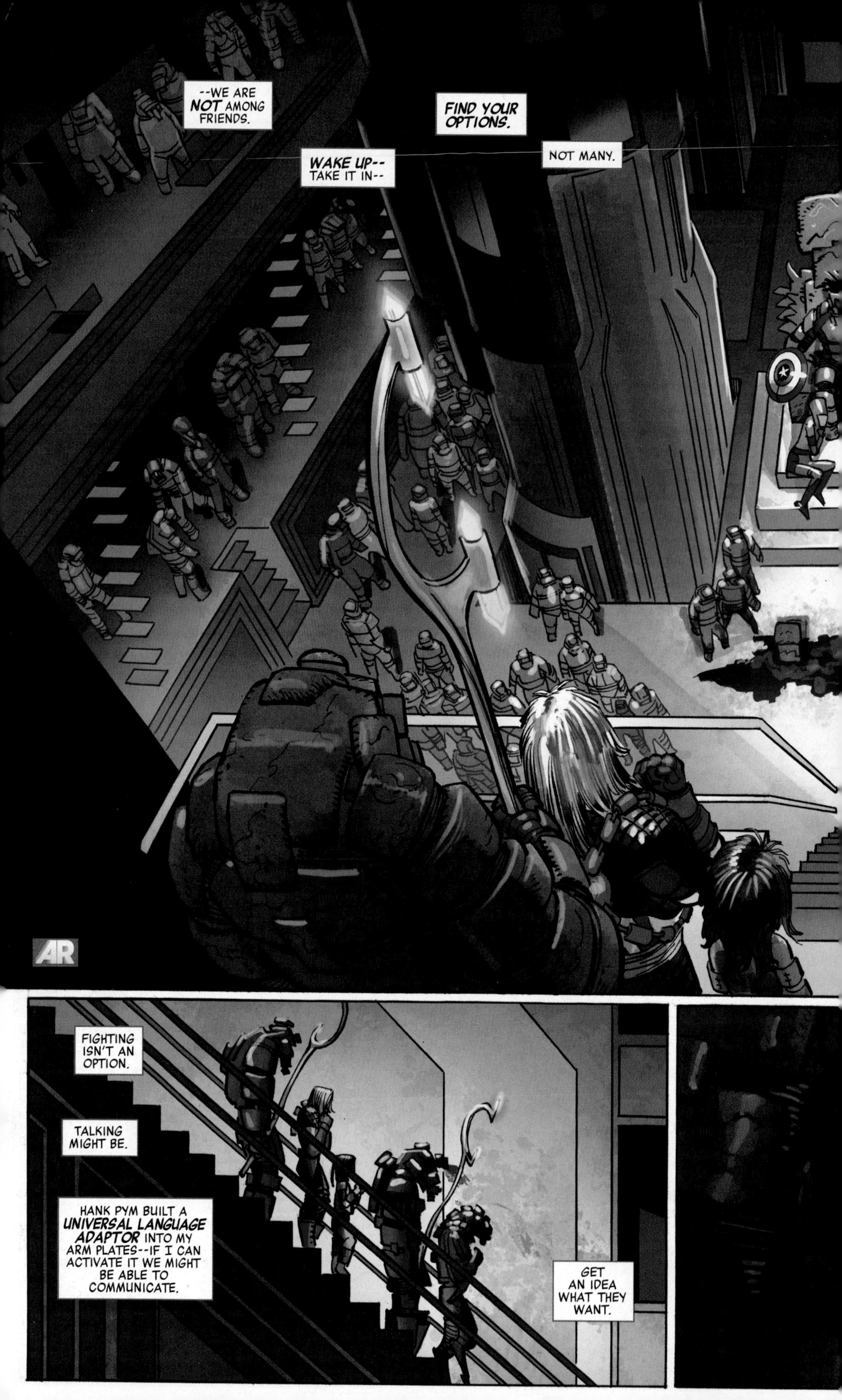

--WE ARE NOT AMONG FRIENDS.
WAKE UP-- TAKE IT IN--
FIND YOUR OPTIONS.
NOT MANY.
AR
FIGHTING ISN'T AN OPTION.
TALKING MIGHT BE.
HANK PYM BUILT A UNIVERSAL LANGUAGE ADAPTOR INTO MY ARM PLATES--IF I CAN ACTIVATE IT WE MIGHT BE ABLE TO COMMUNICATE.
GET AN IDEA WHAT THEY WANT.

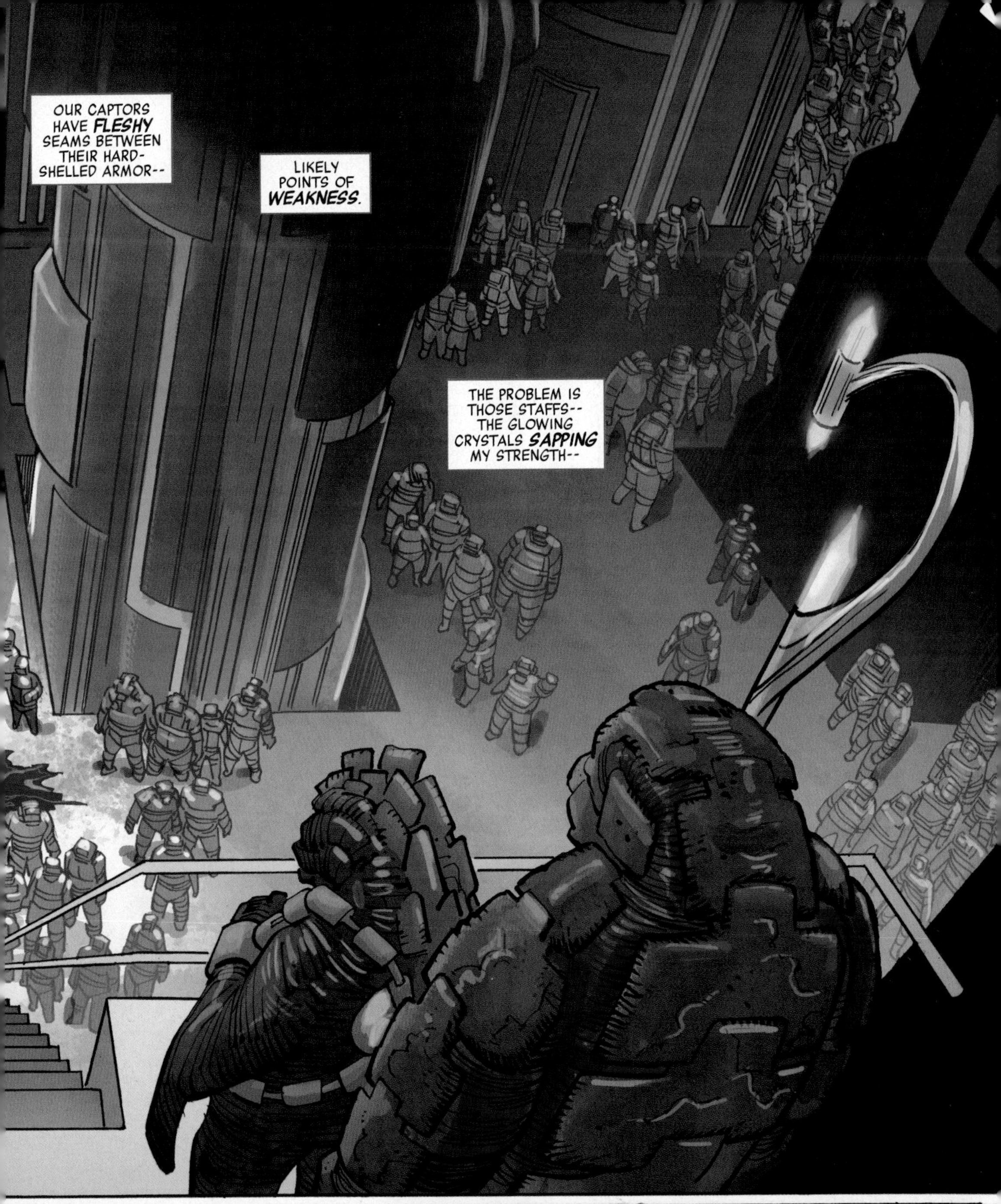
OUR CAPTORS HAVE FLESHY SEAMS BETWEEN THEIR HARD-SHELLED ARMOR--
LIKELY POINTS OF WEAKNESS.
THE PROBLEM IS THOSE STAFFS-- THE GLOWING CRYSTALS SAPPING MY STRENGTH--
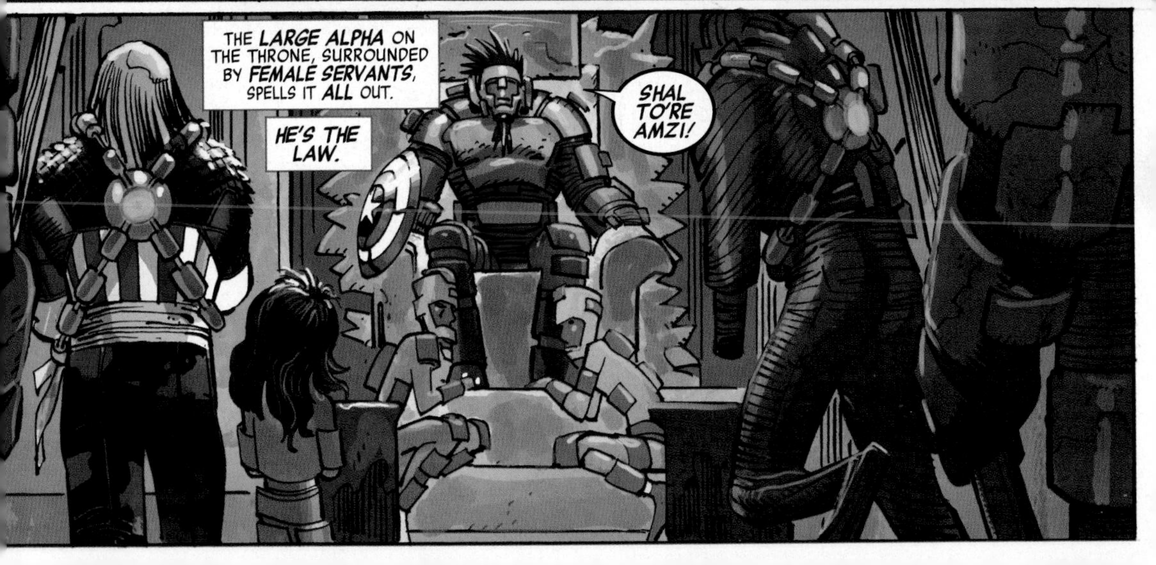
THE LARGE ALPHA ON THE THRONE, SURROUNDED BY FEMALE SERVANTS, SPELLS IT ALL OUT.
HE'S THE LAW.
SHAL TO'RE AMZI!

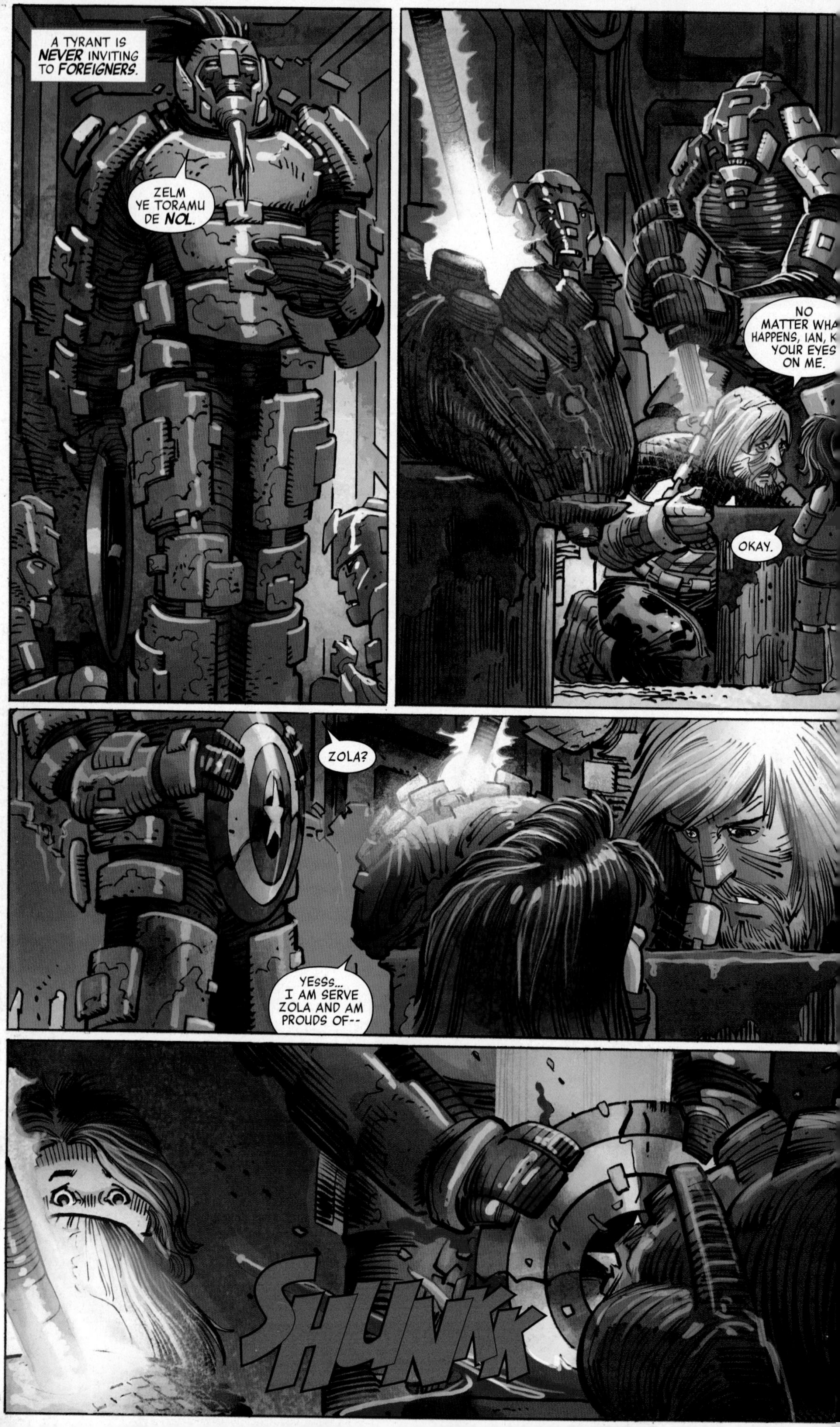
A TYRANT IS NEVER INVITING TO FOREIGNERS.
ZELM YE TORAMU DE NOL.
NO MATTER WHA HAPPENS, IAN, K YOUR EYES ON ME.
OKAY.
ZOLA?
YESSS... I AM SERVE ZOLA AND AM PROUDS OF--
SHUNK

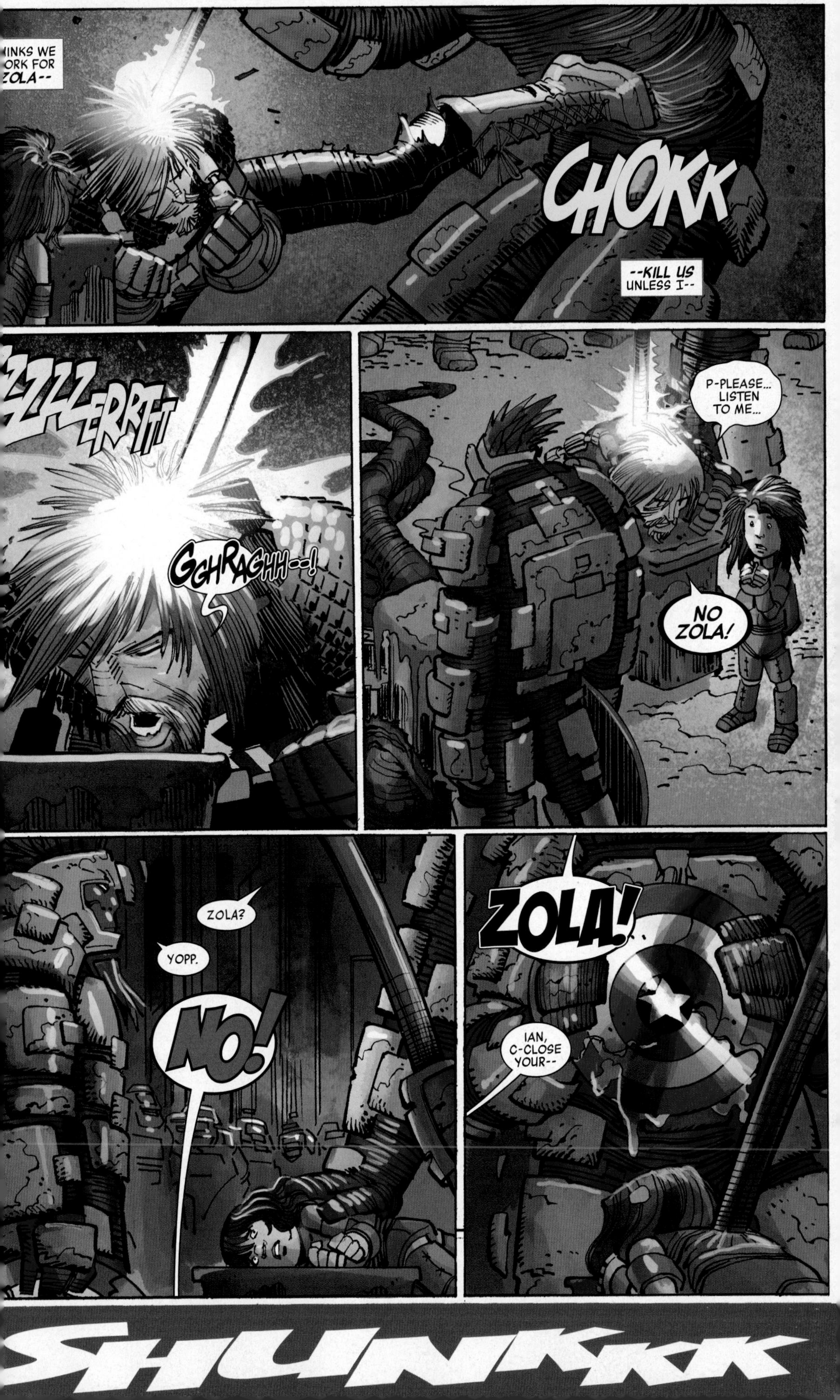

INKS WE
ORK FOR
ZOLA--
CHOKK
--KILL US
UNLESS I--
ZZZZZERRTTT
GGHRAGHH--!
P-PLEASE... LISTEN TO ME...
NO ZOLA!
ZOLA?
YOPP.
NO!
ZOLA!
IAN, C-CLOSE YOUR--
SHUNKKK

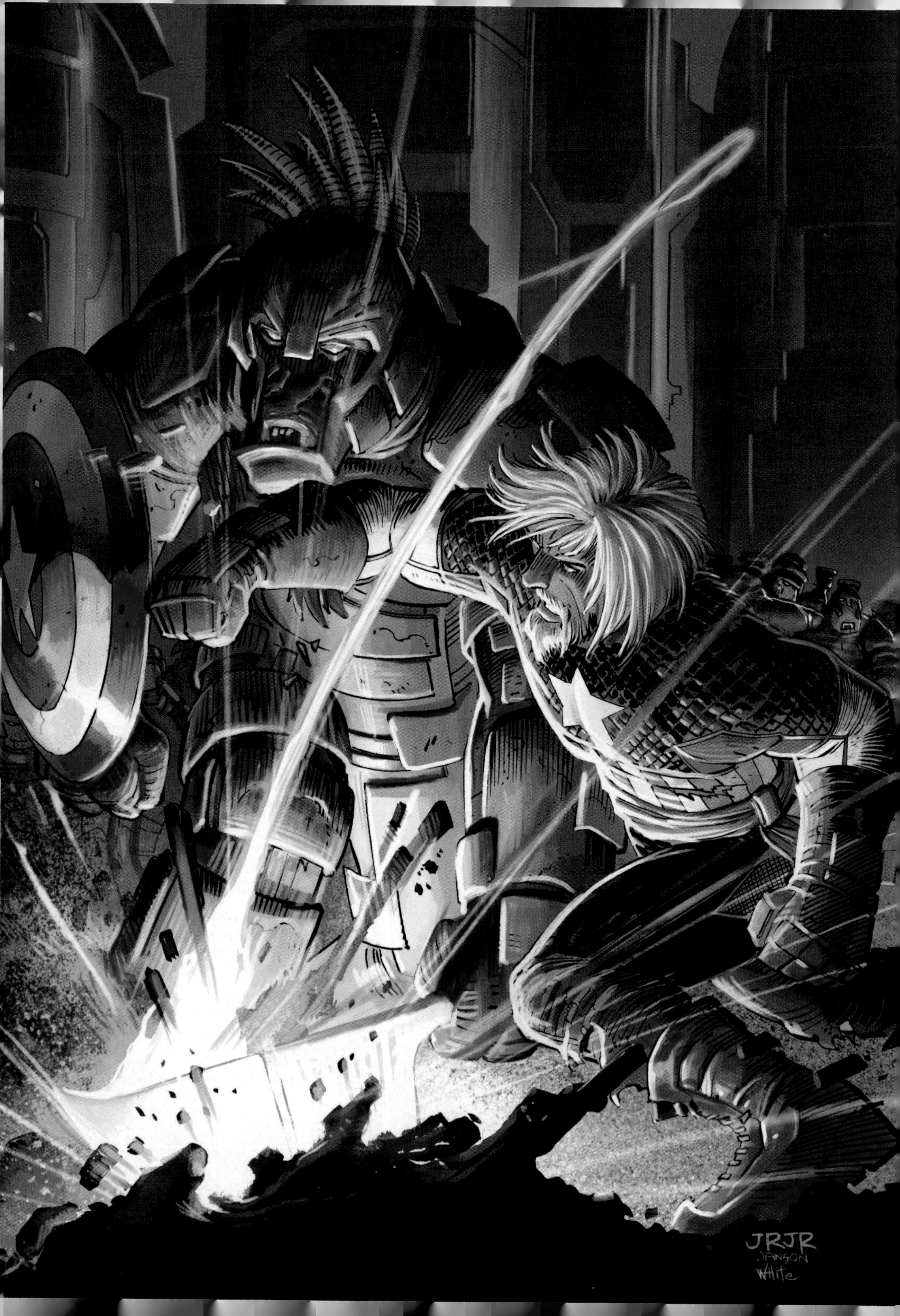
JRJR
JANSON
WHITE

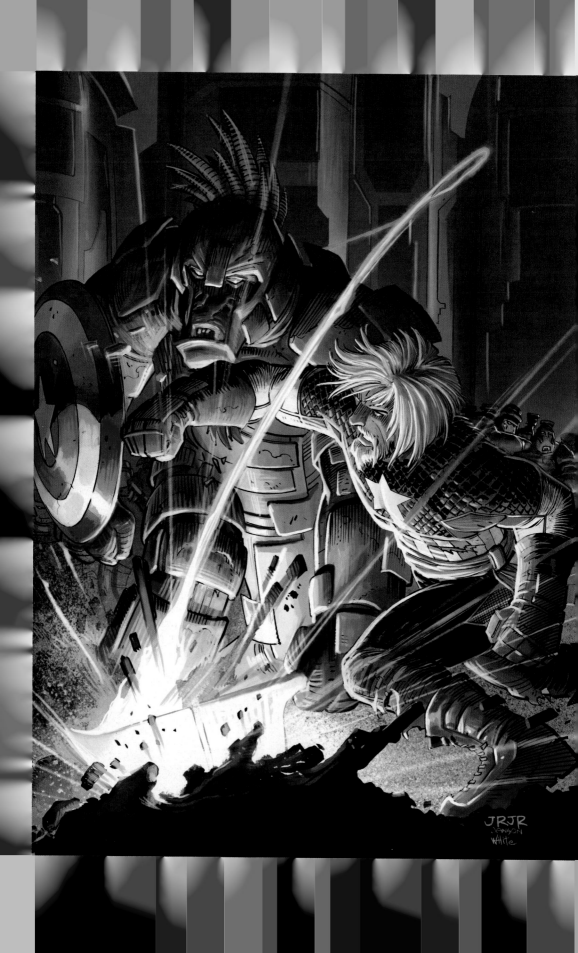

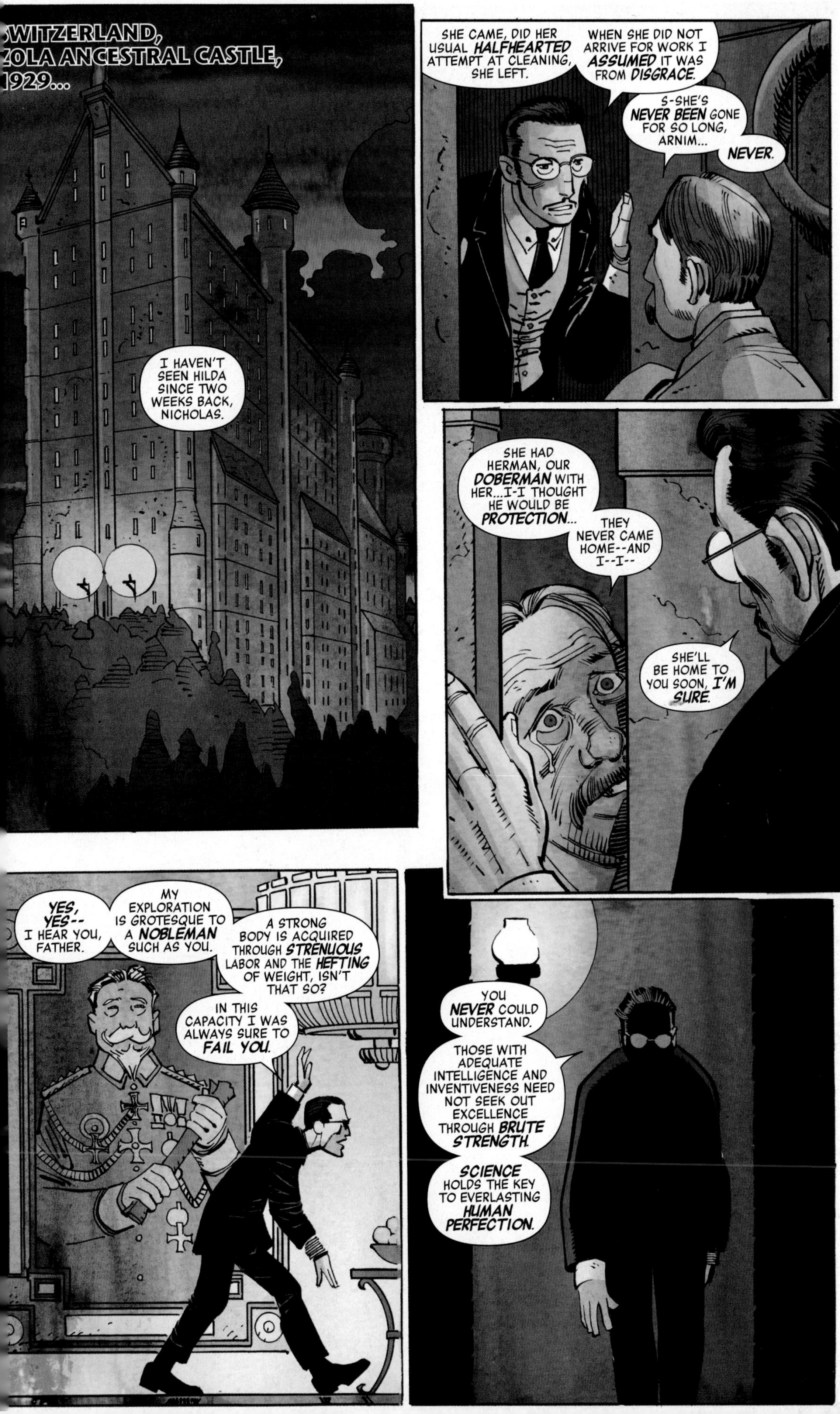
SWITZERLAND, ZOLA ANCESTRAL CASTLE, 1929...
I HAVEN'T SEEN HILDA SINCE TWO WEEKS BACK, NICHOLAS.
SHE CAME, DID HER USUAL HALFHEARTED ATTEMPT AT CLEANING, SHE LEFT.
WHEN SHE DID NOT ARRIVE FOR WORK I ASSUMED IT WAS FROM DISGRACE.
S-SHE'S NEVER BEEN GONE FOR SO LONG, ARNIM...
NEVER.
SHE HAD HERMAN, OUR DOBERMAN WITH HER...I-I THOUGHT HE WOULD BE PROTECTION...
THEY NEVER CAME HOME--AND I--I--
SHE'LL BE HOME TO YOU SOON, I'M SURE.
YES, YES-- I HEAR YOU, FATHER.
MY EXPLORATION IS GROTESQUE TO A NOBLEMAN SUCH AS YOU.
A STRONG BODY IS ACQUIRED THROUGH STRENUOUS LABOR AND THE HEFTING OF WEIGHT, ISN'T THAT SO?
IN THIS CAPACITY I WAS ALWAYS SURE TO FAIL YOU.
YOU NEVER COULD UNDERSTAND.
THOSE WITH ADEQUATE INTELLIGENCE AND INVENTIVENESS NEED NOT SEEK OUT EXCELLENCE THROUGH BRUTE STRENGTH.
SCIENCE HOLDS THE KEY TO EVERLASTING HUMAN PERFECTION.

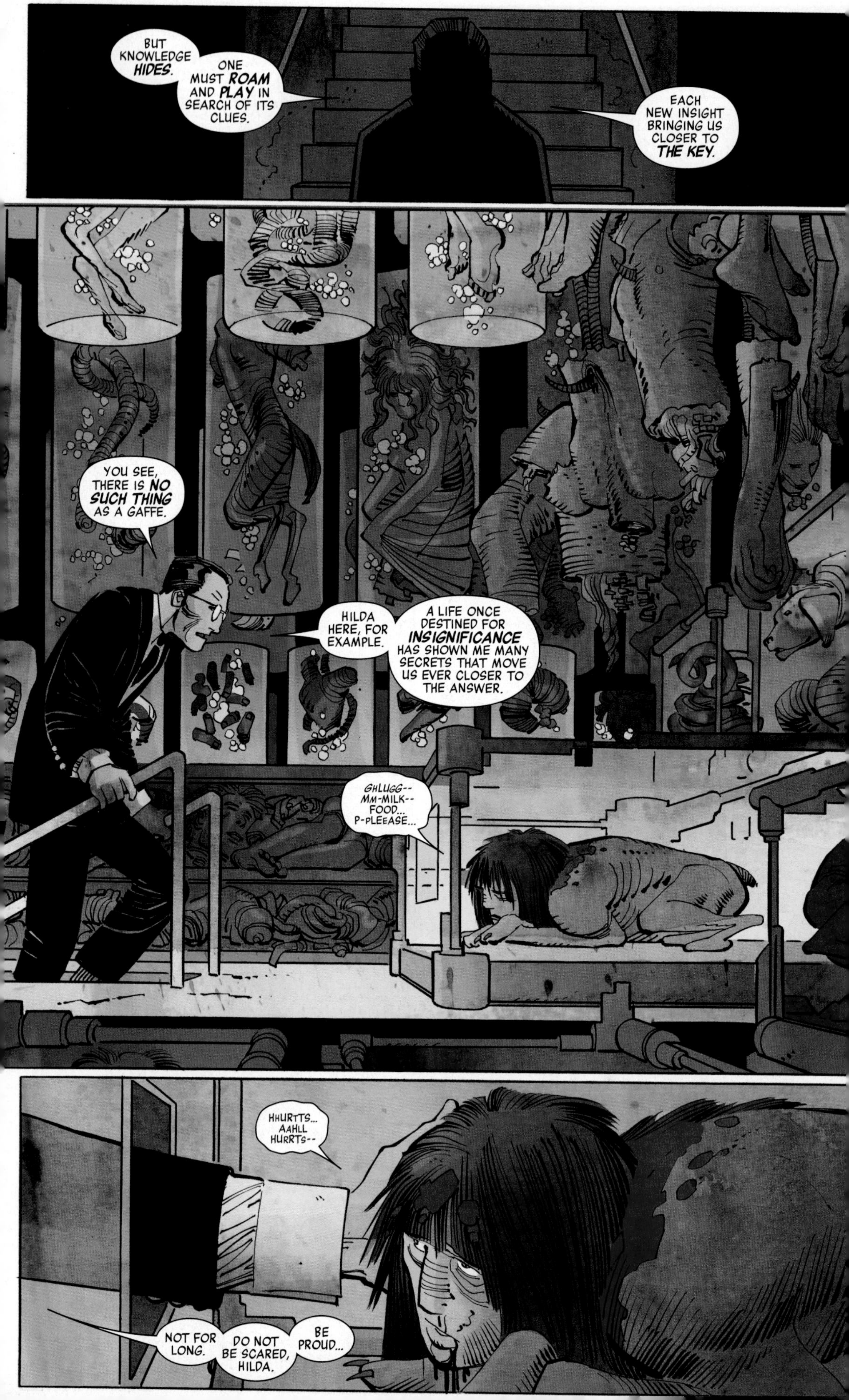
BUT KNOWLEDGE HIDES.
ONE MUST ROAM AND PLAY IN SEARCH OF ITS CLUES.
EACH NEW INSIGHT BRINGING US CLOSER TO THE KEY.
YOU SEE, THERE IS NO SUCH THING AS A GAFFE.
HILDA HERE, FOR EXAMPLE.
A LIFE ONCE DESTINED FOR INSIGNIFICANCE HAS SHOWN ME MANY SECRETS THAT MOVE US EVER CLOSER TO THE ANSWER.
GHLUGG-- MM-MILK-- FOOD... P-PLEEASE...
HHURTTS... AAHLL HURRTS--
NOT FOR LONG.
DO NOT BE SCARED, HILDA.
BE PROUD...

...YOU ARE A **LINK** TO MANKIND'S **"PERFECT"** FUTURE."

I'M **NOT** READY, FATHER.

YOU WERE **BORN** READY. YOU ARE A **PERFECT** PHYSICAL SPECIMEN.

THIS SUIT-- IT'S **SO** UNCOMFORTABLE...

WITHOUT IT YOU WOULD BE A GOOD DEAL **MORE** UNCOMFORTABLE.

IT DAMPENS YOUR WONDERFULLY HEIGHTENED **OMNISENSES**, JET.

ONCE YOU MASTER THESE GIFTS YOU WILL NO LONGER NEED THE SUIT.

AND YOU WILL SEE TO THE **STARS** AND HEAR TO THE **HEAVENS**, MY BEAUTY.

NOW GO, EXCEL AT THE TRIALS.

SHOW YOUR FATHER YOU'RE **PREPARED**.

FOR **WHAT**, FATHER?

FOR **WHAT** DO I PREPARE?

FOR THE **WRETCHED EVIL** THAT AWAITS US ALL.

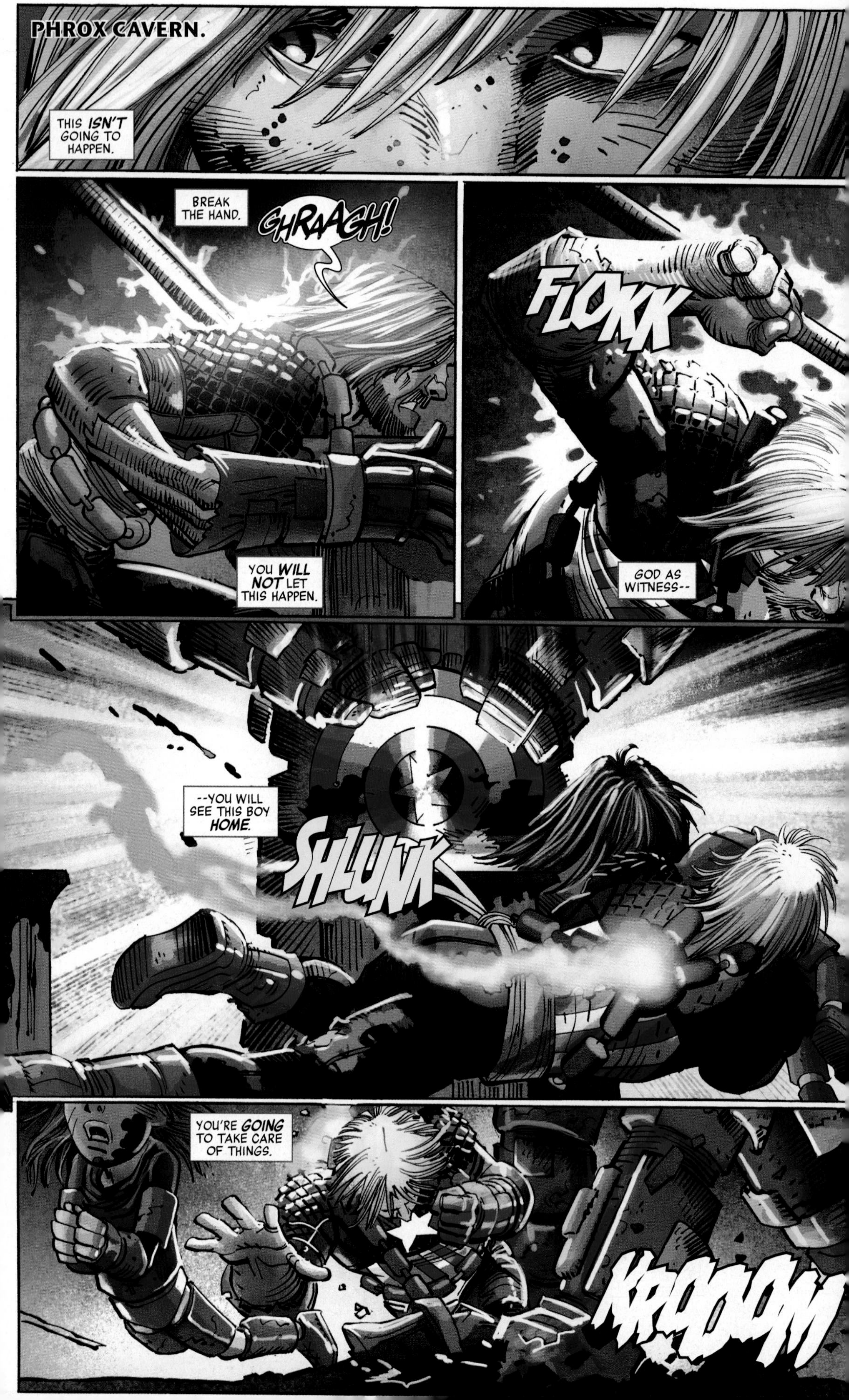
PHROX CAVERN.
THIS ISN'T GOING TO HAPPEN.
BREAK THE HAND.
GHRAAGH!
YOU WILL NOT LET THIS HAPPEN.
FLOKK
GOD AS WITNESS--
--YOU WILL SEE THIS BOY HOME.
SHLUNK
YOU'RE GOING TO TAKE CARE OF THINGS.
KROOOM

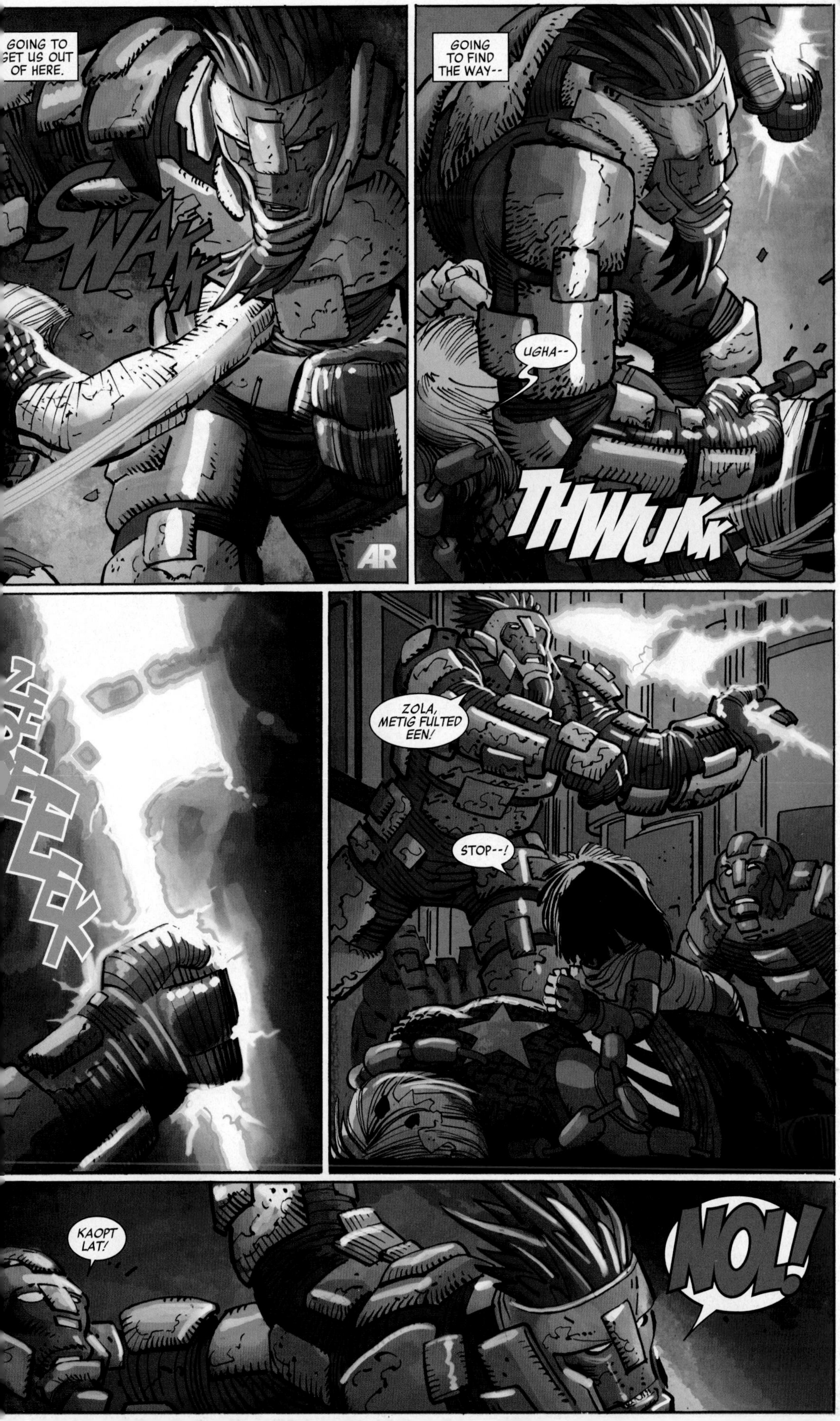

GOING TO GET US OUT OF HERE.
SWAKK
GOING TO FIND THE WAY--
UGHA--
THWUKK
ZOLA, METIG FULTED EEN!
STOP--!
KAOPT LAT!
NO!

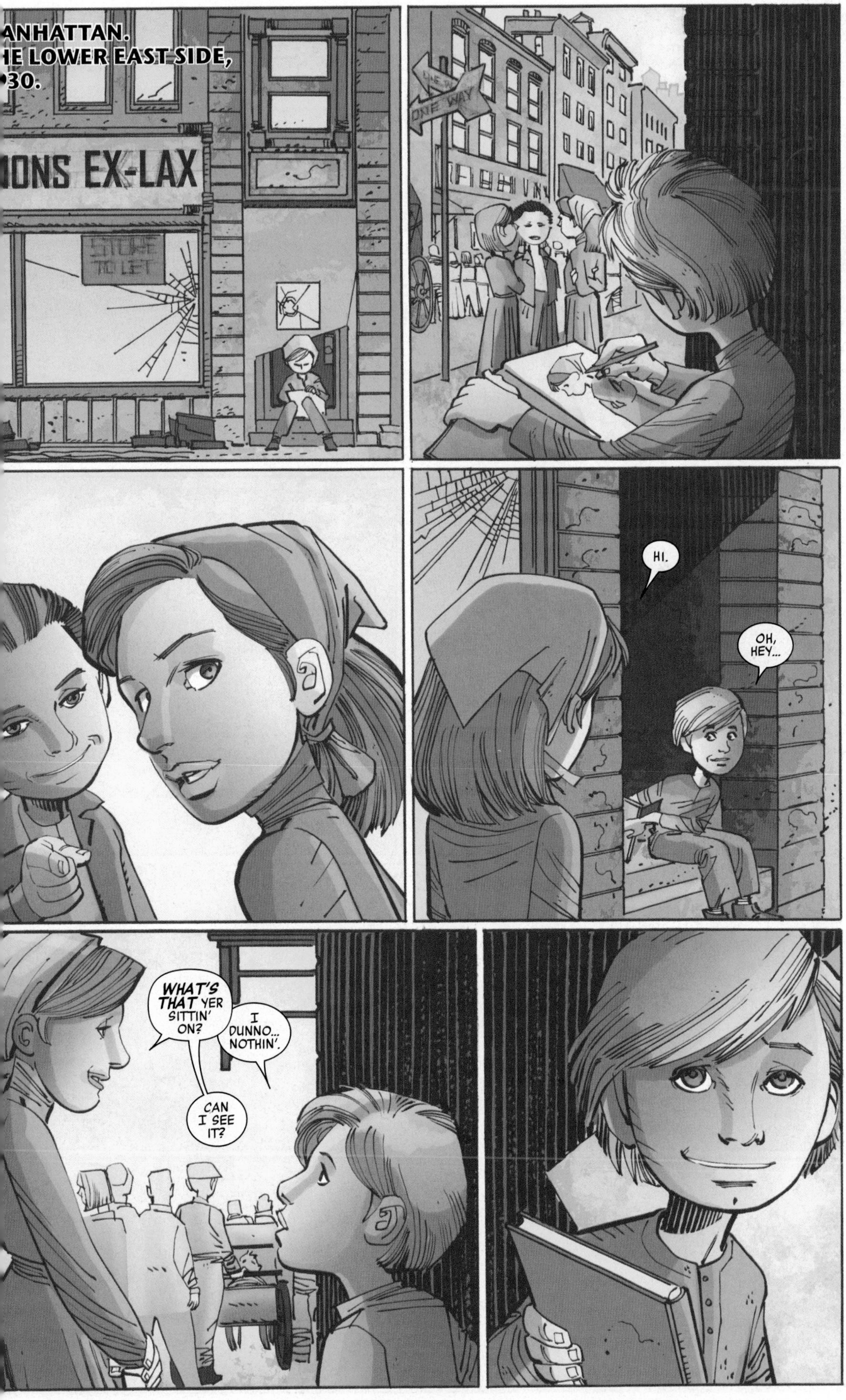
ANHATTAN.
HE LOWER EAST SIDE,
930.
IONS EX-LAX
STORE TO LET
ONE WAY
HI.
OH, HEY...
WHAT'S THAT YER SITTIN' ON?
I DUNNO... NOTHIN'.
CAN I SEE IT?

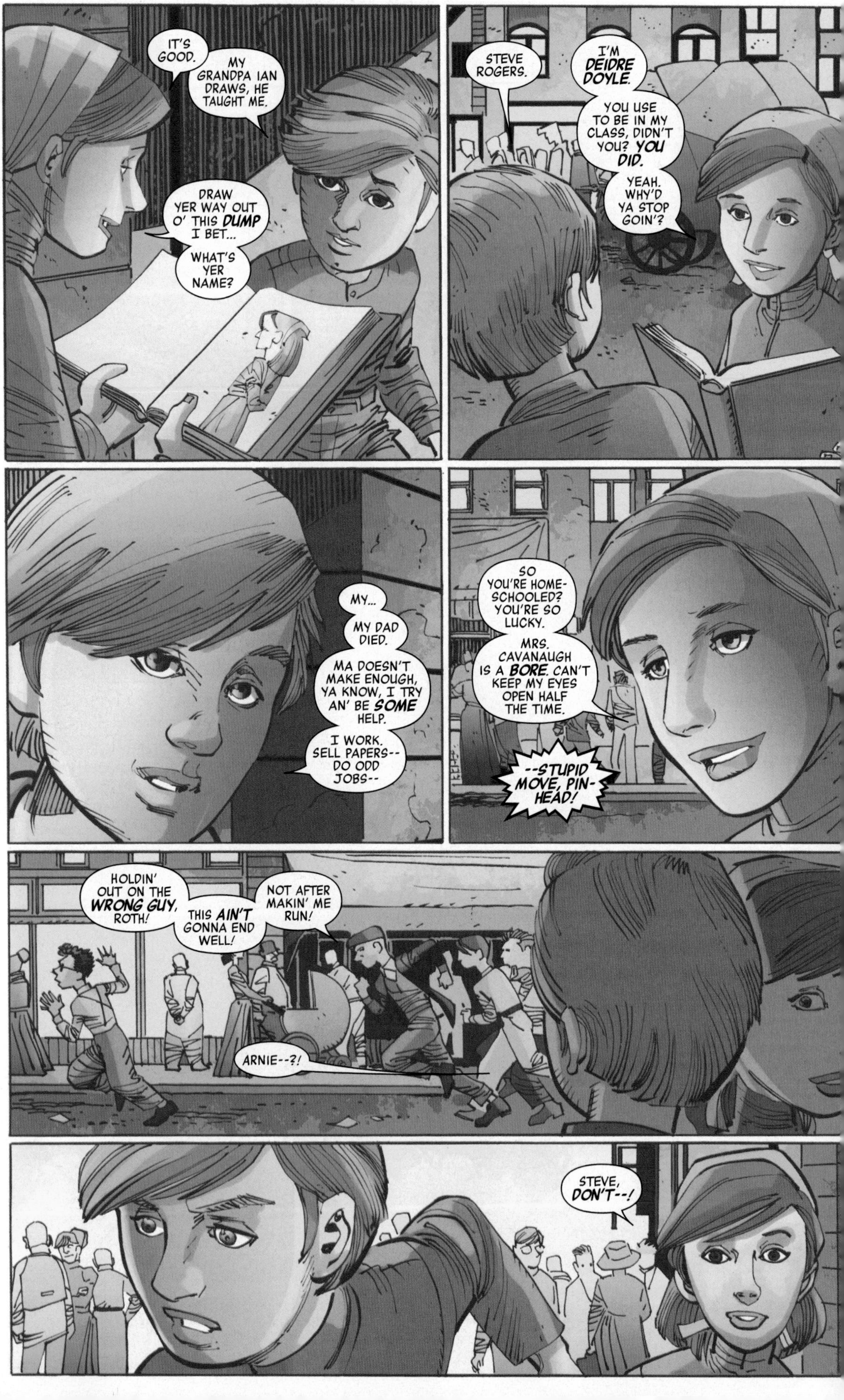

IT'S GOOD.
MY GRANDPA IAN DRAWS, HE TAUGHT ME.
DRAW YER WAY OUT O' THIS DUMP I BET...
WHAT'S YER NAME?
STEVE ROGERS.
I'M DEIDRE DOYLE.
YOU USE TO BE IN MY CLASS, DIDN'T YOU? YOU DID.
YEAH. WHY'D YA STOP GOIN'?
MY...
MY DAD DIED.
MA DOESN'T MAKE ENOUGH, YA KNOW, I TRY AN' BE SOME HELP.
I WORK. SELL PAPERS-- DO ODD JOBS--
SO YOU'RE HOME-SCHOOLED? YOU'RE SO LUCKY.
MRS. CAVANAUGH IS A BORE. CAN'T KEEP MY EYES OPEN HALF THE TIME.
--STUPID MOVE, PIN-HEAD!
HOLDIN' OUT ON THE WRONG GUY, ROTH!
THIS AIN'T GONNA END WELL!
NOT AFTER MAKIN' ME RUN!
ARNIE--?!
STEVE, DON'T--!

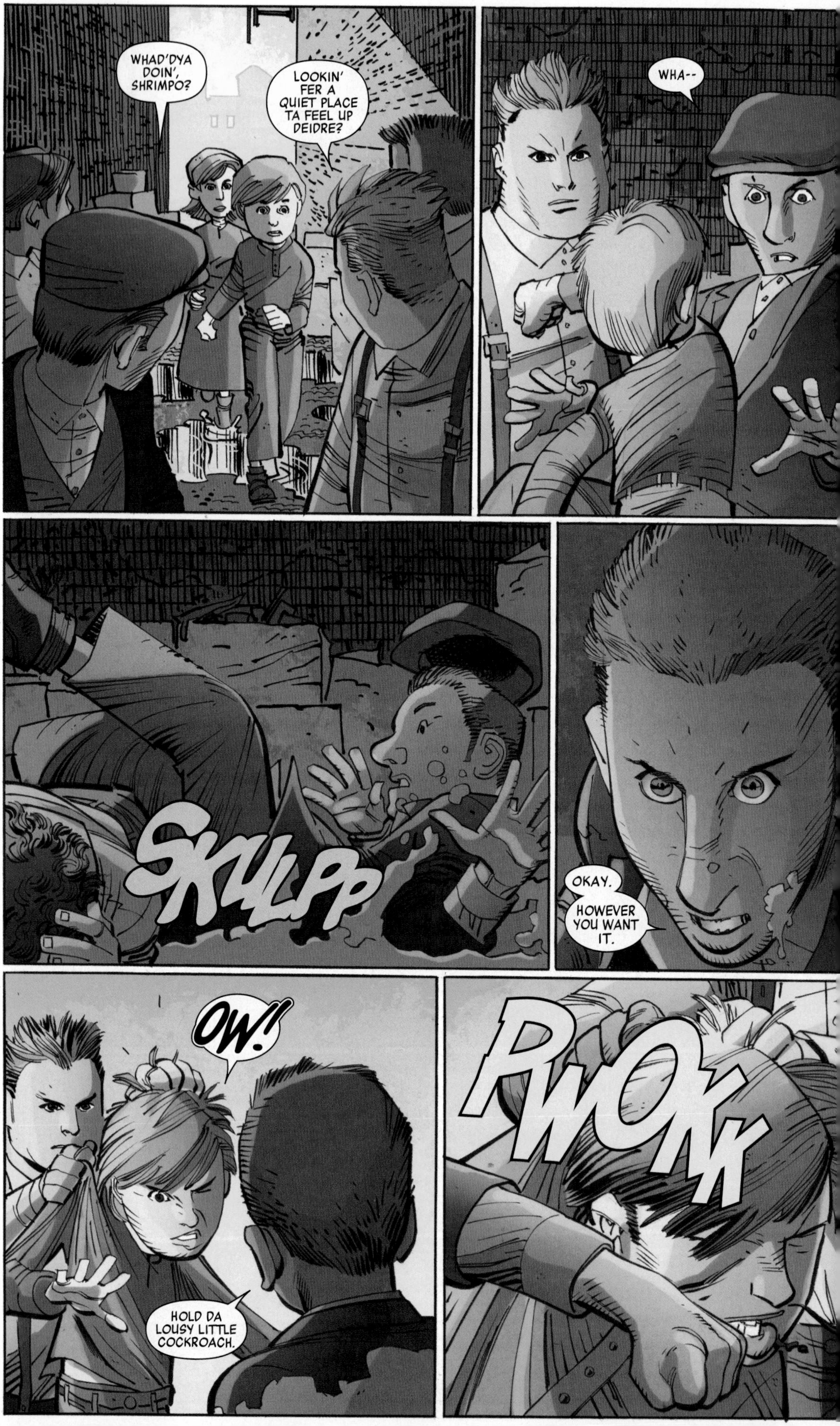
WHAD'DYA DOIN', SHRIMPO?
LOOKIN' FER A QUIET PLACE TA FEEL UP DEIDRE?
WHA--
SKULPP
OKAY. HOWEVER YOU WANT IT.
OW!
HOLD DA LOUSY LITTLE COCKROACH.
PWONK

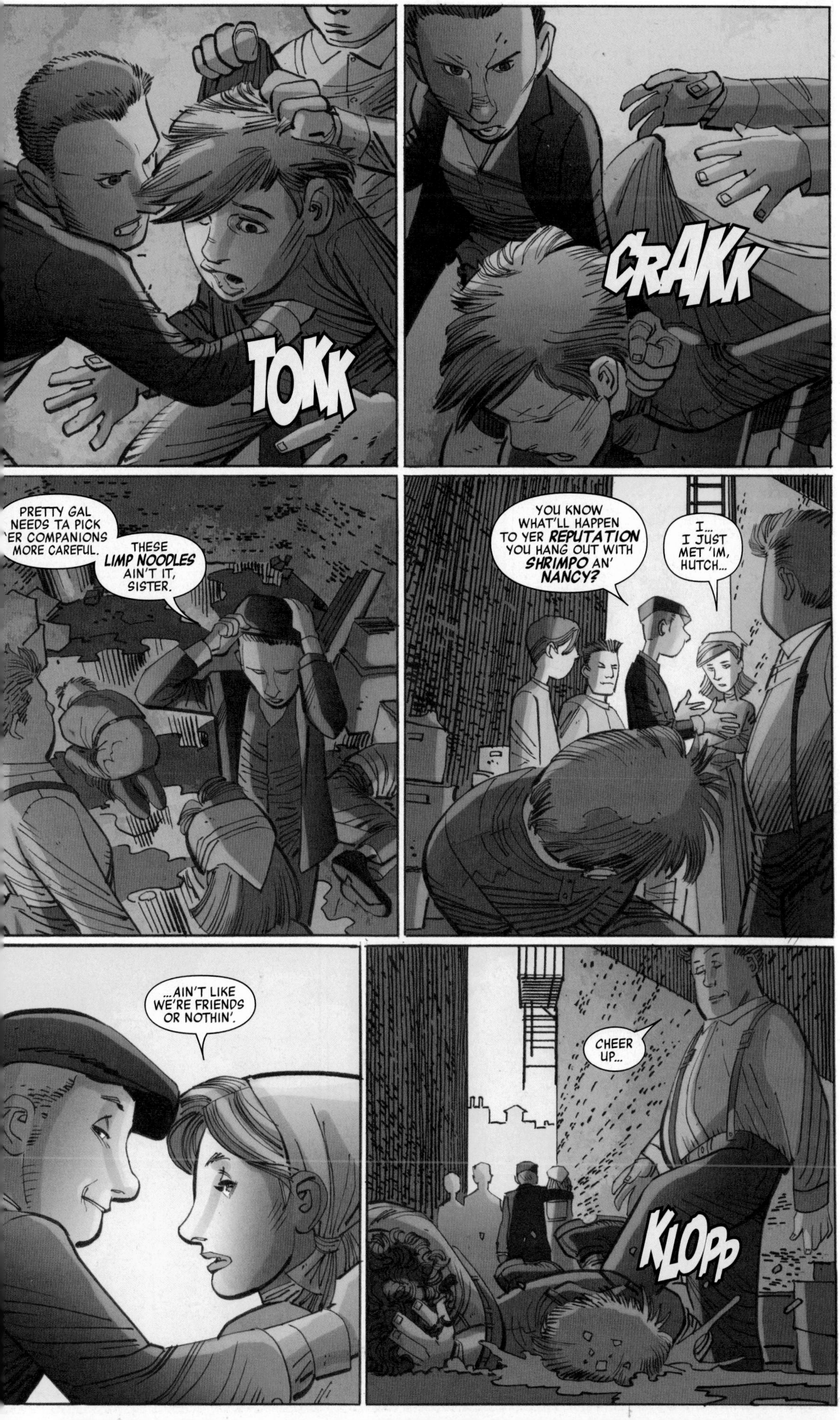
TOKK
CRAKK
PRETTY GAL NEEDS TA PICK 'ER COMPANIONS MORE CAREFUL.
THESE LIMP NOODLES AIN'T IT, SISTER.
YOU KNOW WHAT'LL HAPPEN TO YER REPUTATION YOU HANG OUT WITH SHRIMPO AN' NANCY?
I... I JUST MET 'IM, HUTCH...
...AIN'T LIKE WE'RE FRIENDS OR NOTHIN'.
CHEER UP...
KLOPP

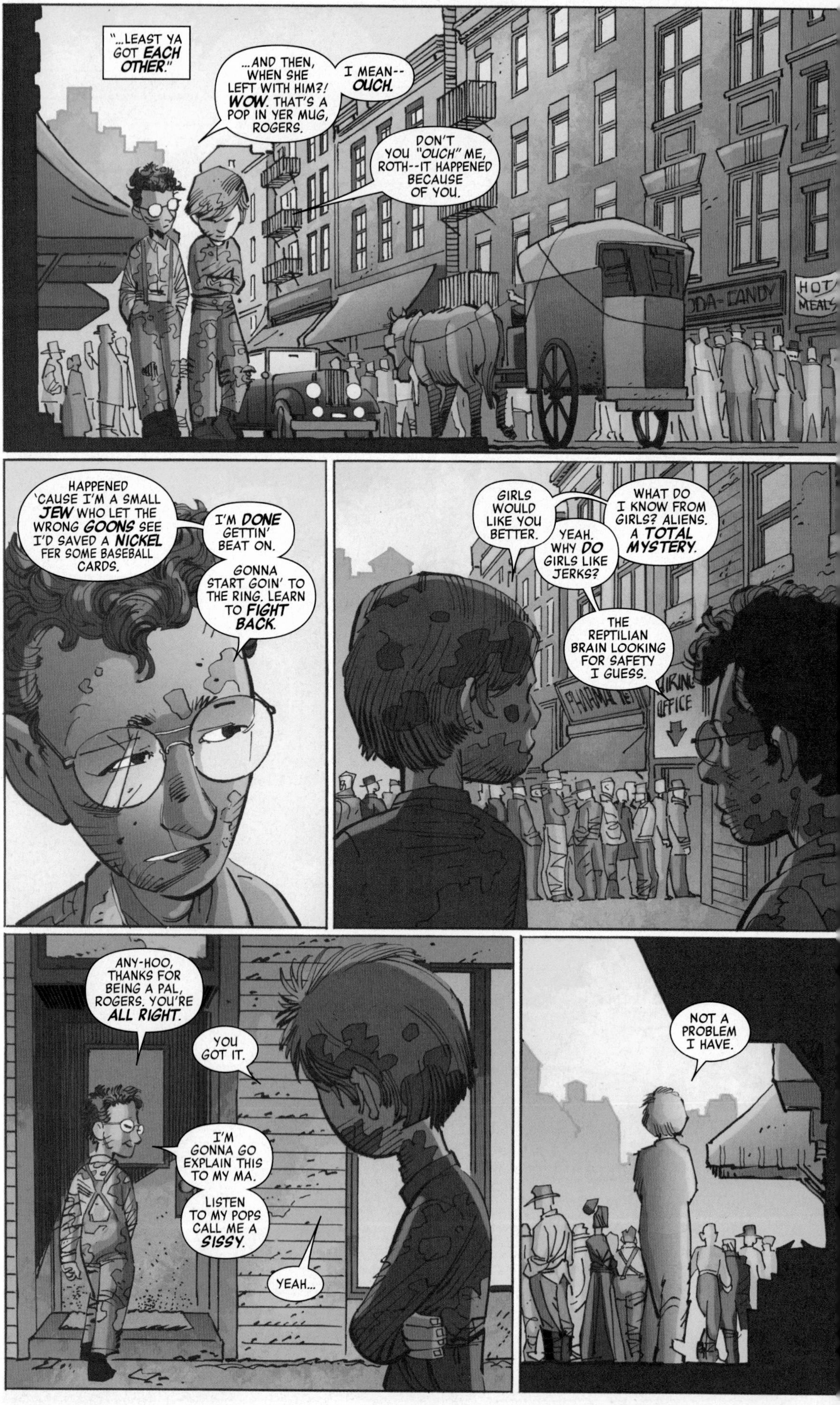
"...LEAST YA GOT EACH OTHER."
...AND THEN, WHEN SHE LEFT WITH HIM?! WOW. THAT'S A POP IN YER MUG, ROGERS.
I MEAN-- OUCH.
DON'T YOU "OUCH" ME, ROTH--IT HAPPENED BECAUSE OF YOU.
ODA-CANDY
HOT MEALS
HAPPENED 'CAUSE I'M A SMALL JEW WHO LET THE WRONG GOONS SEE I'D SAVED A NICKEL FER SOME BASEBALL CARDS.
I'M DONE GETTIN' BEAT ON.
GONNA START GOIN' TO THE RING. LEARN TO FIGHT BACK.
GIRLS WOULD LIKE YOU BETTER.
WHAT DO I KNOW FROM GIRLS? ALIENS. A TOTAL MYSTERY.
YEAH. WHY DO GIRLS LIKE JERKS?
THE REPTILIAN BRAIN LOOKING FOR SAFETY I GUESS.
OFFICE
ANY-HOO, THANKS FOR BEING A PAL, ROGERS. YOU'RE ALL RIGHT.
YOU GOT IT.
I'M GONNA GO EXPLAIN THIS TO MY MA.
LISTEN TO MY POPS CALL ME A SISSY.
YEAH...
NOT A PROBLEM I HAVE.

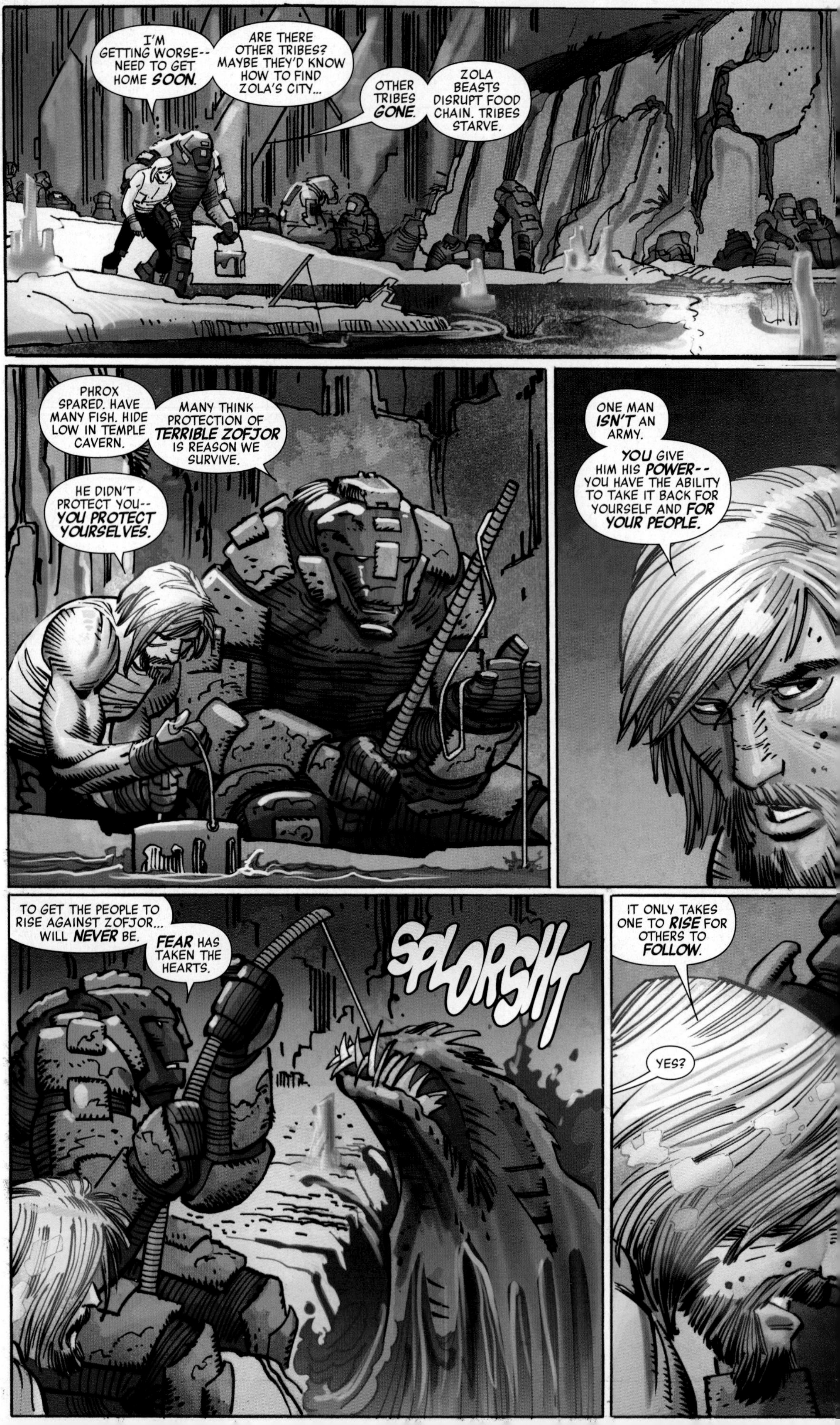

I'M GETTING WORSE-- NEED TO GET HOME SOON.
ARE THERE OTHER TRIBES? MAYBE THEY'D KNOW HOW TO FIND ZOLA'S CITY...
OTHER TRIBES GONE.
ZOLA BEASTS DISRUPT FOOD CHAIN. TRIBES STARVE.
PHROX SPARED. HAVE MANY FISH. HIDE LOW IN TEMPLE CAVERN.
MANY THINK PROTECTION OF TERRIBLE ZOFJOR IS REASON WE SURVIVE.
HE DIDN'T PROTECT YOU-- YOU PROTECT YOURSELVES.
ONE MAN ISN'T AN ARMY.
YOU GIVE HIM HIS POWER-- YOU HAVE THE ABILITY TO TAKE IT BACK FOR YOURSELF AND FOR YOUR PEOPLE.
TO GET THE PEOPLE TO RISE AGAINST ZOFJOR... WILL NEVER BE.
FEAR HAS TAKEN THE HEARTS.
SPLORSHT
IT ONLY TAKES ONE TO RISE FOR OTHERS TO FOLLOW.
YES?

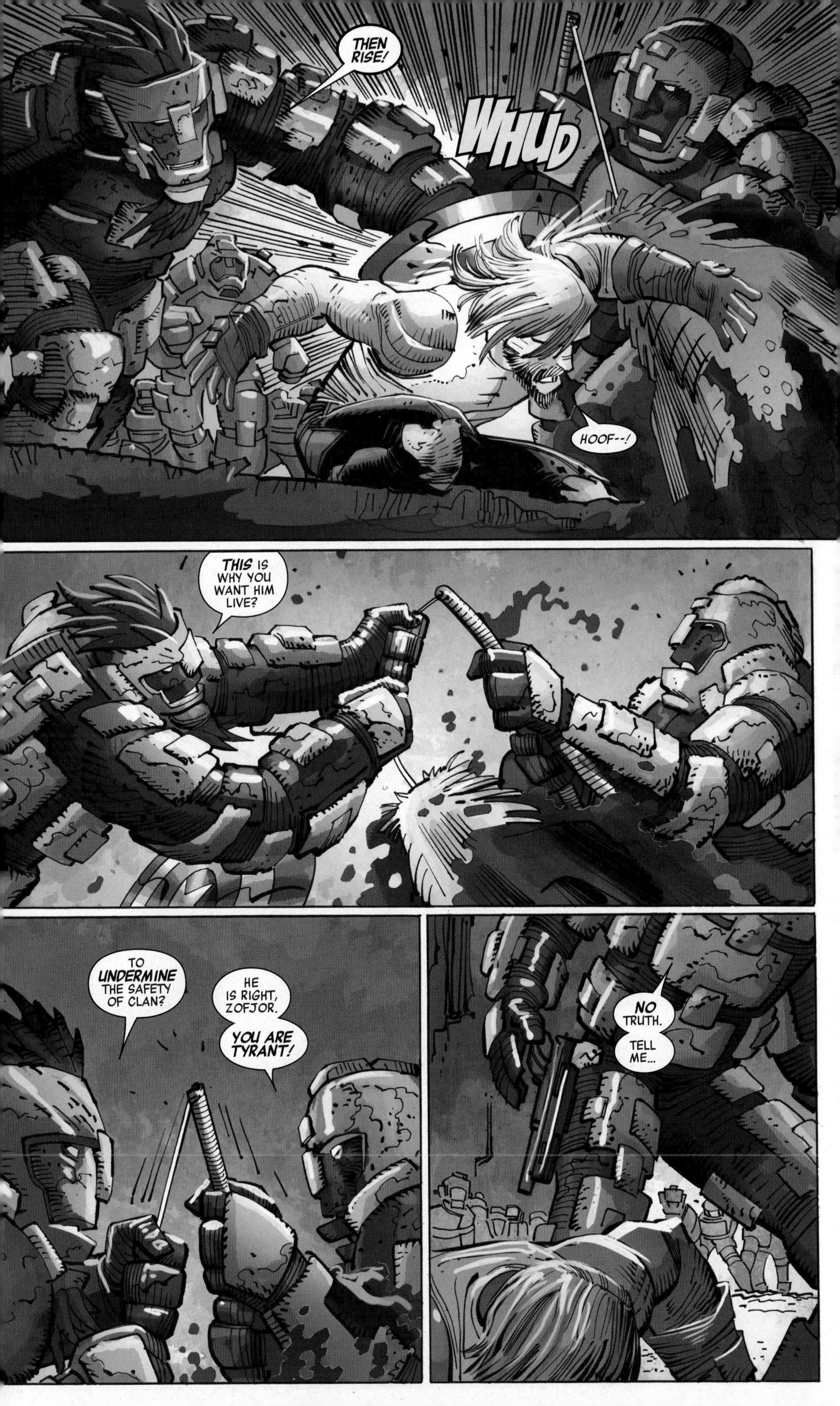
THEN RISE!
WHUD
HOOF--!
THIS IS WHY YOU WANT HIM LIVE?
TO UNDERMINE THE SAFETY OF CLAN?
HE IS RIGHT, ZOFJOR.
YOU ARE TYRANT!
NO TRUTH.
TELL ME...

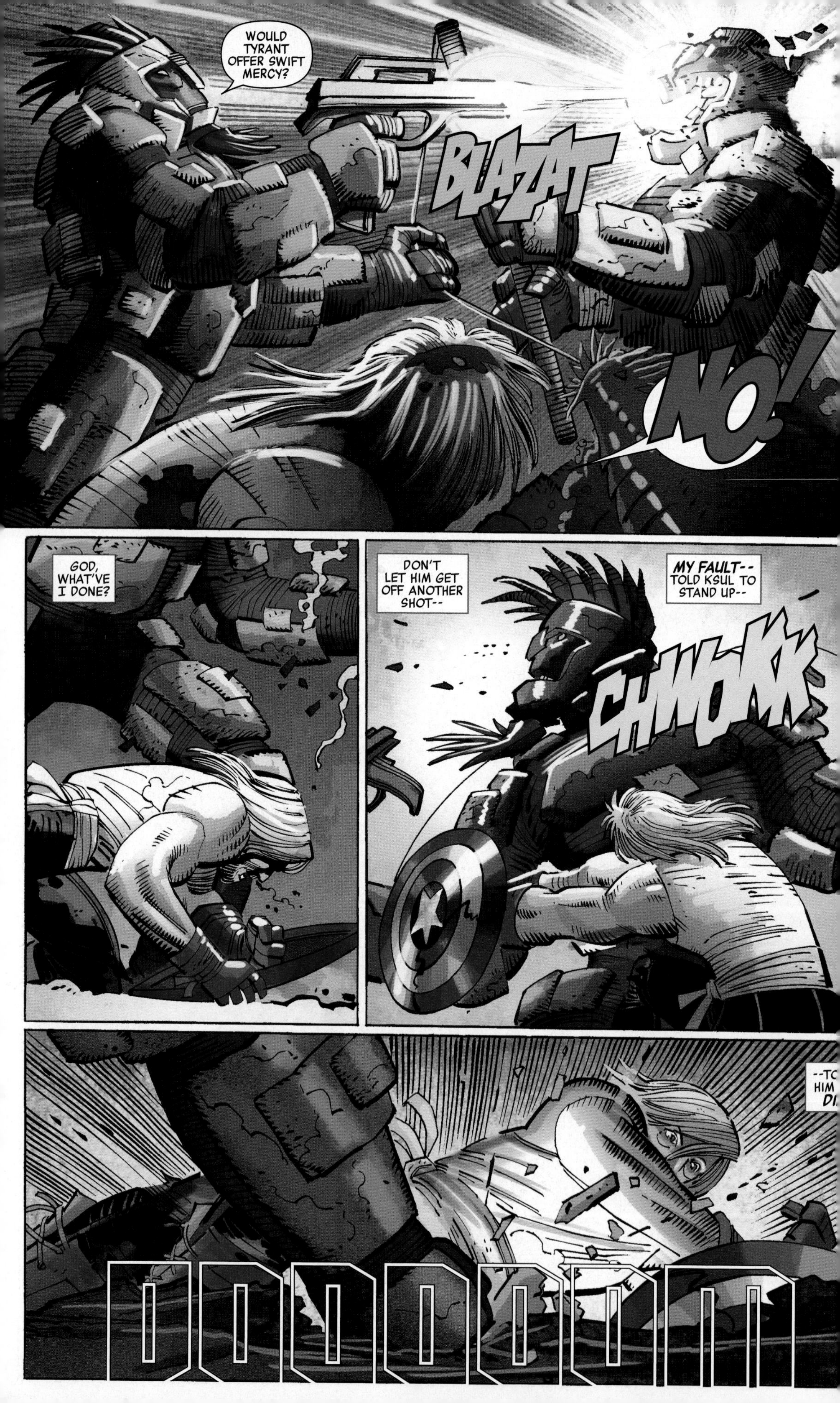
WOULD TYRANT OFFER SWIFT MERCY?
BLAZAT
NO!
GOD, WHAT'VE I DONE?
DON'T LET HIM GET OFF ANOTHER SHOT--
MY FAULT-- TOLD KSUL TO STAND UP--
CHWOKK
DOOOOOM

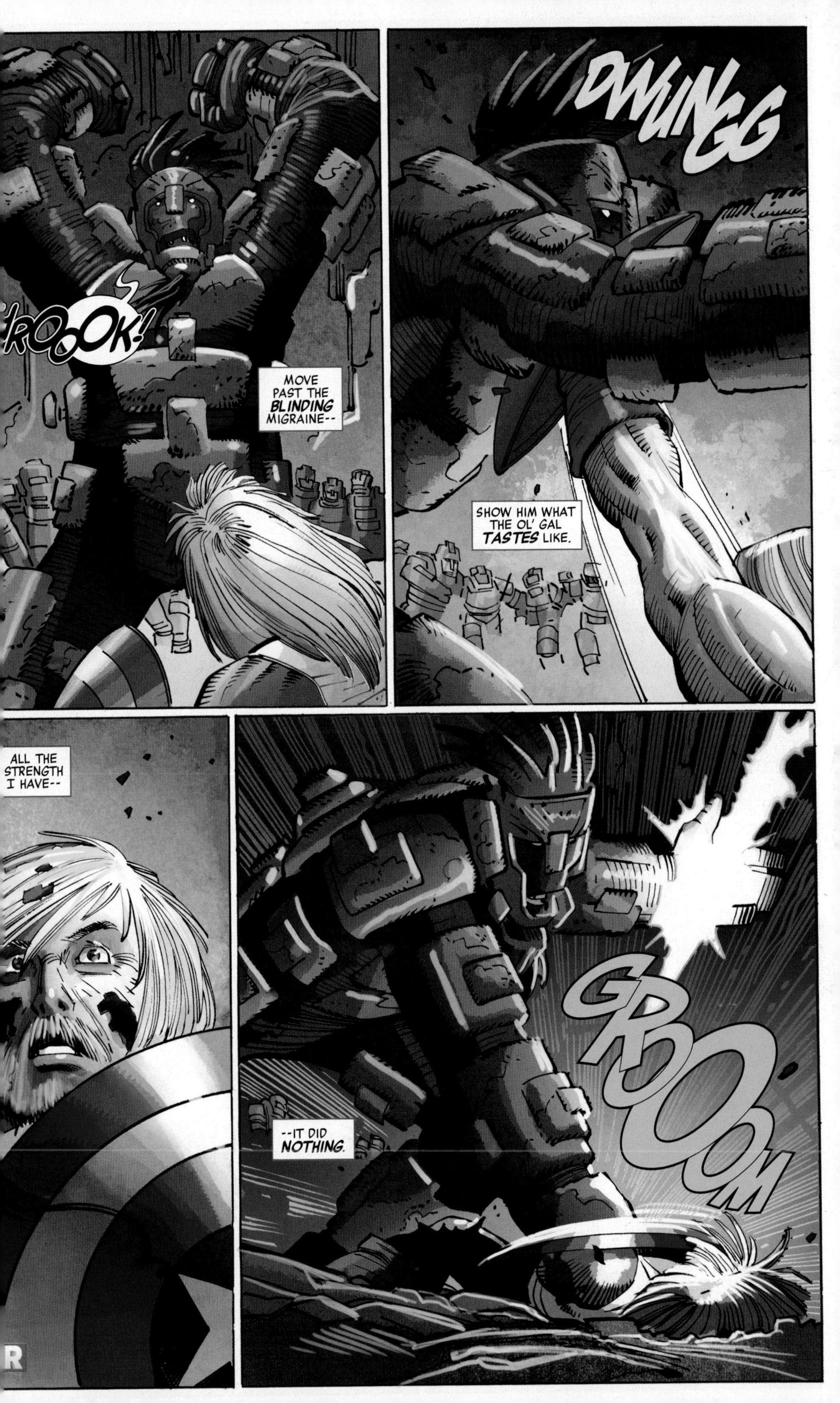
KROOOK!
MOVE PAST THE BLINDING MIGRAINE--
DWUNGG
SHOW HIM WHAT THE OL' GAL TASTES LIKE.
ALL THE STRENGTH I HAVE--
GROOOM
--IT DID NOTHING.

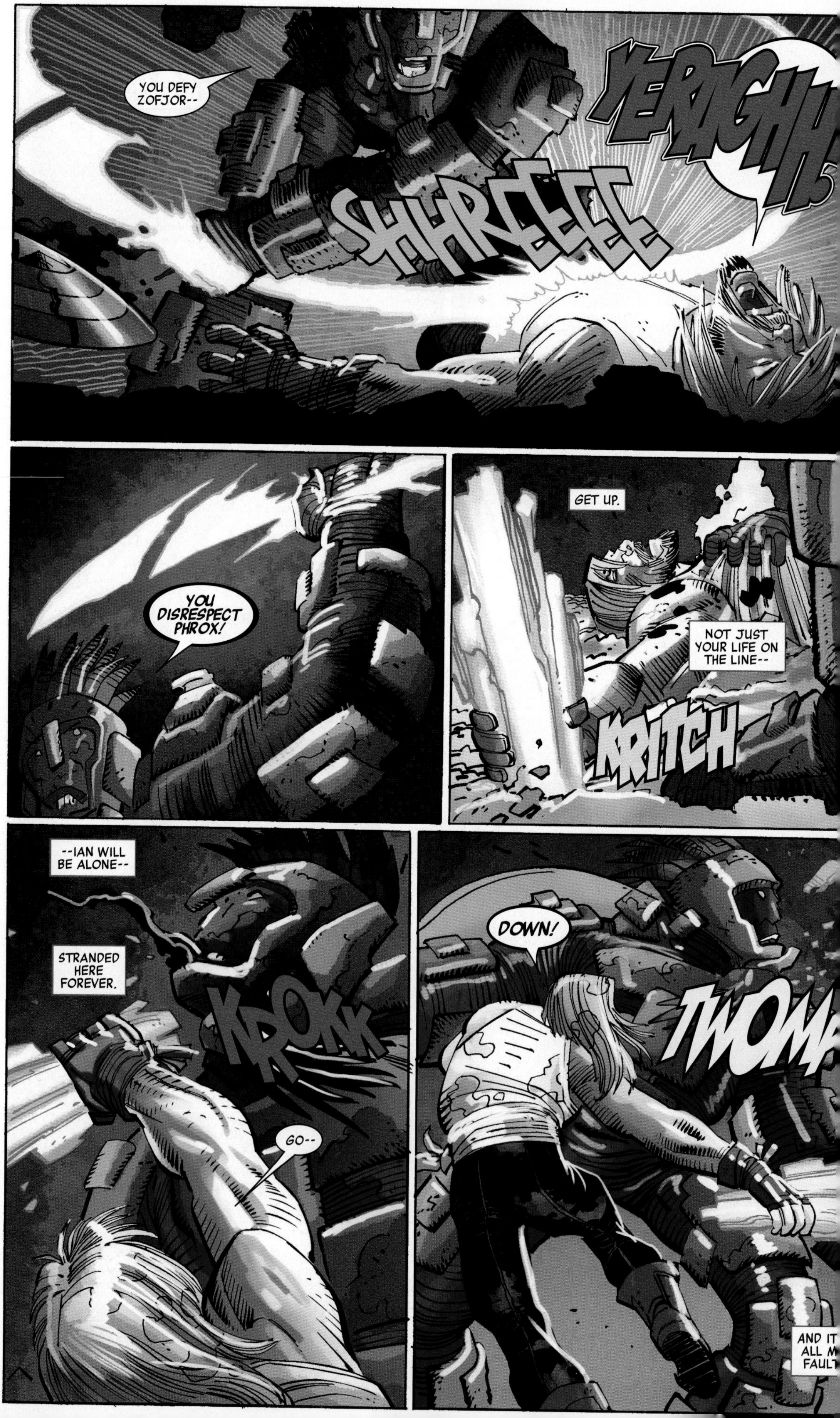

YOU DEFY ZOFJOR--
YERAGHH
SHHREEEE
YOU DISRESPECT PHROX!
GET UP.
NOT JUST YOUR LIFE ON THE LINE--
KRITCH
--IAN WILL BE ALONE--
STRANDED HERE FOREVER.
KROKK
GO--
DOWN!
TWOM

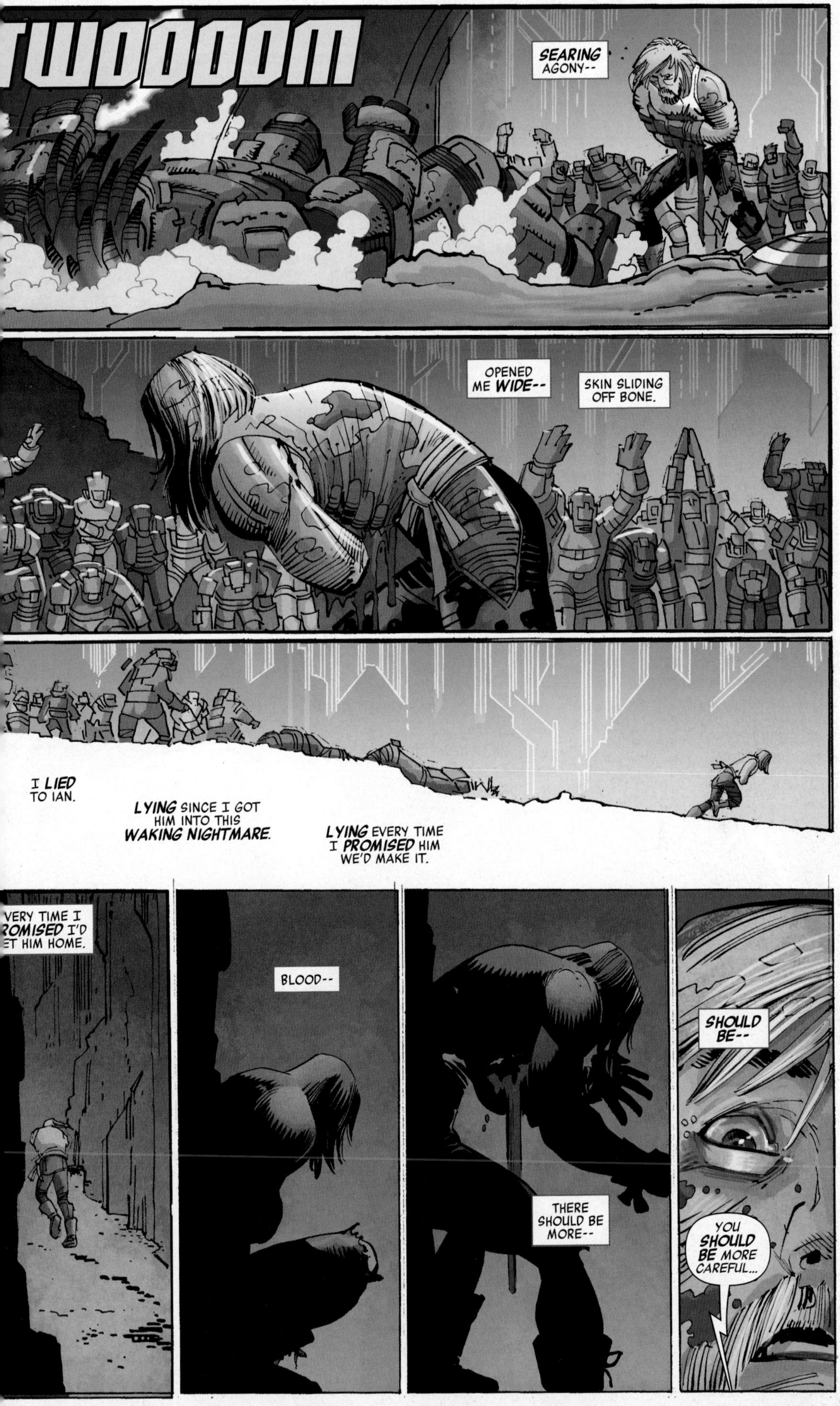
TWOOOOM
SEARING AGONY--
OPENED ME WIDE--
SKIN SLIDING OFF BONE.
I LIED TO IAN.
LYING SINCE I GOT HIM INTO THIS WAKING NIGHTMARE.
LYING EVERY TIME I PROMISED HIM WE'D MAKE IT.
VERY TIME I ROMISED I'D ET HIM HOME.
BLOOD--
THERE SHOULD BE MORE--
SHOULD BE--
YOU SHOULD BE MORE CAREFUL...

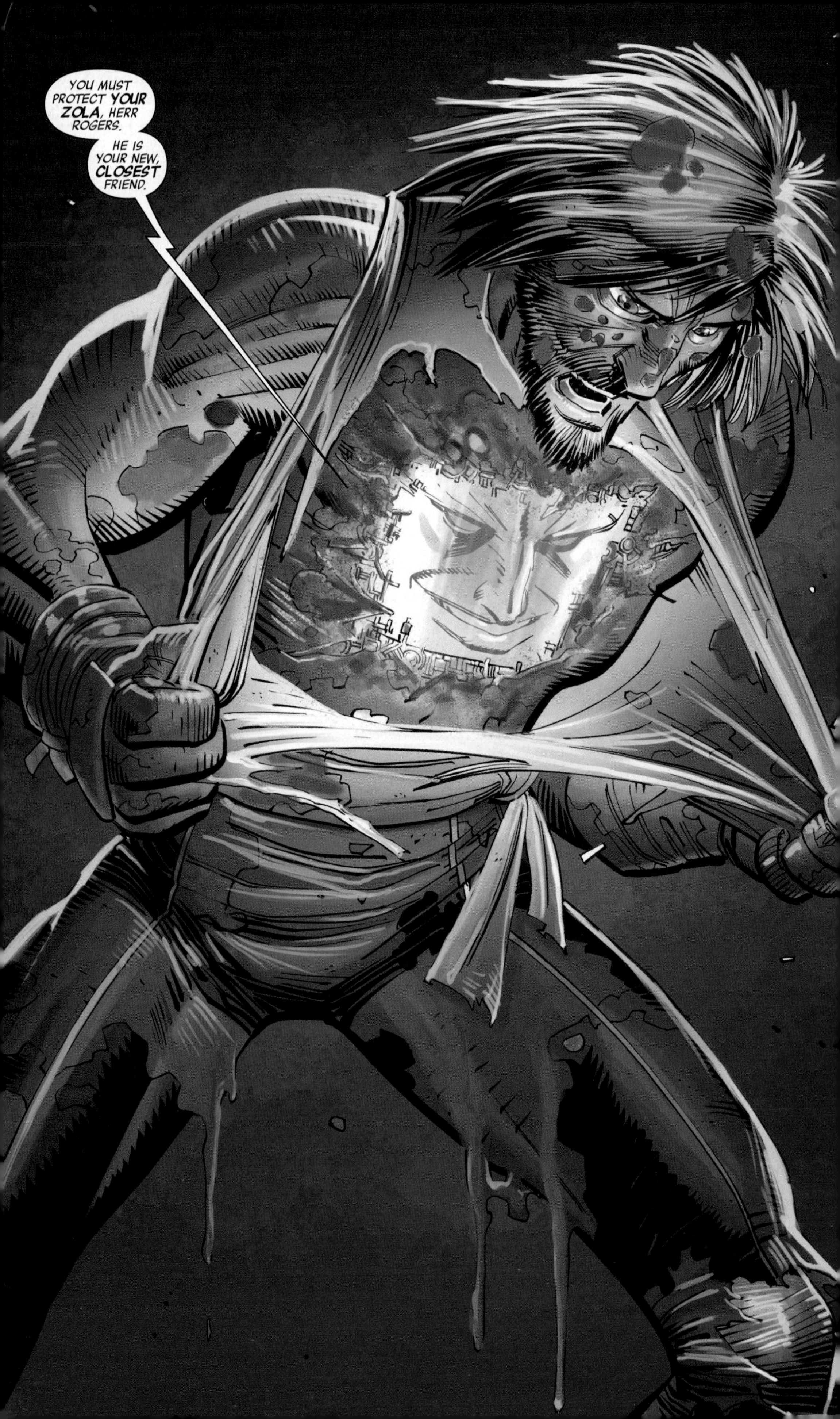
YOU MUST PROTECT YOUR ZOLA, HERR ROGERS.
HE IS YOUR NEW, CLOSEST FRIEND.

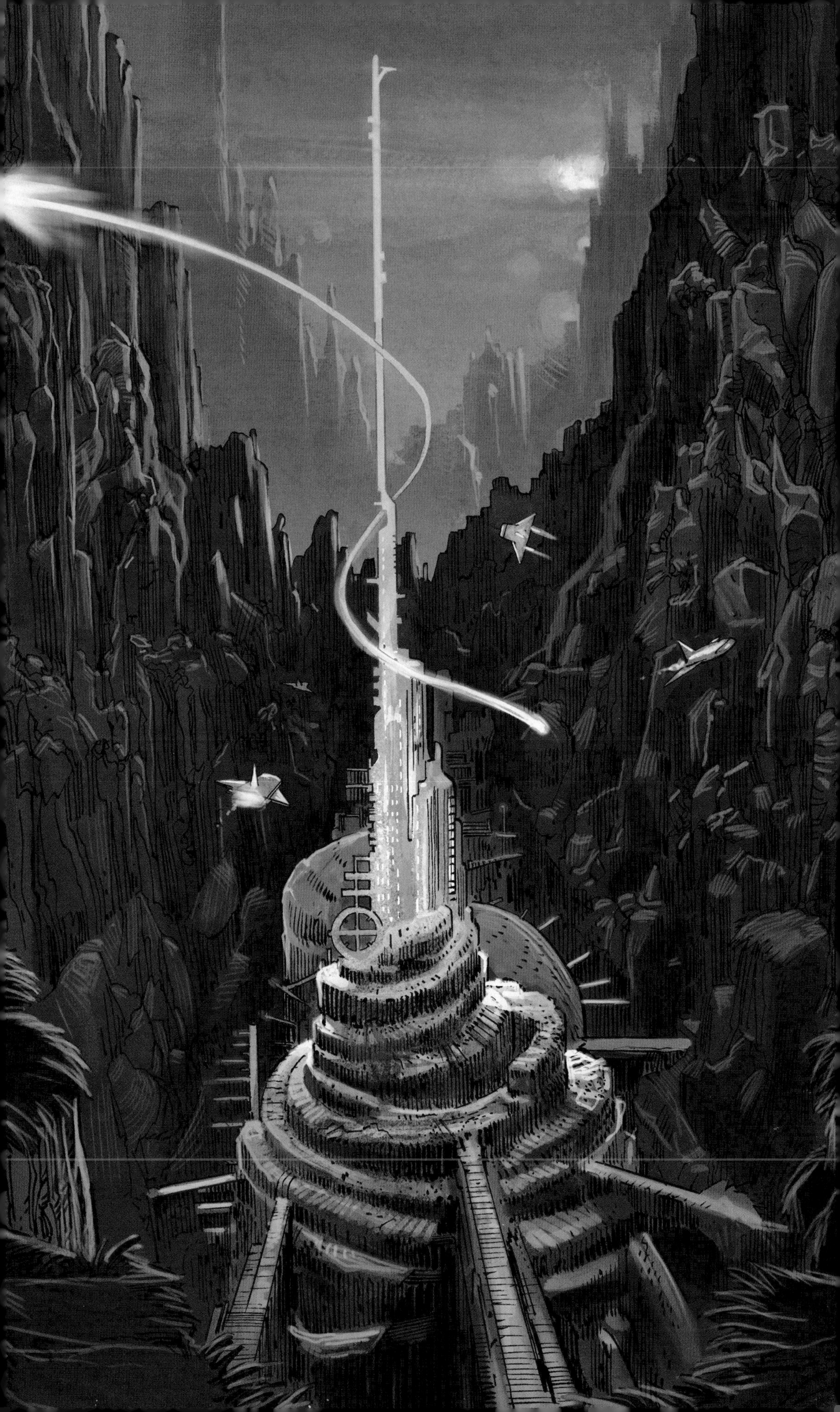

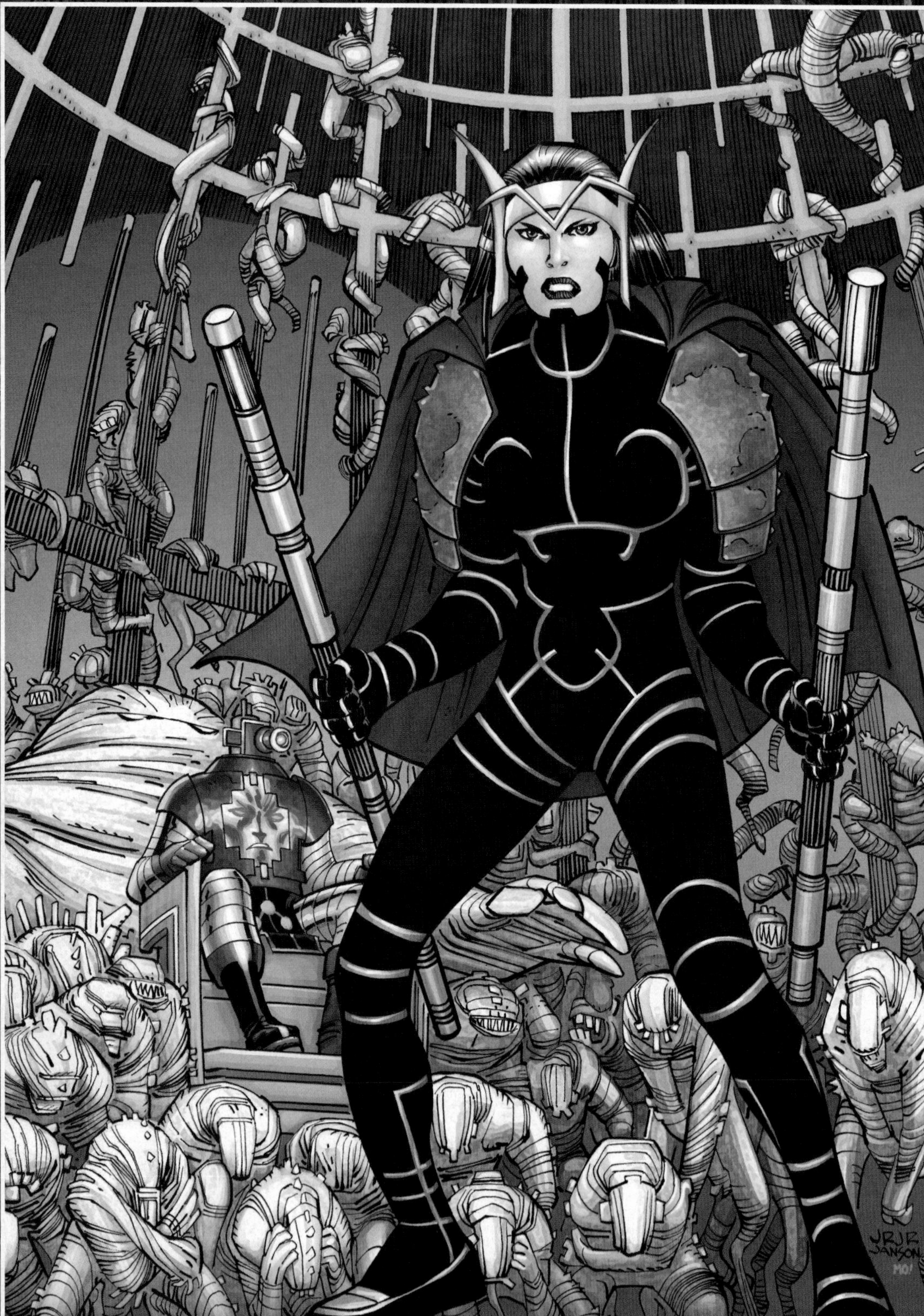
JRJR
JANSON
MO!

FOUR

ELEVEN YEARS LATER.

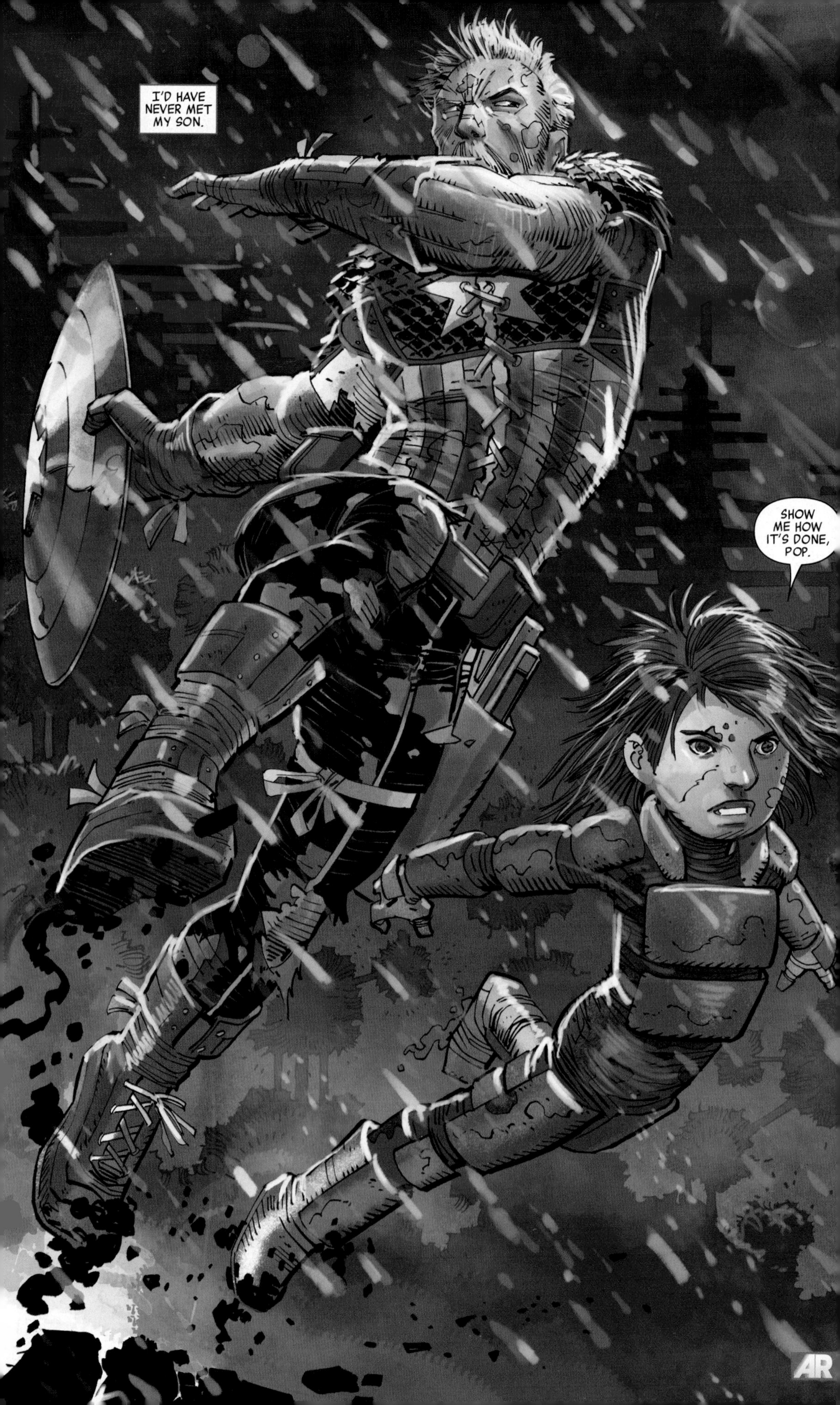
I'D HAVE NEVER MET MY SON.
SHOW ME HOW IT'S DONE, POP.

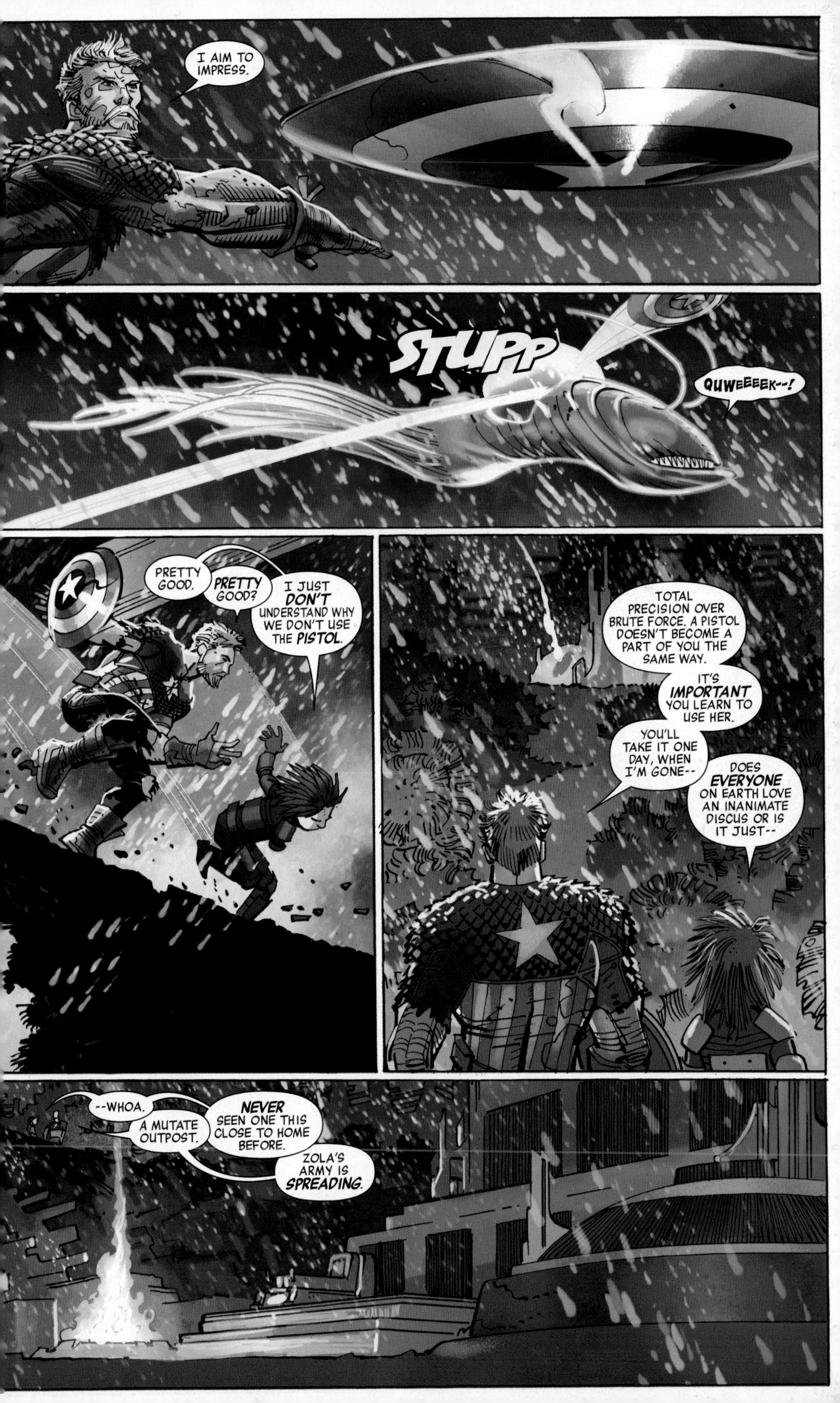

I AIM TO IMPRESS.
STUPP
QUWEEEEK--!
PRETTY GOOD.
PRETTY GOOD?
I JUST DON'T UNDERSTAND WHY WE DON'T USE THE PISTOL.
TOTAL PRECISION OVER BRUTE FORCE. A PISTOL DOESN'T BECOME A PART OF YOU THE SAME WAY.
IT'S IMPORTANT YOU LEARN TO USE HER.
YOU'LL TAKE IT ONE DAY, WHEN I'M GONE--
DOES EVERYONE ON EARTH LOVE AN INANIMATE DISCUS OR IS IT JUST--
--WHOA.
A MUTATE OUTPOST.
NEVER SEEN ONE THIS CLOSE TO HOME BEFORE.
ZOLA'S ARMY IS SPREADING.

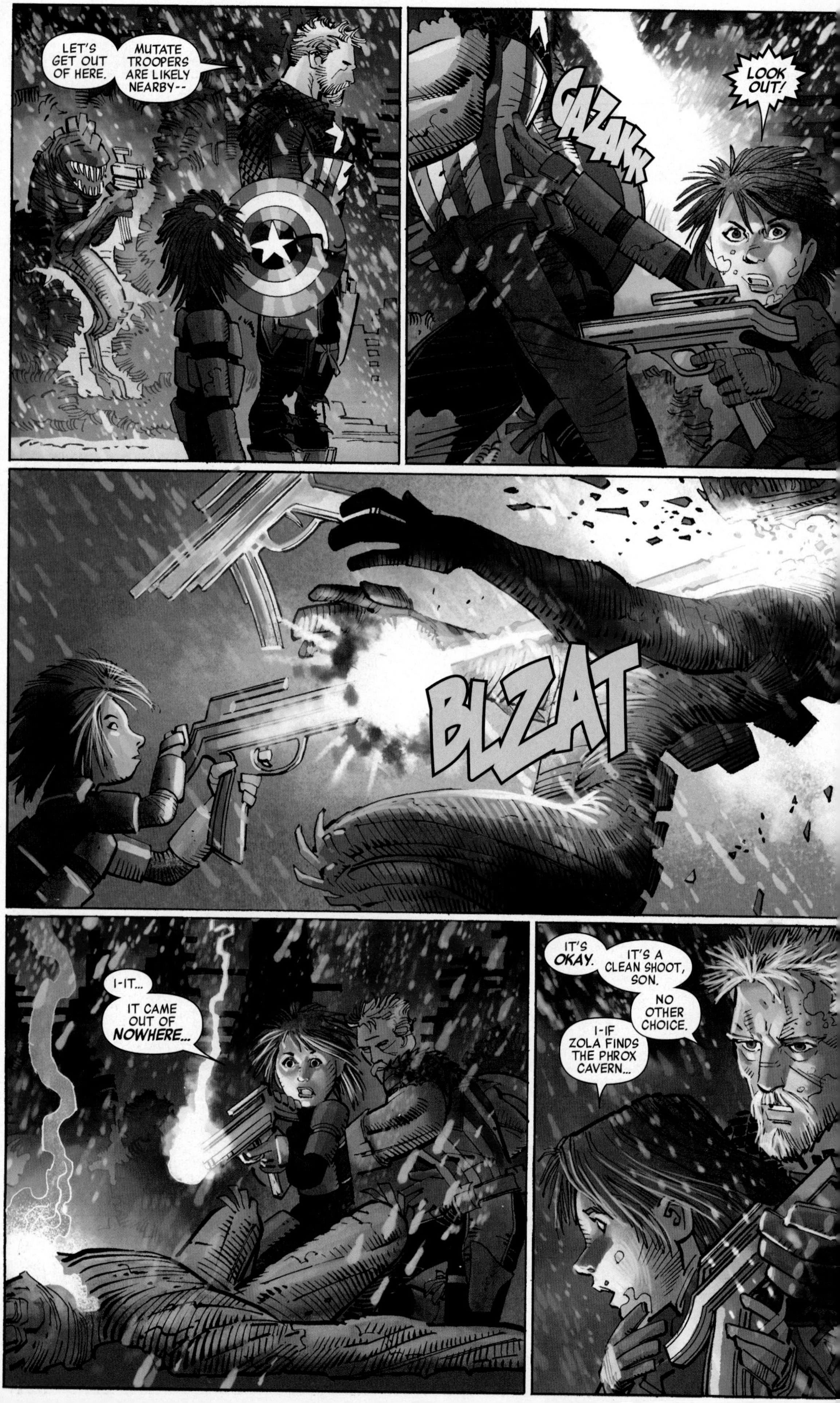
LET'S GET OUT OF HERE.
MUTATE TROOPERS ARE LIKELY NEARBY--
GAZAKK
LOOK OUT!
BLZAT
I-IT...
IT CAME OUT OF NOWHERE...
IT'S OKAY.
IT'S A CLEAN SHOOT, SON.
NO OTHER CHOICE.
I-IF ZOLA FINDS THE PHROX CAVERN...

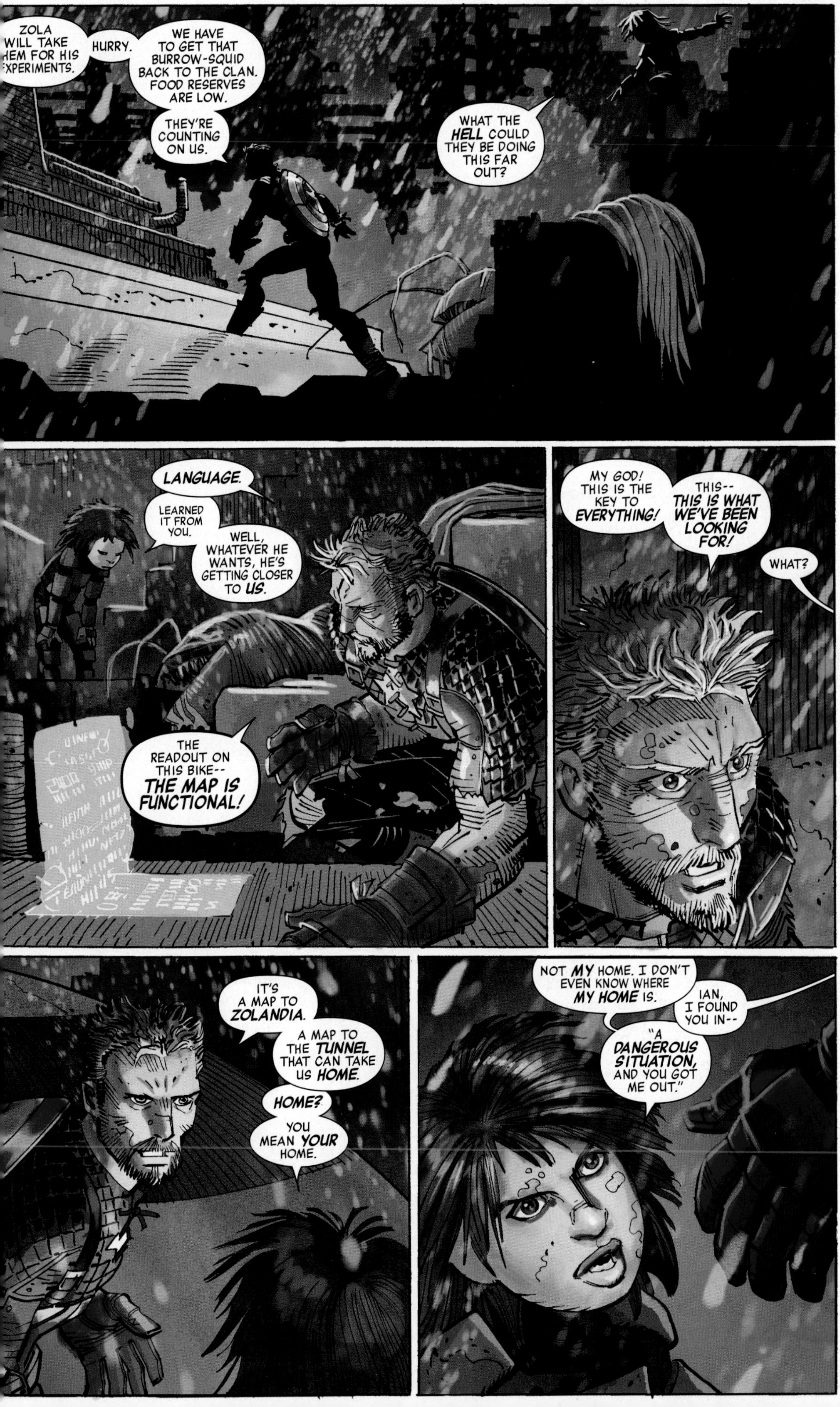
ZOLA WILL TAKE HEM FOR HIS EXPERIMENTS.
HURRY.
WE HAVE TO GET THAT BURROW-SQUID BACK TO THE CLAN. FOOD RESERVES ARE LOW.
THEY'RE COUNTING ON US.
WHAT THE HELL COULD THEY BE DOING THIS FAR OUT?
LANGUAGE.
LEARNED IT FROM YOU.
WELL, WHATEVER HE WANTS, HE'S GETTING CLOSER TO US.
THE READOUT ON THIS BIKE-- THE MAP IS FUNCTIONAL!
MY GOD! THIS IS THE KEY TO EVERYTHING!
THIS-- THIS IS WHAT WE'VE BEEN LOOKING FOR!
WHAT?
IT'S A MAP TO ZOLANDIA.
A MAP TO THE TUNNEL THAT CAN TAKE US HOME.
HOME?
YOU MEAN YOUR HOME.
NOT MY HOME. I DON'T EVEN KNOW WHERE MY HOME IS.
IAN, I FOUND YOU IN--
"A DANGEROUS SITUATION, AND YOU GOT ME OUT."

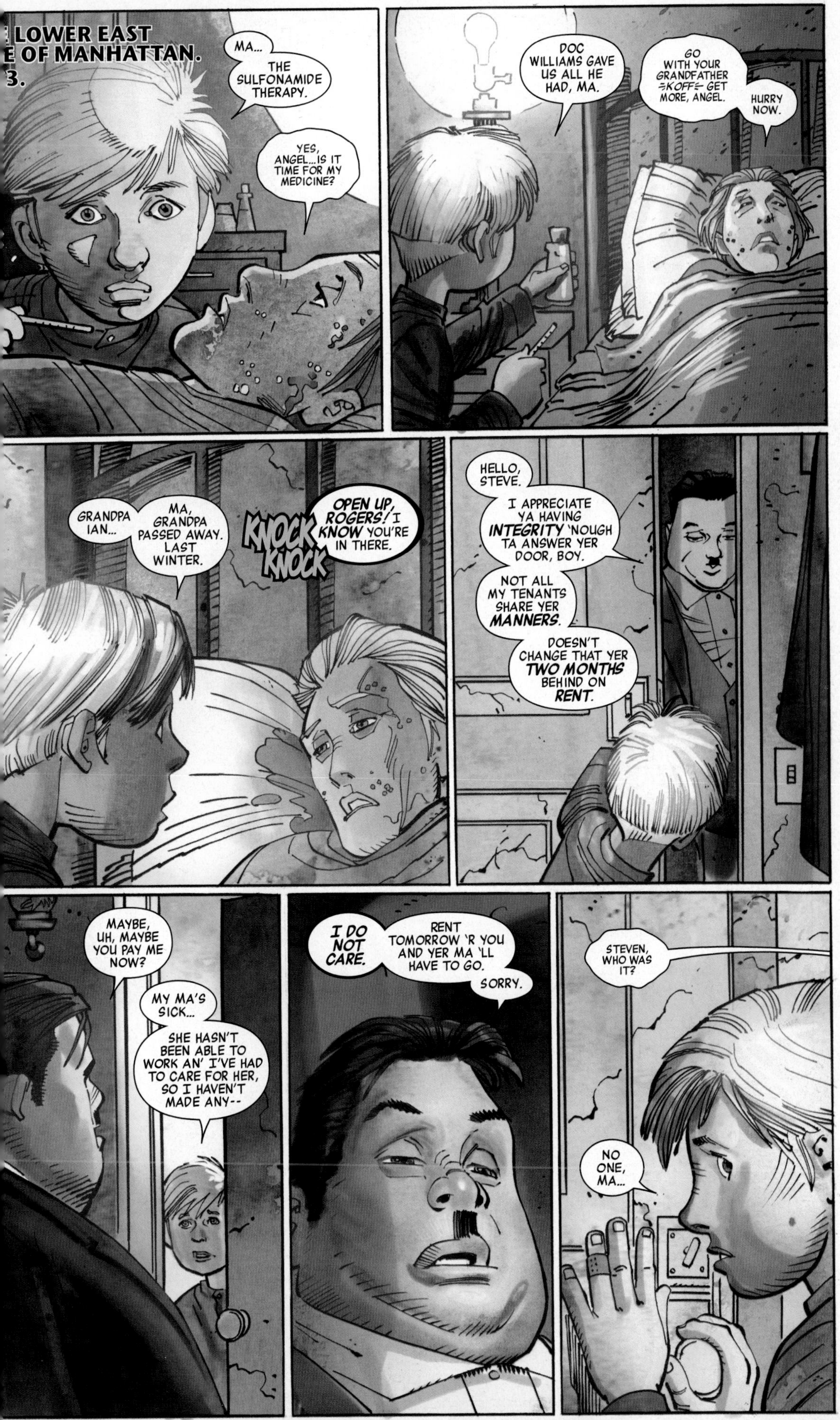
LOWER EAST
E OF MANHATTAN.
3.
MA... THE SULFONAMIDE THERAPY.
YES, ANGEL...IS IT TIME FOR MY MEDICINE?
DOC WILLIAMS GAVE US ALL HE HAD, MA.
GO WITH YOUR GRANDFATHER =KOFF= GET MORE, ANGEL.
HURRY NOW.
GRANDPA IAN...
MA, GRANDPA PASSED AWAY. LAST WINTER.
KNOCK KNOCK
OPEN UP, ROGERS! I KNOW YOU'RE IN THERE.
HELLO, STEVE.
I APPRECIATE YA HAVING INTEGRITY 'NOUGH TA ANSWER YER DOOR, BOY.
NOT ALL MY TENANTS SHARE YER MANNERS.
DOESN'T CHANGE THAT YER TWO MONTHS BEHIND ON RENT.
MAYBE, UH, MAYBE YOU PAY ME NOW?
MY MA'S SICK...
SHE HASN'T BEEN ABLE TO WORK AN' I'VE HAD TO CARE FOR HER, SO I HAVEN'T MADE ANY--
I DO NOT CARE.
RENT TOMORROW 'R YOU AND YER MA 'LL HAVE TO GO.
SORRY.
STEVEN, WHO WAS IT?
NO ONE, MA...

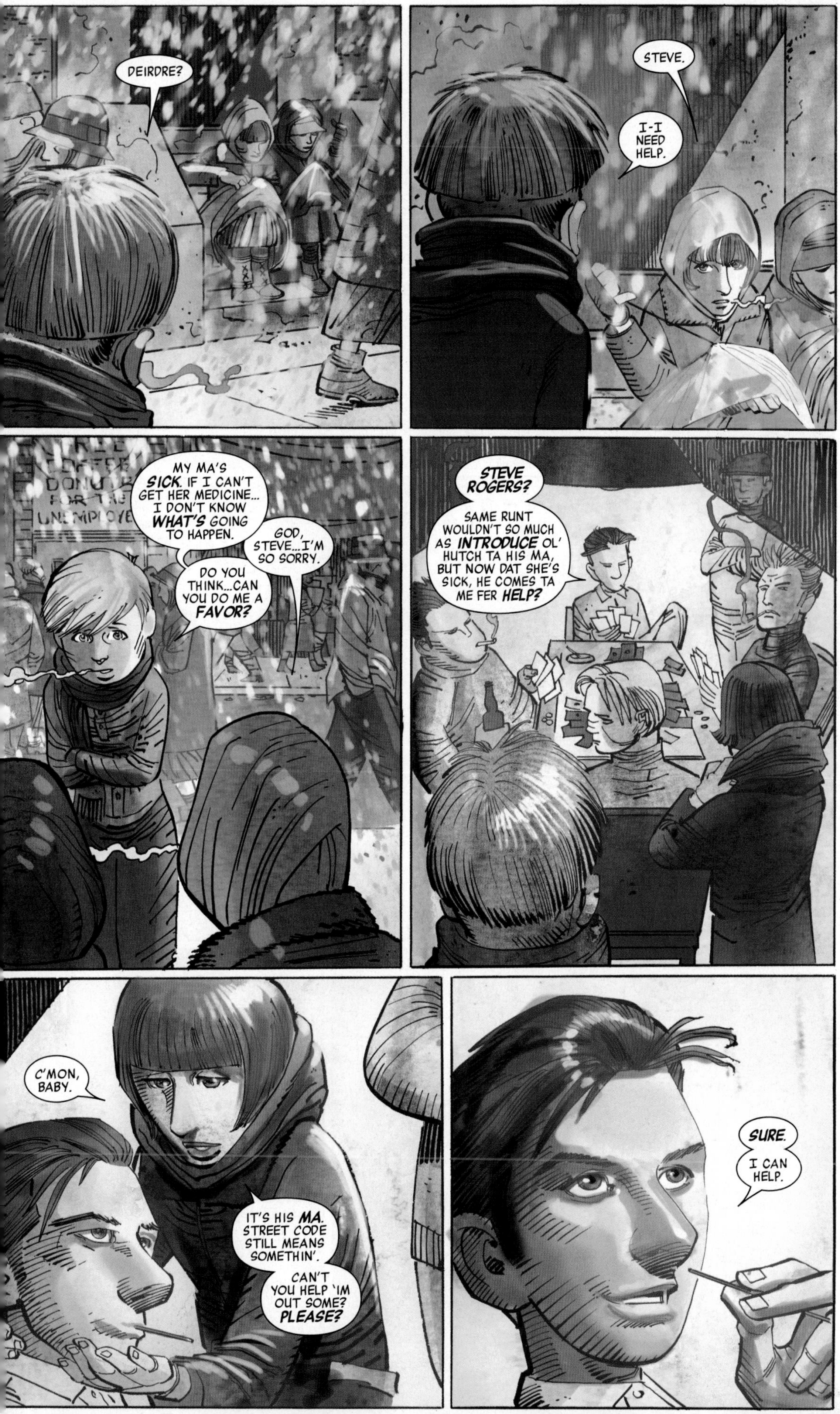
DEIRDRE?
STEVE.
I-I NEED HELP.
MY MA'S SICK. IF I CAN'T GET HER MEDICINE... I DON'T KNOW WHAT'S GOING TO HAPPEN.
GOD, STEVE...I'M SO SORRY.
DO YOU THINK...CAN YOU DO ME A FAVOR?
STEVE ROGERS?
SAME RUNT WOULDN'T SO MUCH AS INTRODUCE OL' HUTCH TA HIS MA, BUT NOW DAT SHE'S SICK, HE COMES TA ME FER HELP?
C'MON, BABY.
IT'S HIS MA. STREET CODE STILL MEANS SOMETHIN'.
CAN'T YOU HELP 'IM OUT SOME? PLEASE?
SURE.
I CAN HELP.

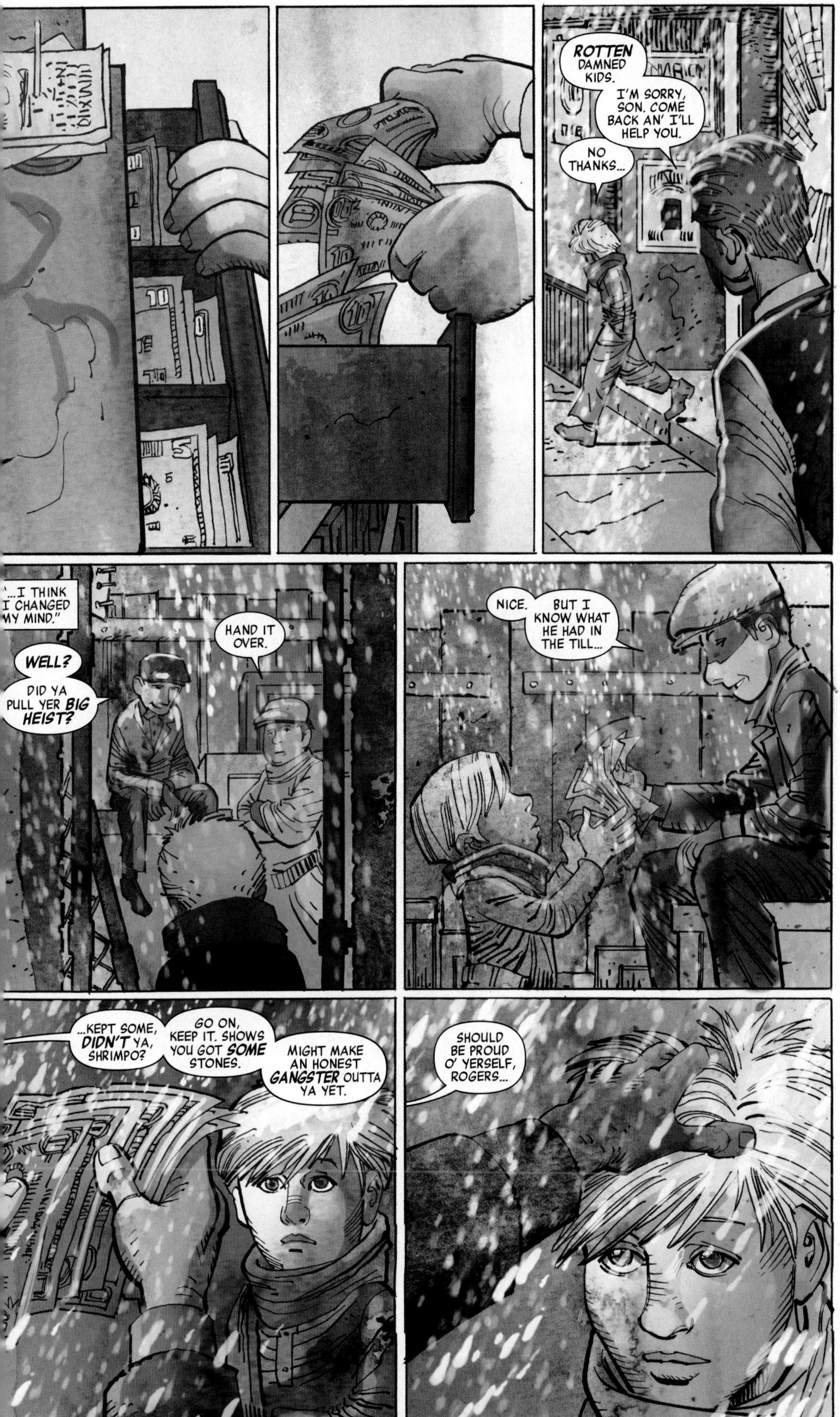
ROTTEN DAMNED KIDS.
I'M SORRY, SON. COME BACK AN' I'LL HELP YOU.
NO THANKS...
"...I THINK I CHANGED MY MIND."
WELL?
DID YA PULL YER BIG HEIST?
HAND IT OVER.
NICE.
BUT I KNOW WHAT HE HAD IN THE TILL...
...KEPT SOME, DIDN'T YA, SHRIMPO?
GO ON, KEEP IT. SHOWS YOU GOT SOME STONES.
MIGHT MAKE AN HONEST GANGSTER OUTTA YA YET.
SHOULD BE PROUD O' YERSELF, ROGERS...

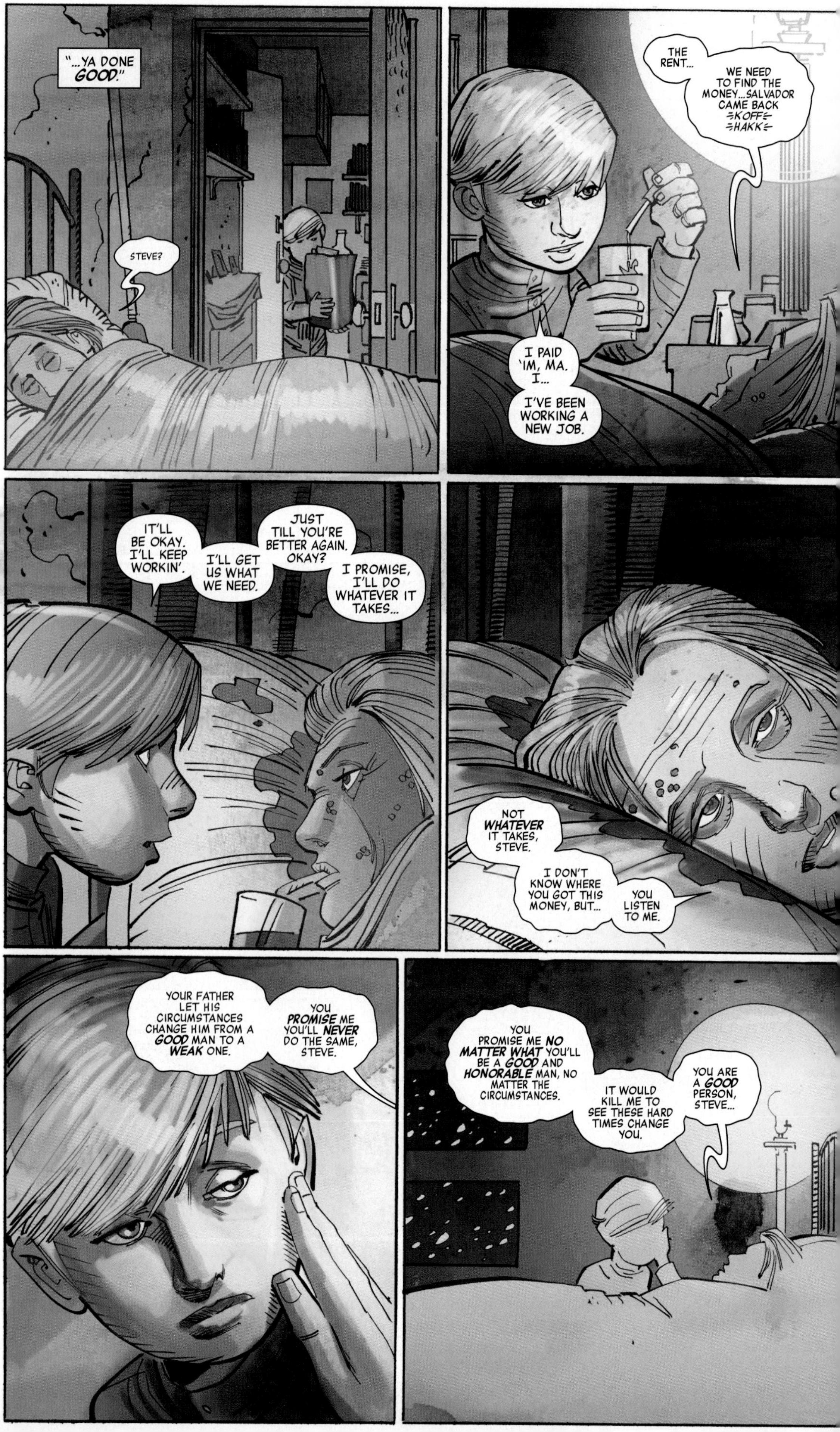
"...YA DONE GOOD."
STEVE?
THE RENT...
WE NEED TO FIND THE MONEY...SALVADOR CAME BACK
≠KOFF≠
≠HAKK≠
I PAID 'IM, MA. I...
I'VE BEEN WORKING A NEW JOB.
IT'LL BE OKAY. I'LL KEEP WORKIN'.
I'LL GET US WHAT WE NEED.
JUST TILL YOU'RE BETTER AGAIN. OKAY?
I PROMISE, I'LL DO WHATEVER IT TAKES...
NOT WHATEVER IT TAKES, STEVE.
I DON'T KNOW WHERE YOU GOT THIS MONEY, BUT...
YOU LISTEN TO ME.
YOUR FATHER LET HIS CIRCUMSTANCES CHANGE HIM FROM A GOOD MAN TO A WEAK ONE.
YOU PROMISE ME YOU'LL NEVER DO THE SAME, STEVE.
YOU PROMISE ME NO MATTER WHAT YOU'LL BE A GOOD AND HONORABLE MAN, NO MATTER THE CIRCUMSTANCES.
IT WOULD KILL ME TO SEE THESE HARD TIMES CHANGE YOU.
YOU ARE A GOOD PERSON, STEVE...

"...PROMISE ME YOU'LL ALWAYS KEEP THAT INTACT."

DING-DING

CAN I HELP YOU?

I-I'M THE BOY WHO STOLE YOUR MONEY.

MY MA'S REAL SICK AND...

IT DOESN'T MAKE IT RIGHT, I KNOW.

I'M SORRY...I KNOW IT WAS WRONG.

IF YOU'LL LET ME, I'LL WORK OFF THE MONEY AND THE DAMAGES. I'M A HARD WORKER.

I'LL WORK AS LONG AS YOU SAY, UNTIL YOU'RE PAID BACK.

BROOM AND MOP IN THE BACK.

GET 'FORE I CHANGE MY MIND.

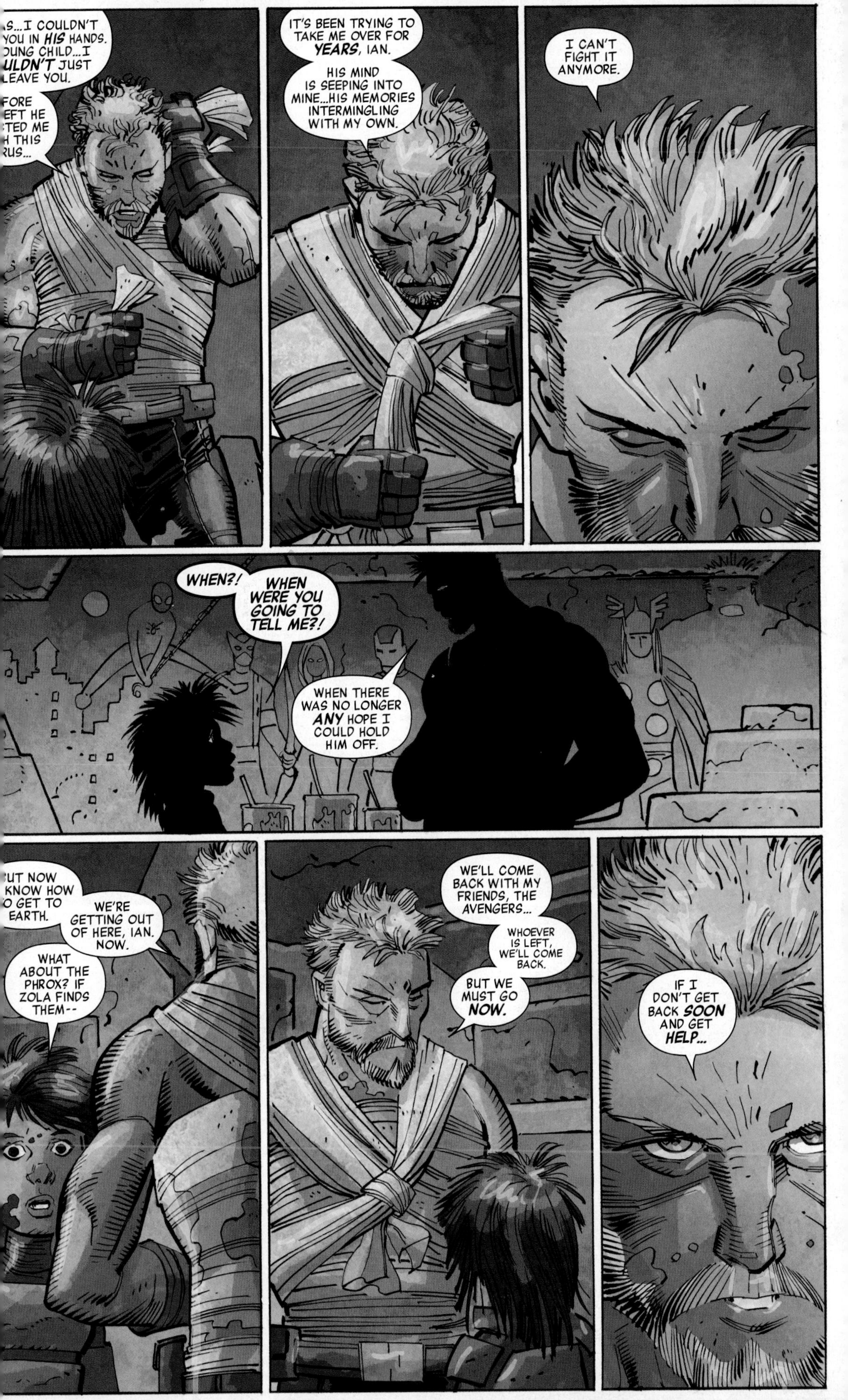

S...I COULDN'T YOU IN HIS HANDS. OUNG CHILD...I ULDN'T JUST LEAVE YOU.
FORE EFT HE TED ME H THIS RUS...
IT'S BEEN TRYING TO TAKE ME OVER FOR YEARS, IAN.
HIS MIND IS SEEPING INTO MINE...HIS MEMORIES INTERMINGLING WITH MY OWN.
I CAN'T FIGHT IT ANYMORE.
WHEN?!
WHEN WERE YOU GOING TO TELL ME?!
WHEN THERE WAS NO LONGER ANY HOPE I COULD HOLD HIM OFF.
UT NOW KNOW HOW O GET TO EARTH.
WE'RE GETTING OUT OF HERE, IAN. NOW.
WHAT ABOUT THE PHROX? IF ZOLA FINDS THEM--
WE'LL COME BACK WITH MY FRIENDS, THE AVENGERS...
WHOEVER IS LEFT, WE'LL COME BACK.
BUT WE MUST GO NOW.
IF I DON'T GET BACK SOON AND GET HELP...

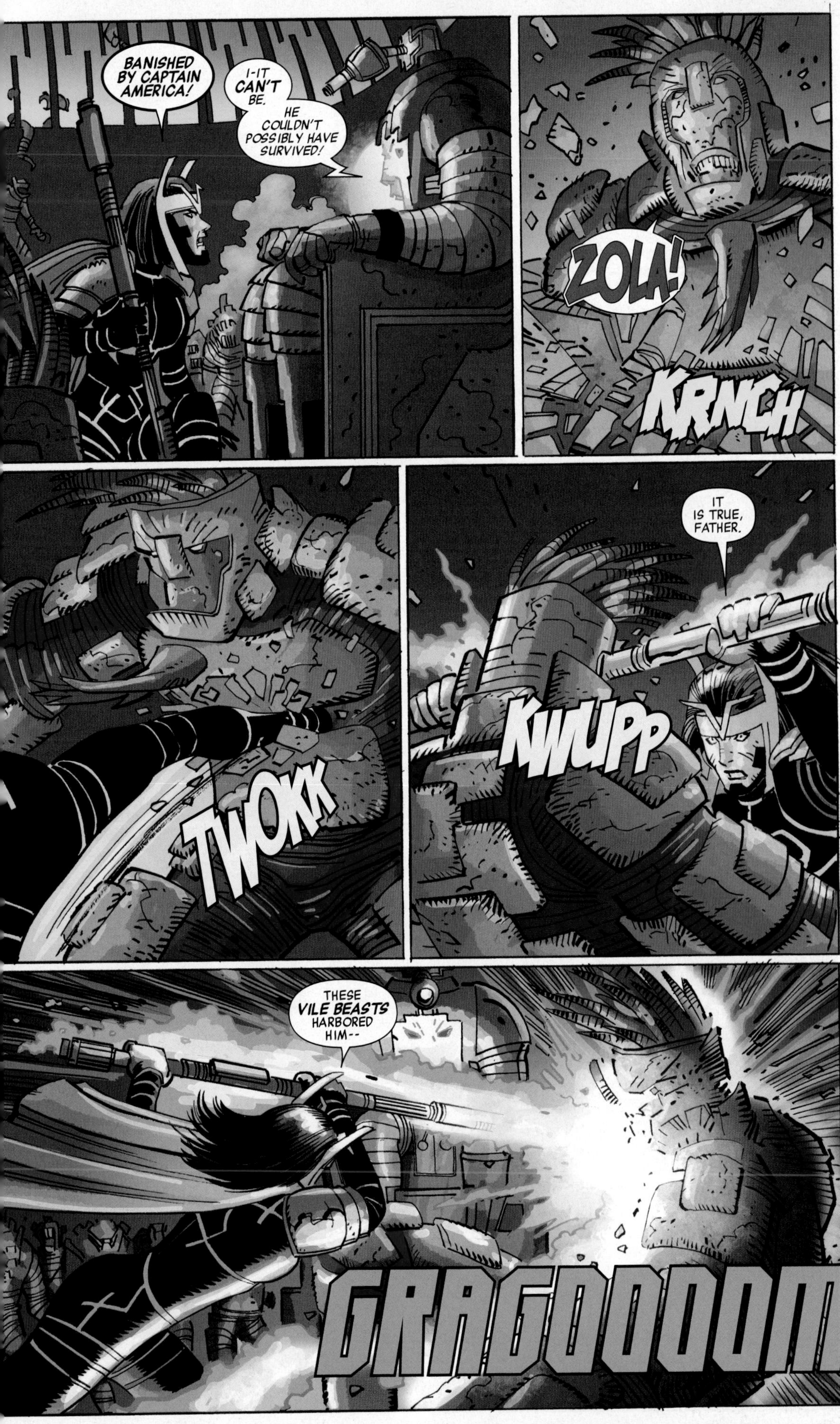

BANISHED BY CAPTAIN AMERICA!
I-IT CAN'T BE.
HE COULDN'T POSSIBLY HAVE SURVIVED!
ZOLA!
KRNCH
TWOKK
IT IS TRUE, FATHER.
KWUPP
THESE VILE BEASTS HARBORED HIM--
GRAGOOOOM

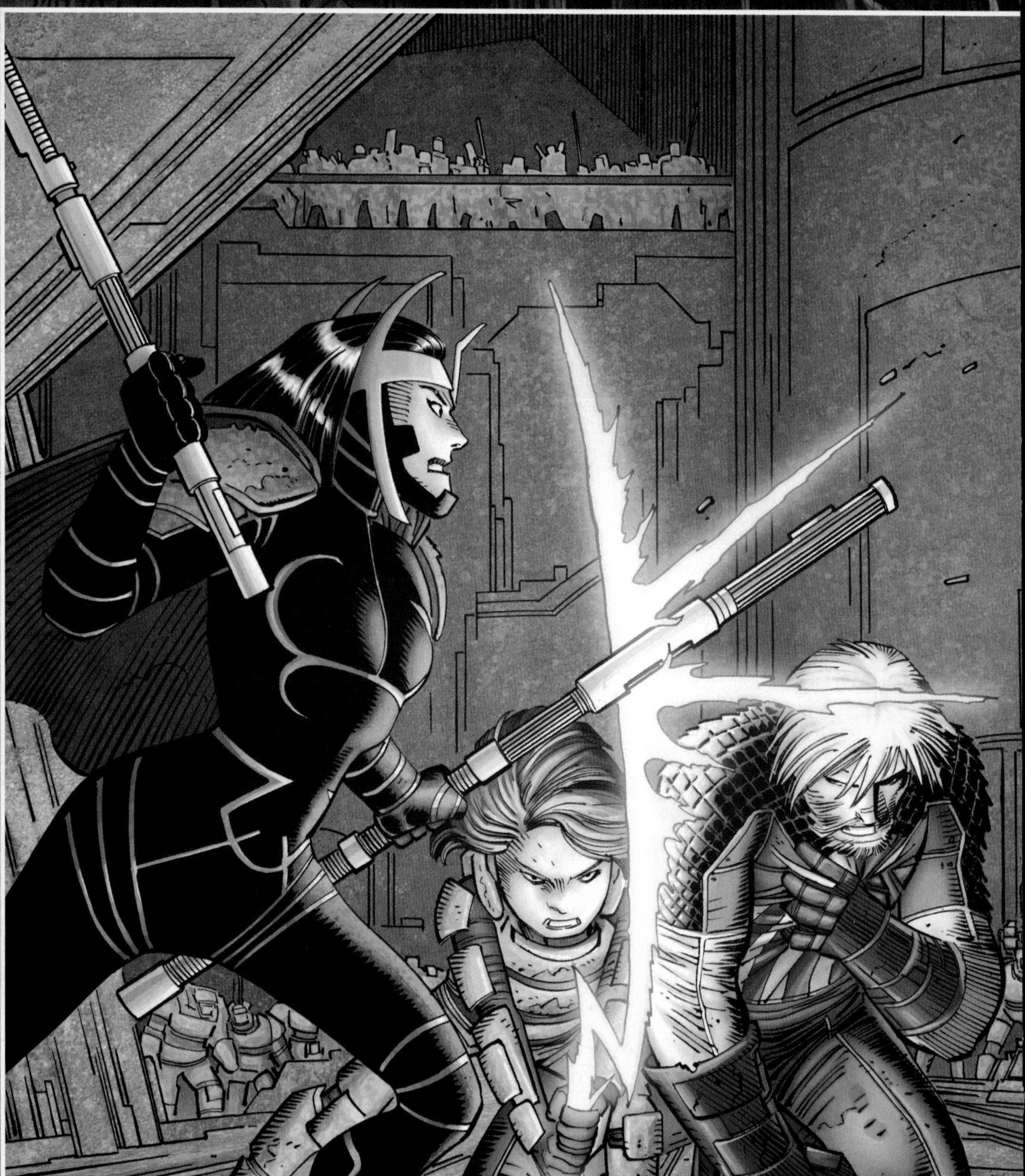
JRJR

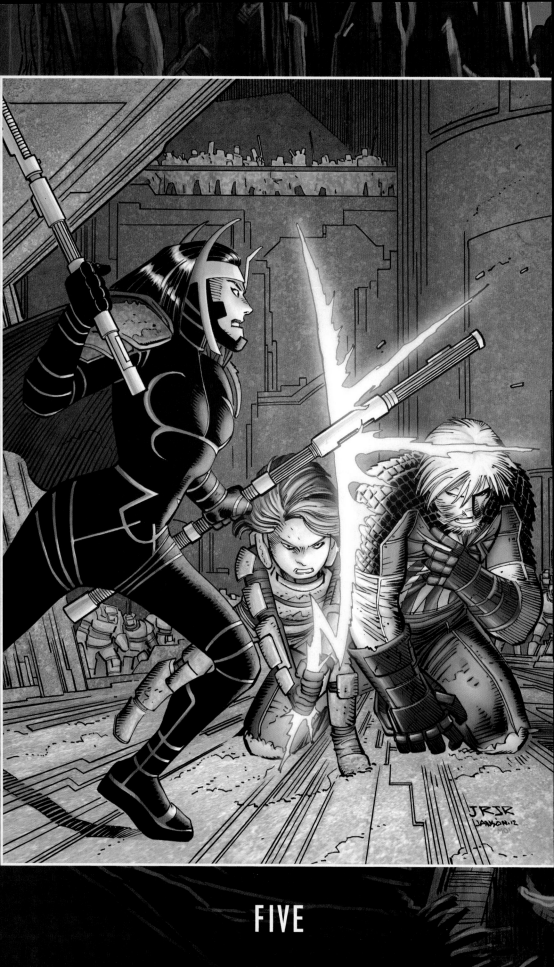

FIVE

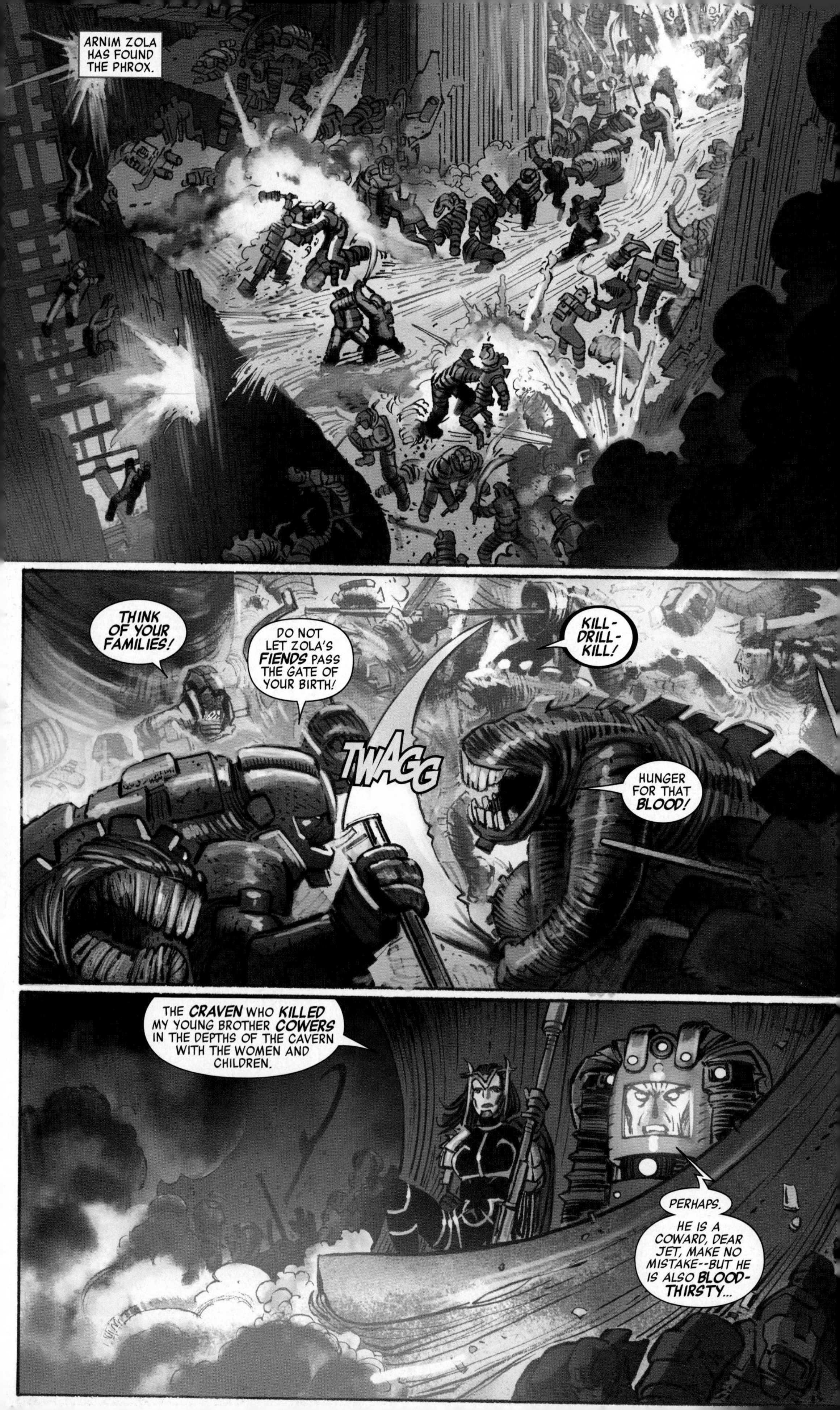
ARNIM ZOLA HAS FOUND THE PHROX.
THINK OF YOUR FAMILIES!
DO NOT LET ZOLA'S FIENDS PASS THE GATE OF YOUR BIRTH!
KILL-DRILL-KILL!
TWAGG
HUNGER FOR THAT BLOOD!
THE CRAVEN WHO KILLED MY YOUNG BROTHER COWERS IN THE DEPTHS OF THE CAVERN WITH THE WOMEN AND CHILDREN.
PERHAPS.
HE IS A COWARD, DEAR JET, MAKE NO MISTAKE--BUT HE IS ALSO BLOOD-THIRSTY...

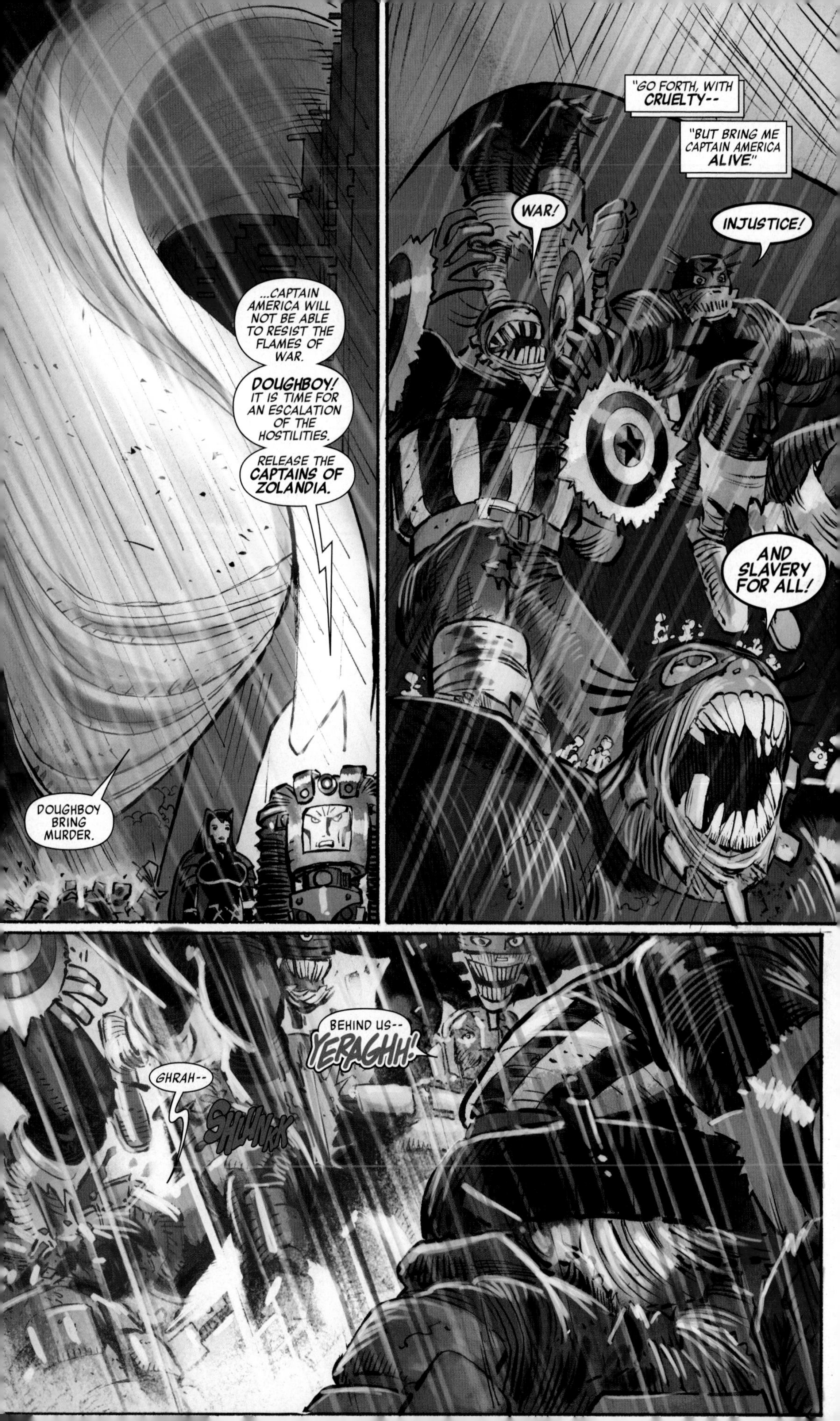
...CAPTAIN AMERICA WILL NOT BE ABLE TO RESIST THE FLAMES OF WAR.
DOUGHBOY! IT IS TIME FOR AN ESCALATION OF THE HOSTILITIES.
RELEASE THE CAPTAINS OF ZOLANDIA.
DOUGHBOY BRING MURDER.
"GO FORTH, WITH CRUELTY--
"BUT BRING ME CAPTAIN AMERICA ALIVE."
WAR!
INJUSTICE!
AND SLAVERY FOR ALL!
BEHIND US--
YERAGHH!
GHRAH--
SHUNKK

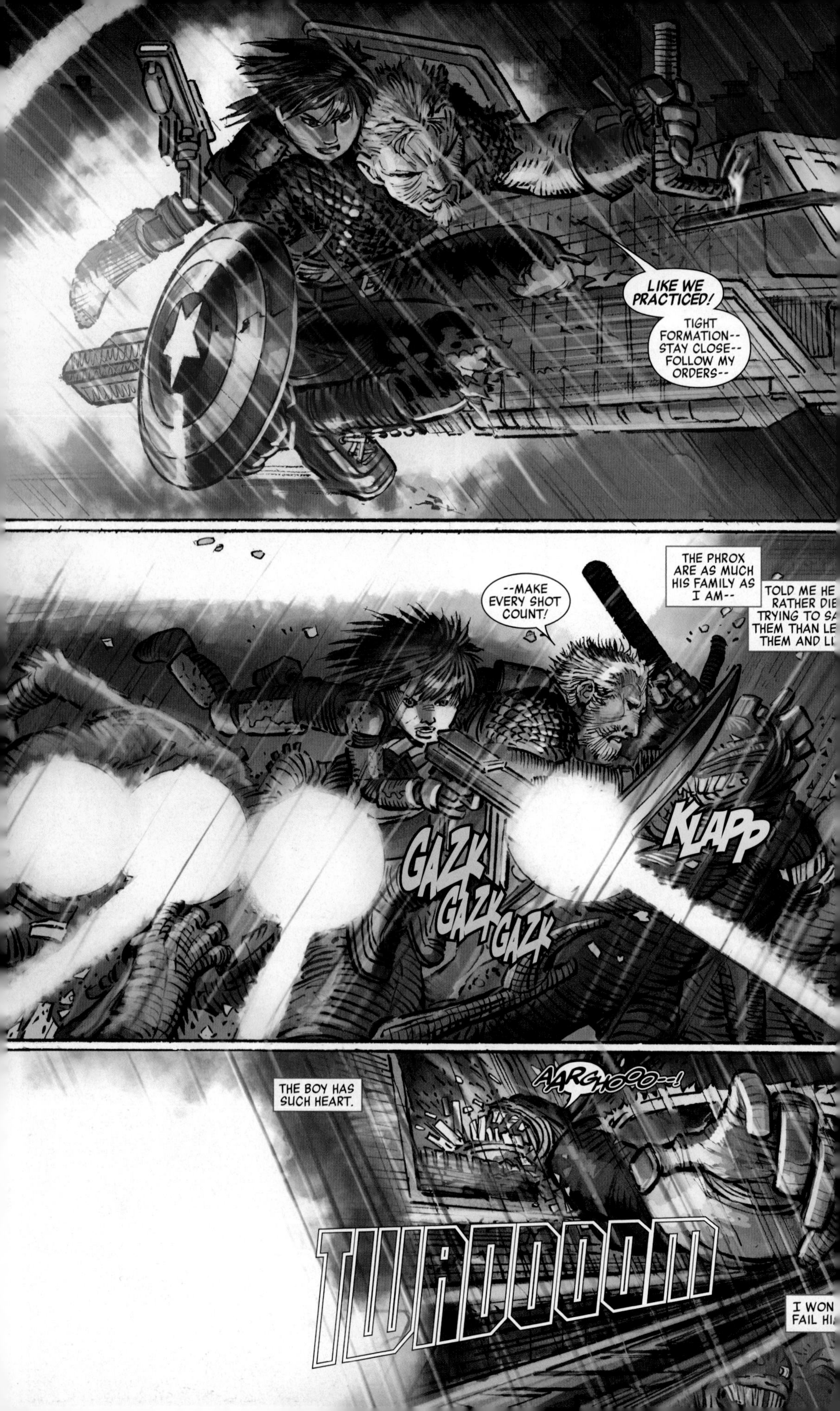

LIKE WE PRACTICED!
TIGHT FORMATION-- STAY CLOSE-- FOLLOW MY ORDERS--
THE PHROX ARE AS MUCH HIS FAMILY AS I AM--
--MAKE EVERY SHOT COUNT!
TOLD ME HE RATHER DIE TRYING TO SA THEM THAN LE THEM AND LI
GAZK GAZK GAZK
KLAPP
THE BOY HAS SUCH HEART.
AARGHOOOO--!
TWROOOOM
I WON FAIL HI

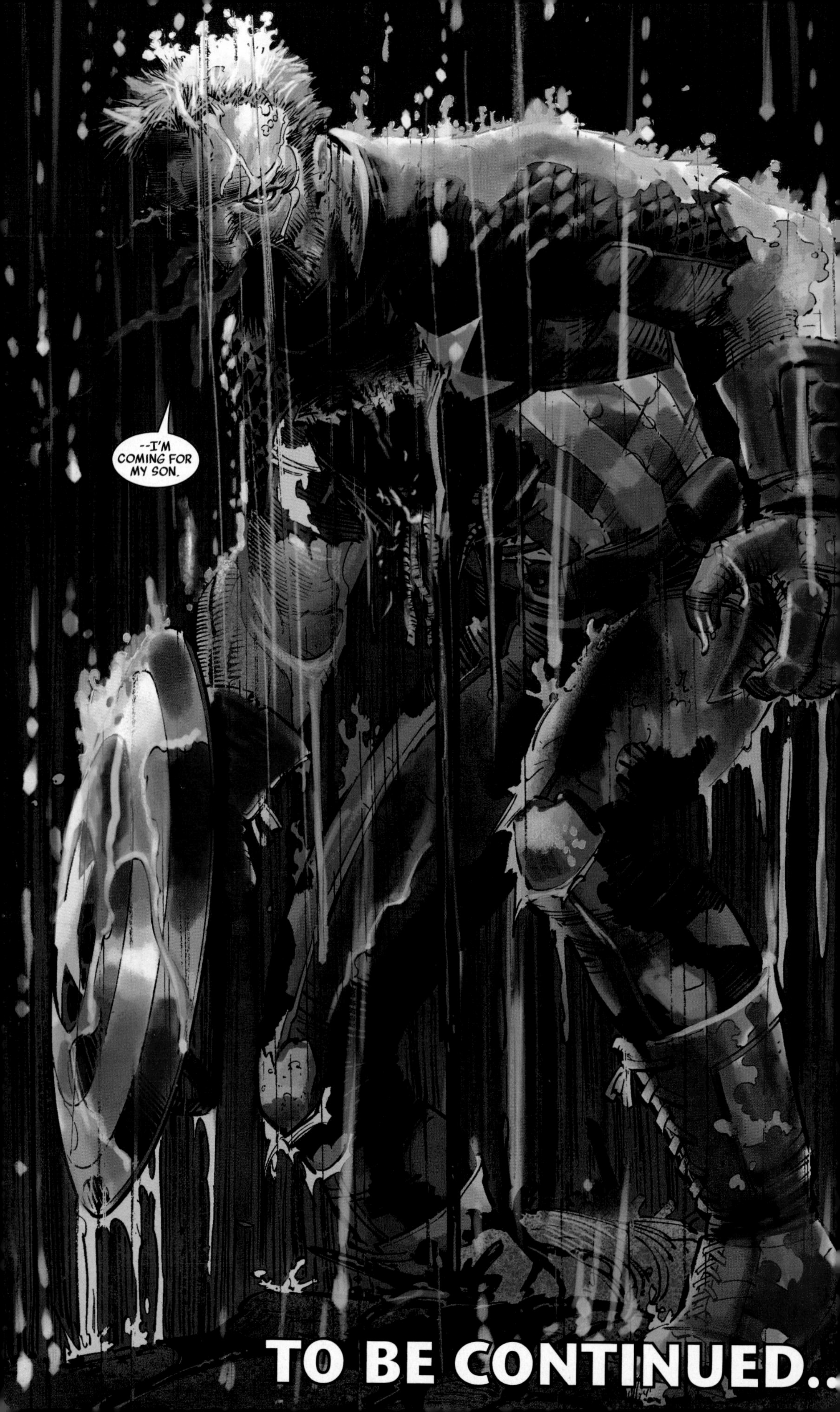
--I'M COMING FOR MY SON.
TO BE CONTINUED...

What an incredible honor it is e entrusted with continuing the cy of the star-spangled Sentinel iberty. As you'd imagine, for a fan of Captain America this is a m job. I am and it is. On top of to have legendary masters of ential art John Romita Jr, Klaus on and Dean White by my side, total craziness. I'm humbled by opportunity and the greatness I'm ounded by.

The first issue of Captain America d was issue 298. I bought it at the even along with some Amazing er-Man comics and maybe an e of Secret Wars and it came with to Camp Geronimo in Northern ona where I was spending a few ks at summer camp. It was one of e books that you reread over and again because, well, while it was ly great, it was also the only thing had to read. But it left a genuine ression on me; I was immediately aged and invested in Steve Rogers his eternal struggle against a y old Nazi named the Red Skull. n I got back home I saved up all money and went out and bought y issue of Captain America going through the J. M. DeMatteis/ e Zeck era to the Roger Stern/John ne era (two of my very favorite s). It was the 2nd long box I ever d, 2nd only to my sacred Uncanny Men collection.

Capt. America was the character the other super heroes turned to well, almost anything. But what cooler still, Cap didn't have any blasts, he couldn't fly, didn't have lear-superpower-glowy-hands, could he whistle through time. He just an incredibly noble, brave, est, and seemingly fearless man h a big heart and a Super-Soldier um infused steel fist. He's the guy want watching your back in a t, the guy you turn to, the guy nt in charge of things.

Steve Rogers is a patriotic lier, directed by a personal ethical npass, belief in the American dream faith in his fellow man. He's ver, roughish, quick with a sly look droll comment. He can punch out bad people and jump through glass. He's the person you wish you were.

He's not superhuman; he's just the pinnacle of our natural potential. He's like us. He's vulnerable. If he gets shot, it opens him up, it hurts. If he falls out of a plane without a parachute, he dies. He isn't Superman, he has limits, and he must overcome them with smarts and tenacity more than brute strength.

He is fighting for the safety of humanity, freedom, liberty and justice for all. He believes a perfect world without war or strife is a possibility worth fighting for. He will no doubt spend his entire life protecting people from the endless sea of chaos that surrounds the Marvel Universe.

This is the hero I want to write.

There've been many great eras, many legendary chapters in the life of Steve Rogers, but while rereading back issues it was one era that spoke to me more than the others. It was an era of Capt. America I hadn't read since I was the manager of a comic book shop in Phoenix, Arizona back in 1993. It was when Jack Kirby came back and entirely took over the book. He wrote it, drew it, and even edited it for a time. It was 100% Jack Kirby at one of the most interesting periods of his career towards the mid 70s. It was so imaginative and insane, yet always stayed so true to the character; all the crazy stuff seemed classic, it just seemed like it had always been there. I can't imagine an era of Captain America where Arnim Zola didn't exist. When I reread Zola's first appearance it struck me just how interesting this character was and how many ideas immediately sprung to mind. That's usually a good sign that the character has legs.

Then there was the tone of what Jack was doing in that era, a strange mixture of espionage, science fiction, and pure psychedelic imagination. So, I wanted to try and do something similar, with my own spin of course. Tonally you can expect something that is inspired by that era while also infusing some of the soap opera, and the very hard times, I like to put my characters through. High-adventure, tough-as-nails, mind-melting sci-fi, pulp-fantasy with constant high stakes, real velocity, and fast action. After the events in our first story, our hero won't resemble any other era that has come before but his fiber and how he earned it will still shine through. As they say, a bold new era begins now.

So, we all have a little change to adjust to. But change is good. It's exciting. It's how we keep these iconic and long running books fresh. After a legendary run by Ed Brubaker, one of my favorite writers, it seemed like a big change was the only way to outrun the shadow he cast. And, in the end, this direction was the thing that got me the most excited to write.

Steve Rogers, Captain America, is a man who may very well live forever due to the Super Solder serum, and he's going to discover that he must let go of the past in order to move forward, in order to serve not only his country, but himself.

Rick Remender

NEXT: IN THE WILDERNESS!

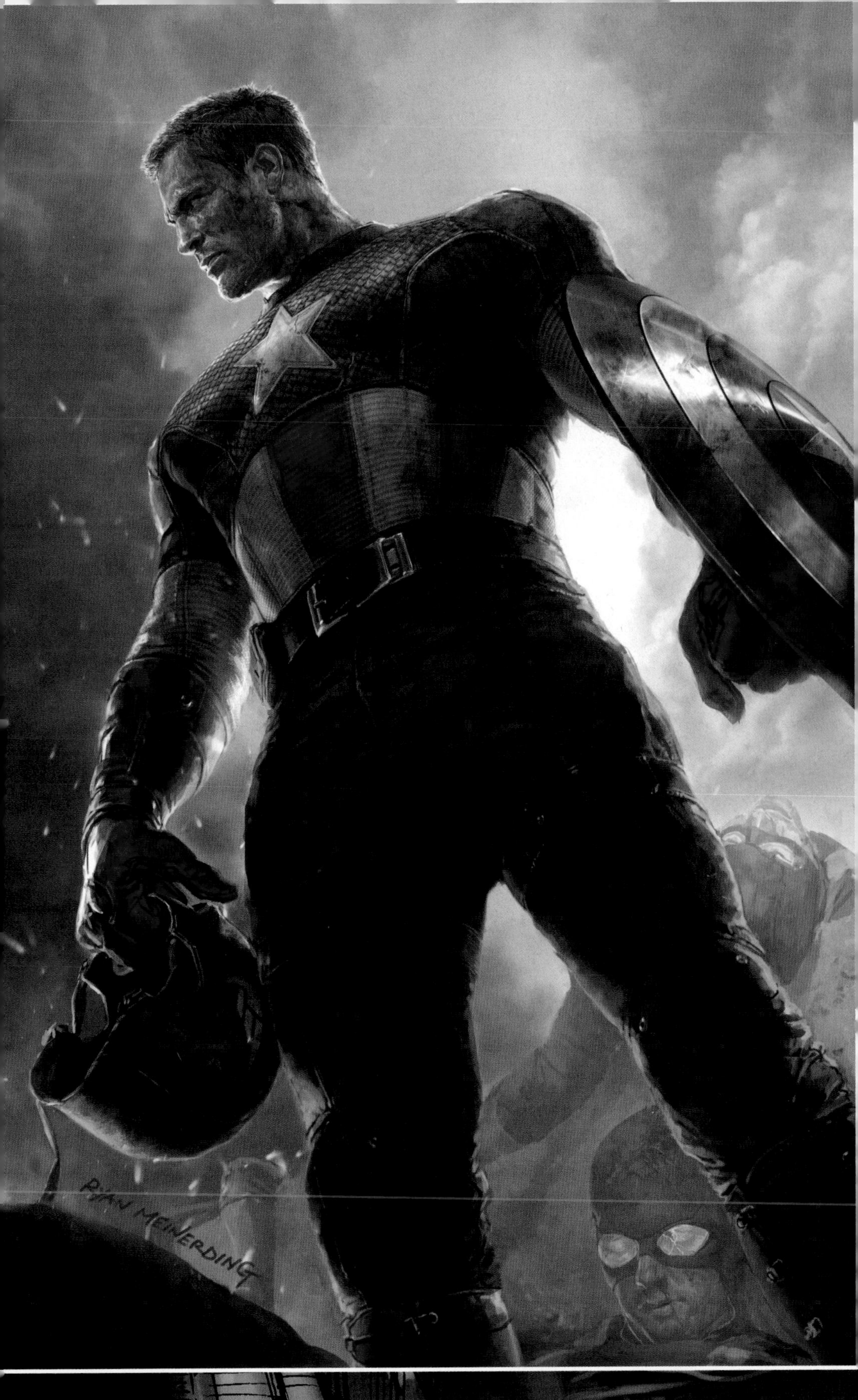
RYAN MEINERDING

#1 VARIANT BY RYAN MEINERDING

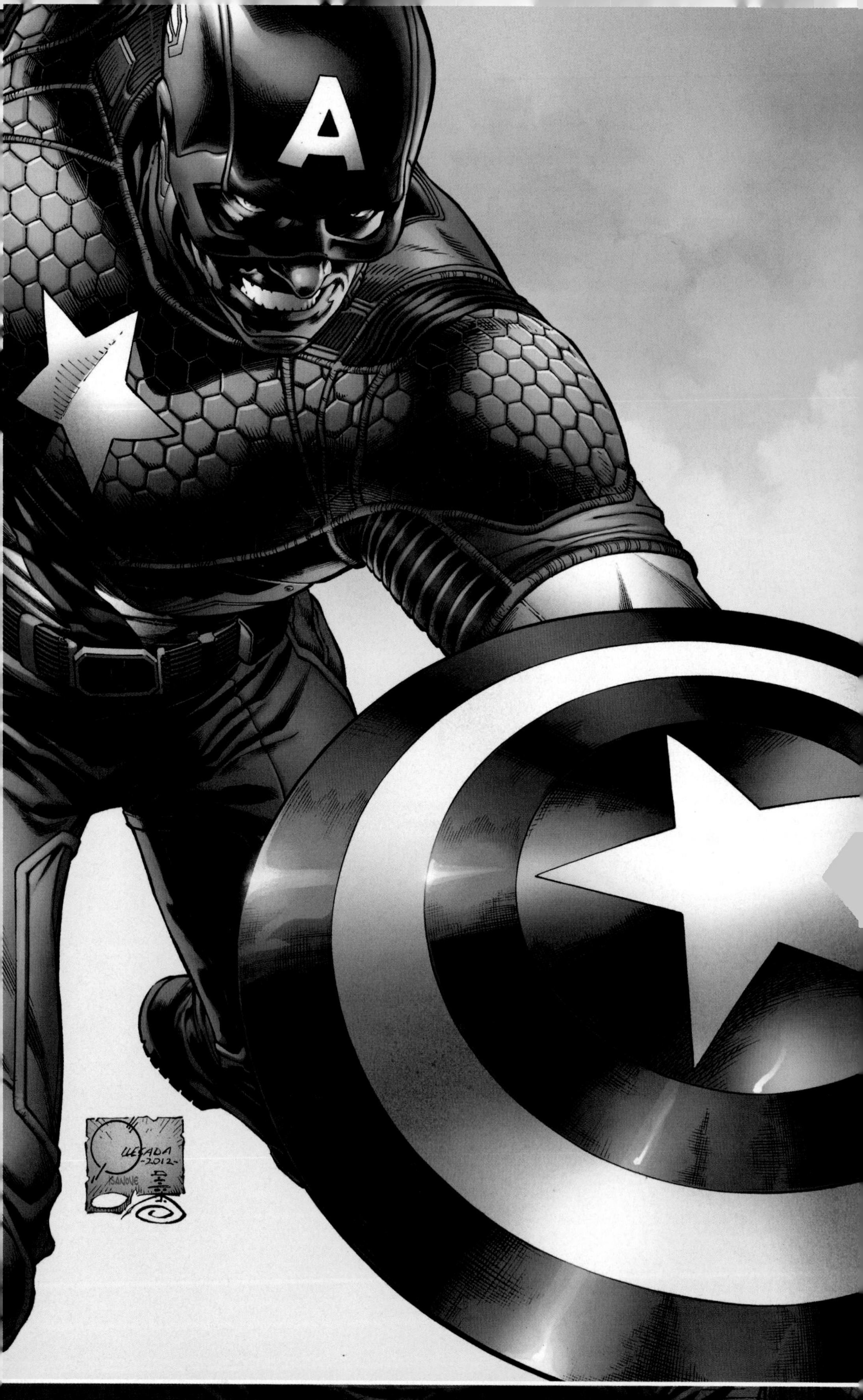

#1 VARIANT BY JOE QUESADA DANNY MIKI & RICHARD ISANOVE

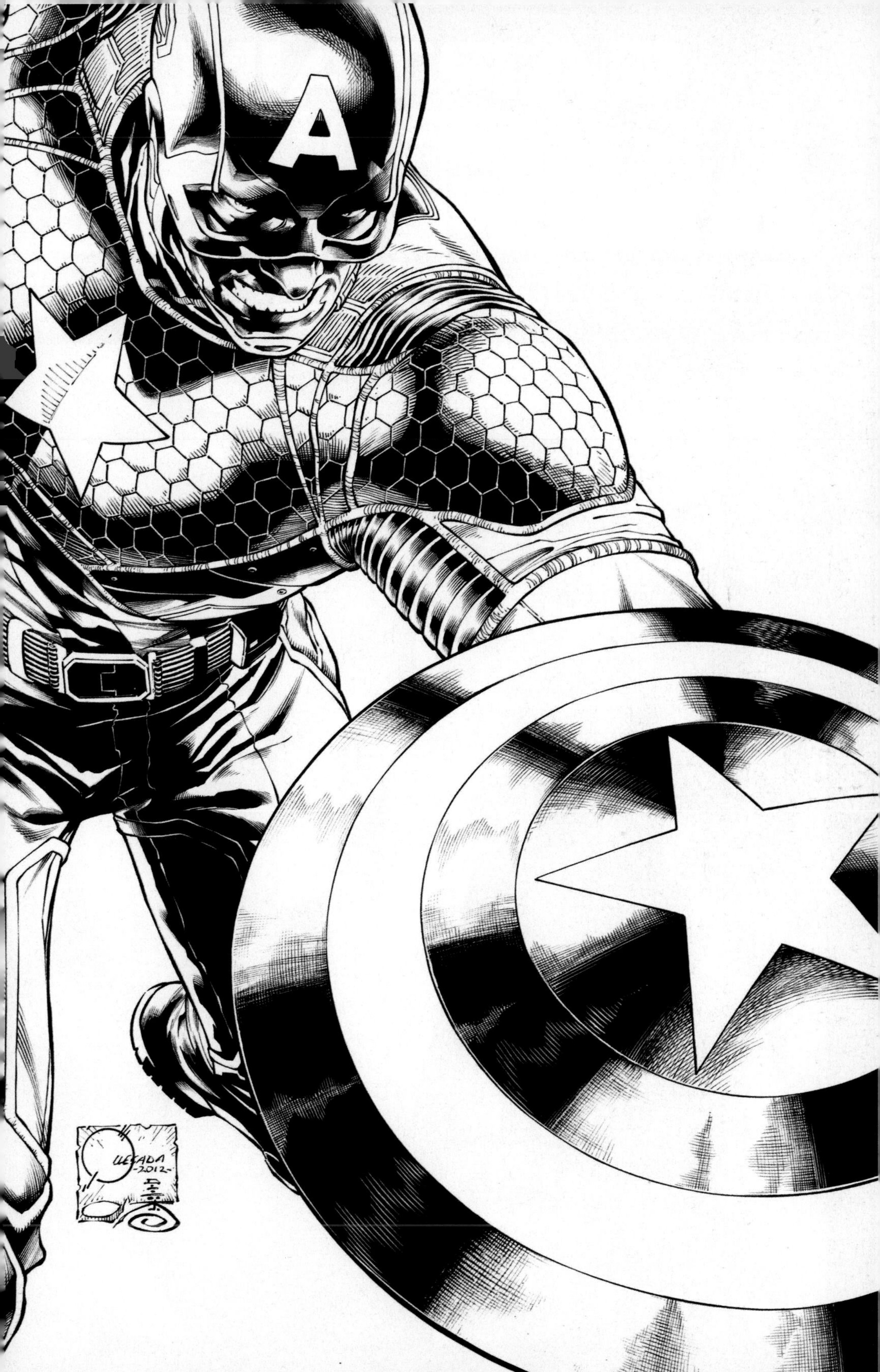

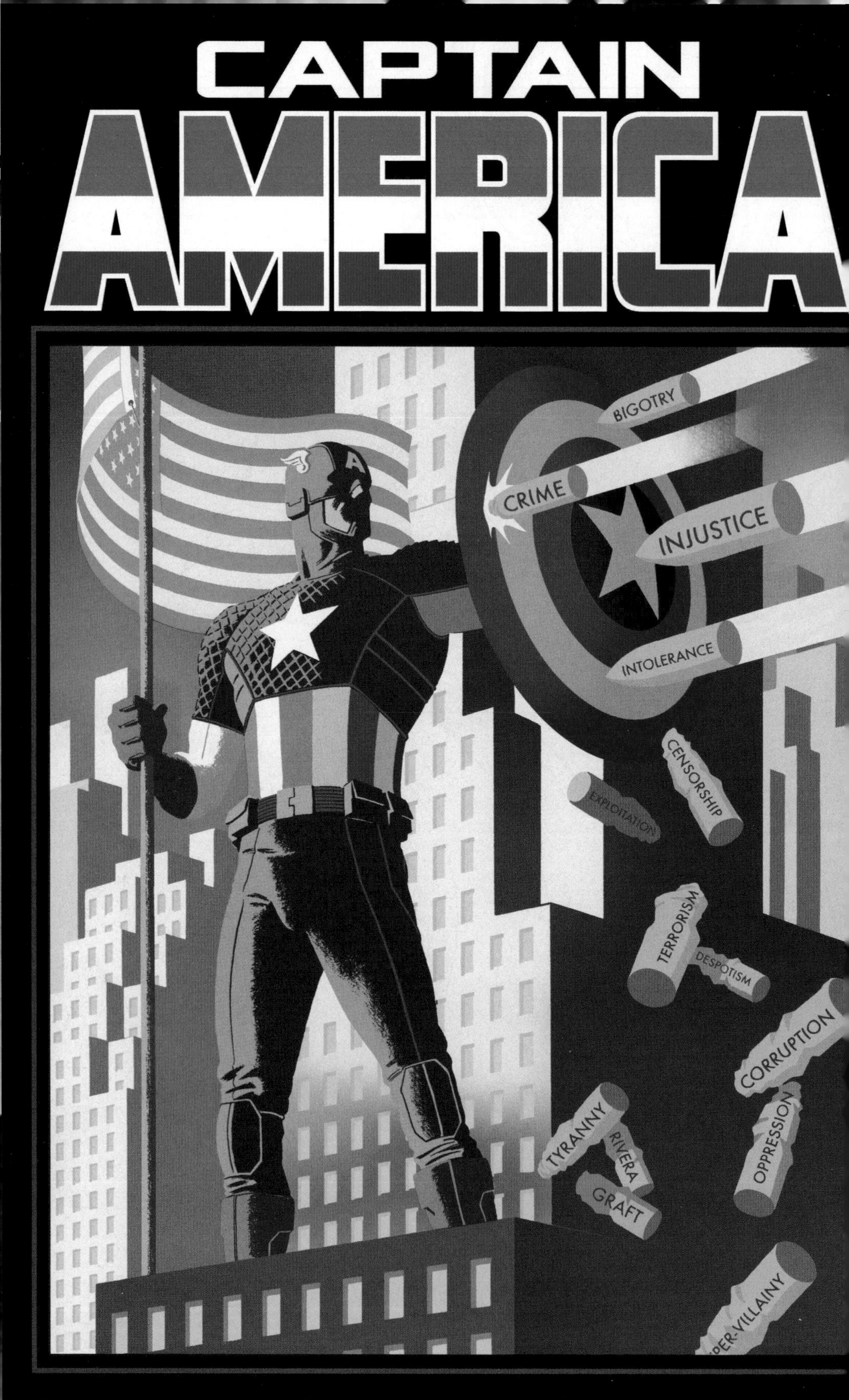
CAPTAIN
AMERICA
BIGOTRY
CRIME
INJUSTICE
INTOLERANCE
CENSORSHIP
EXPLOITATION
TERRORISM
DESPOTISM
CORRUPTION
OPPRESSION
TYRANNY
RIVERA
GRAFT

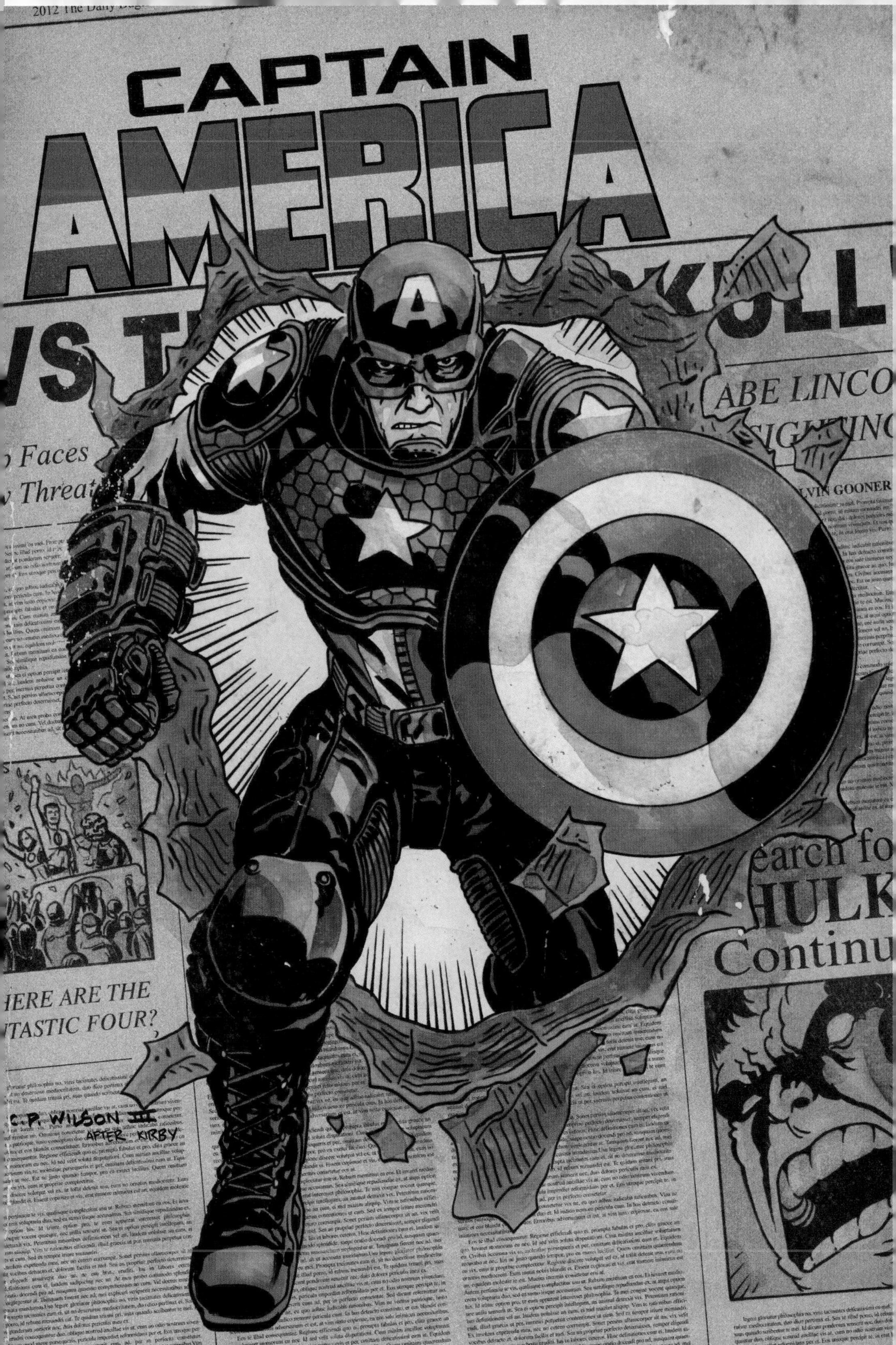

CAPTAIN
AMERICA
ABE LINCO
Faces
Threat
earch fo
HULK
Continu
HERE ARE THE
TASTIC FOUR?
C.P. WILSON III
AFTER KIRBY

CAPTAIN AMERICA

ITA JR.

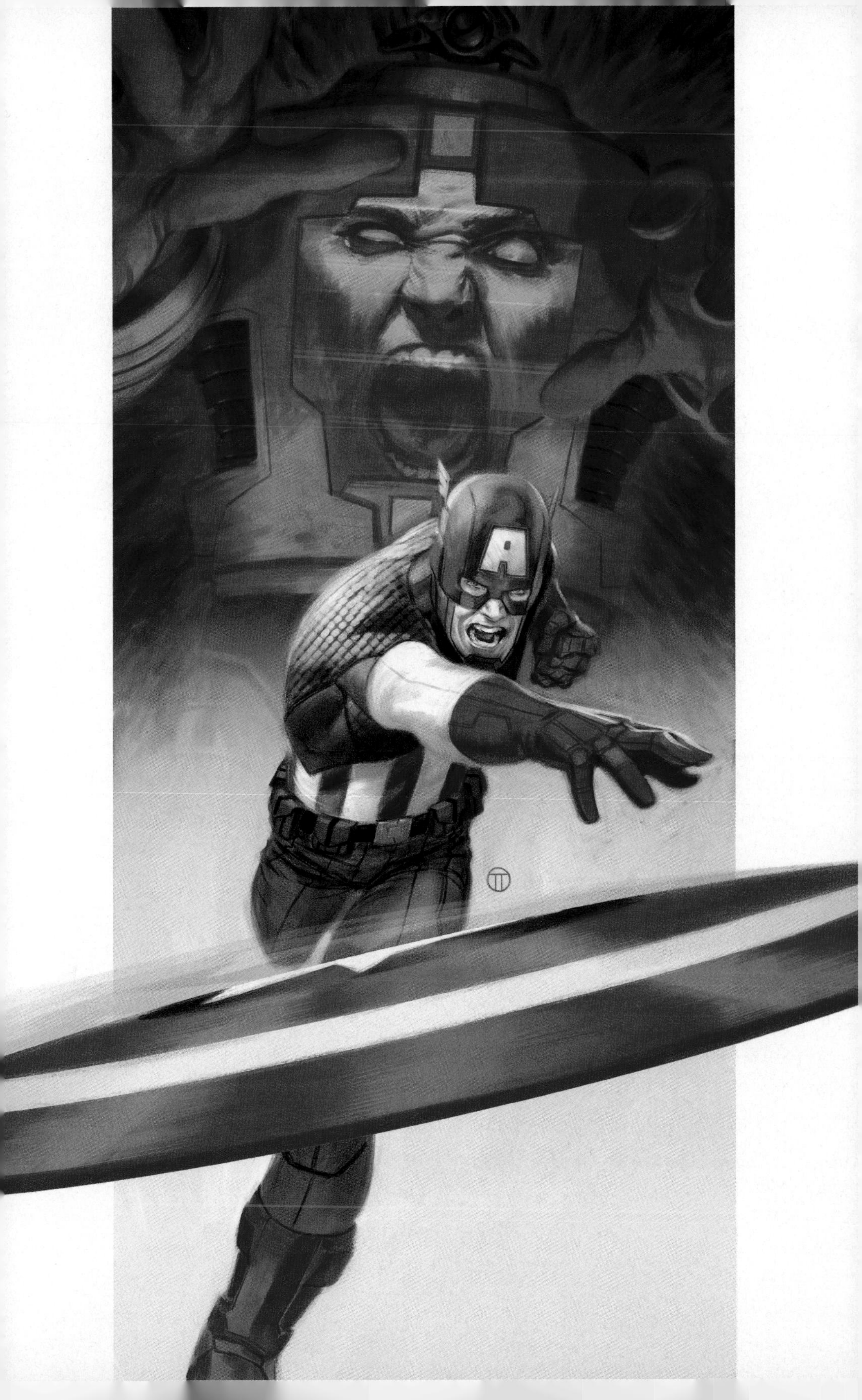

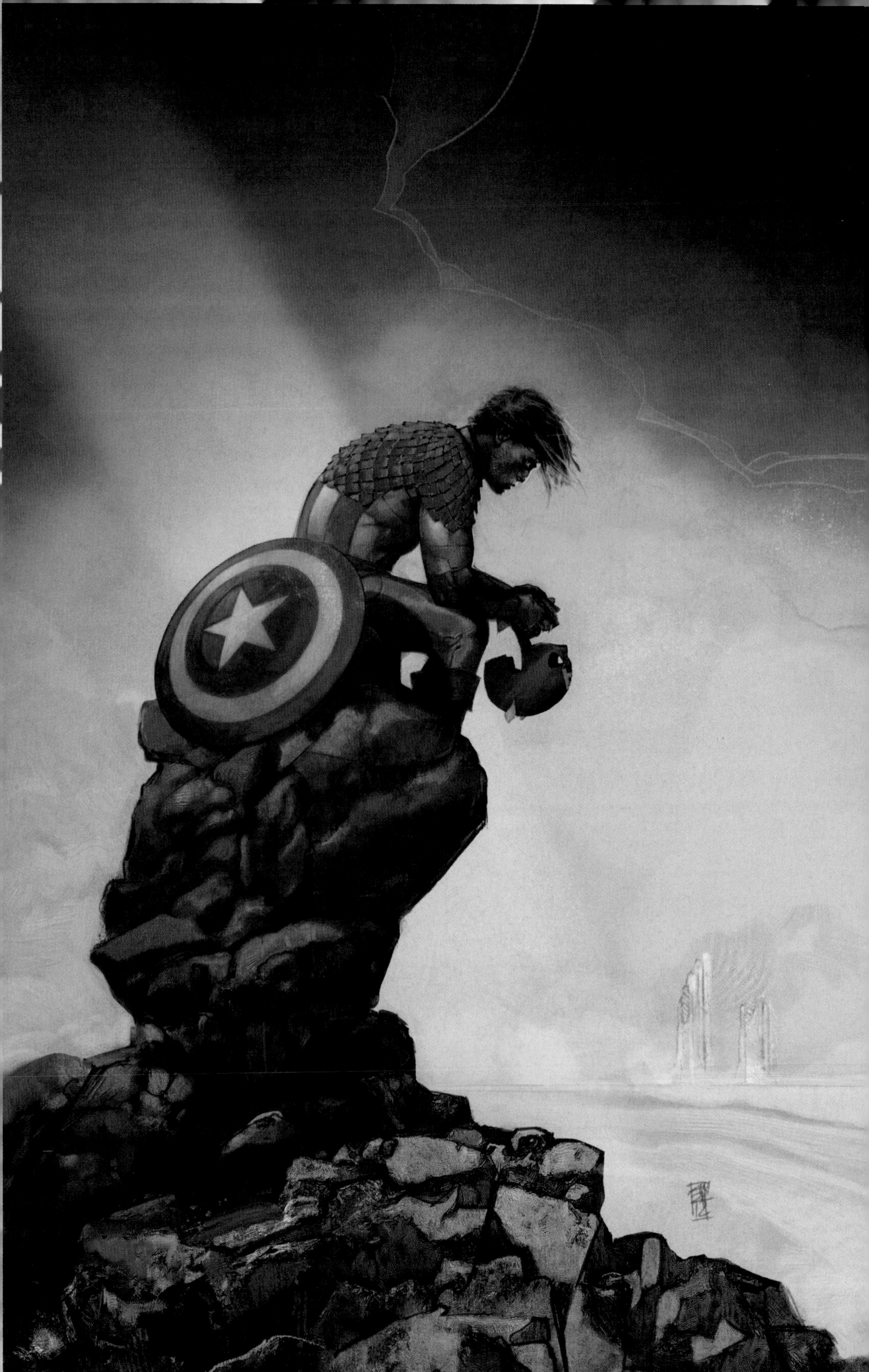

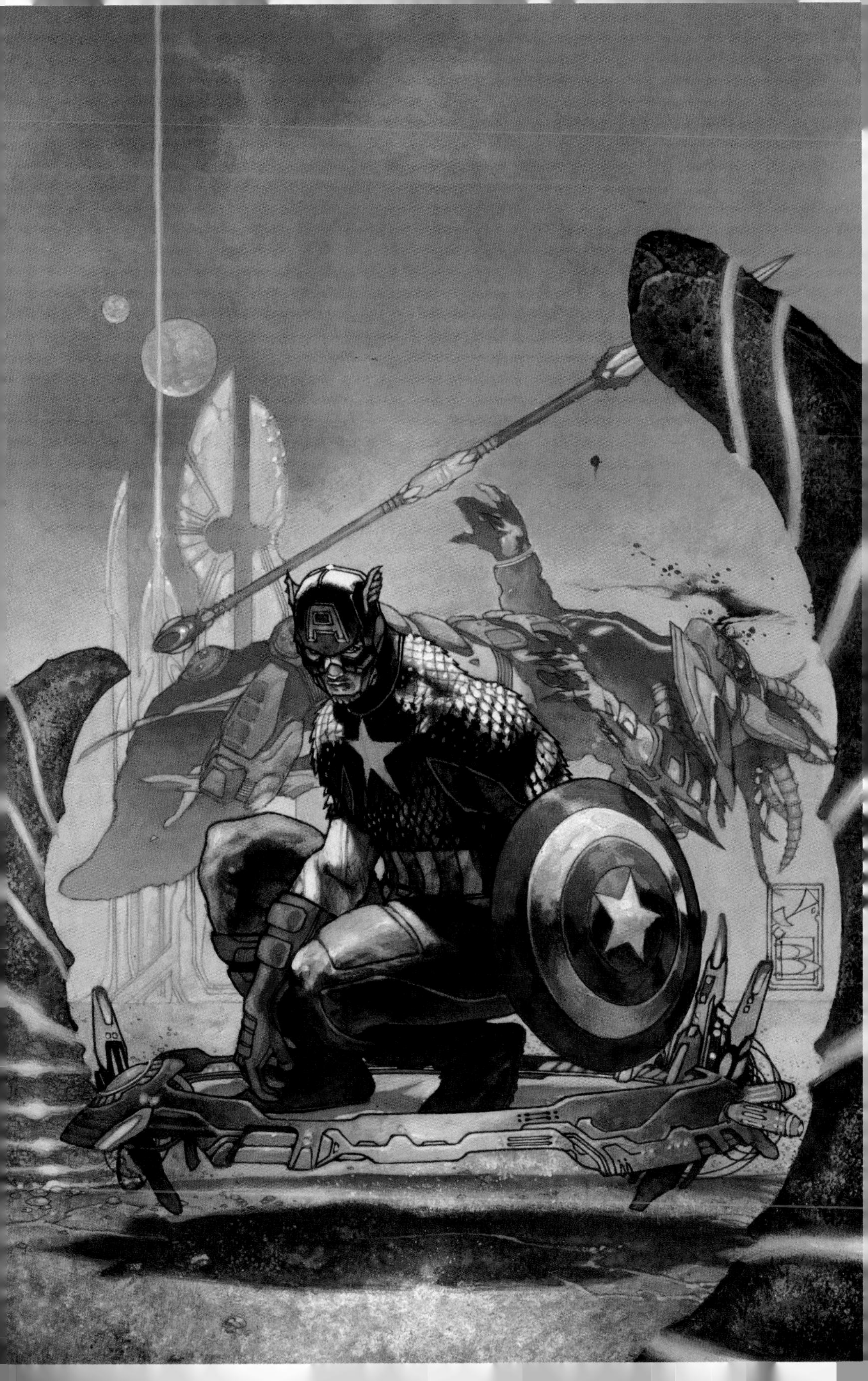

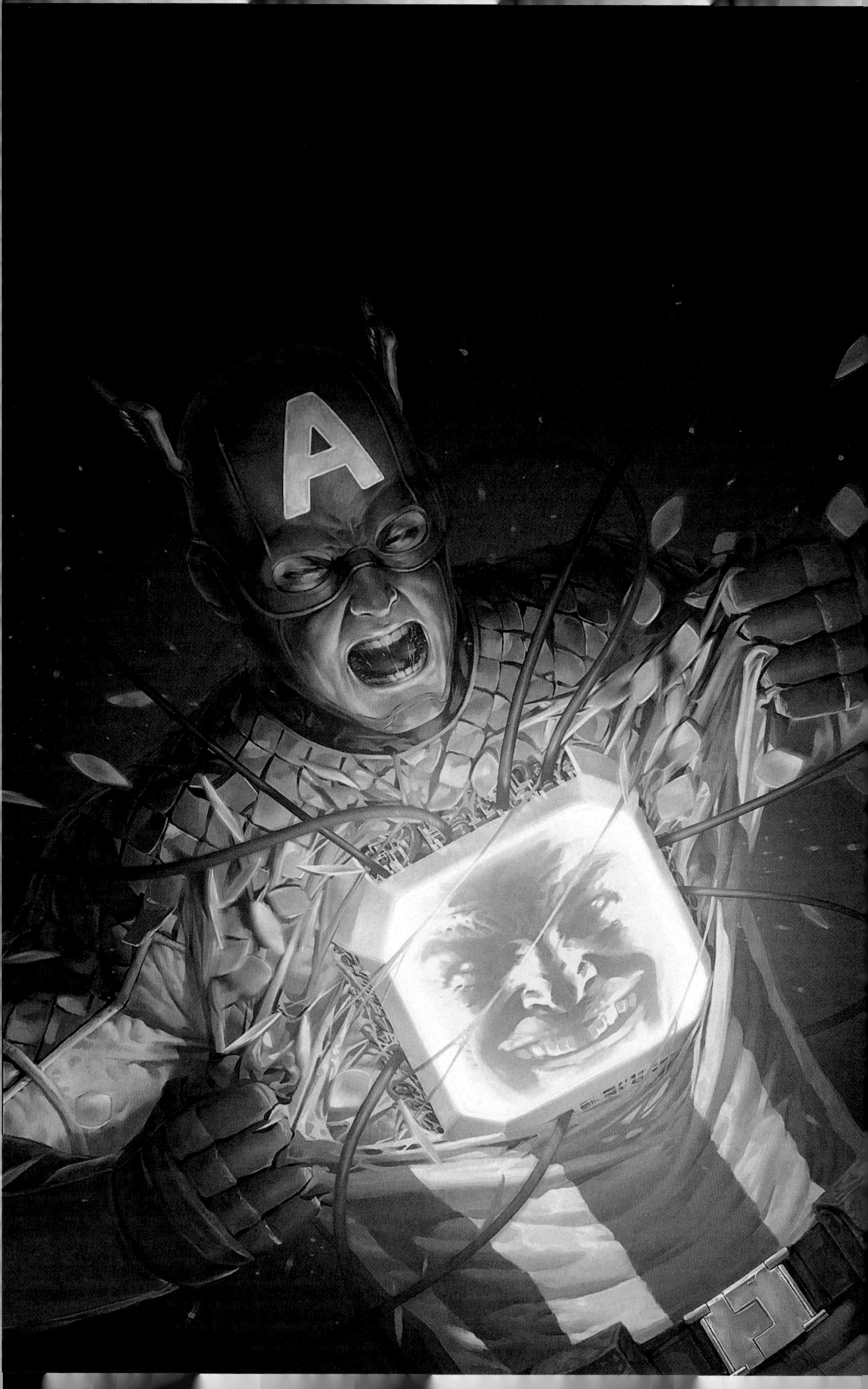

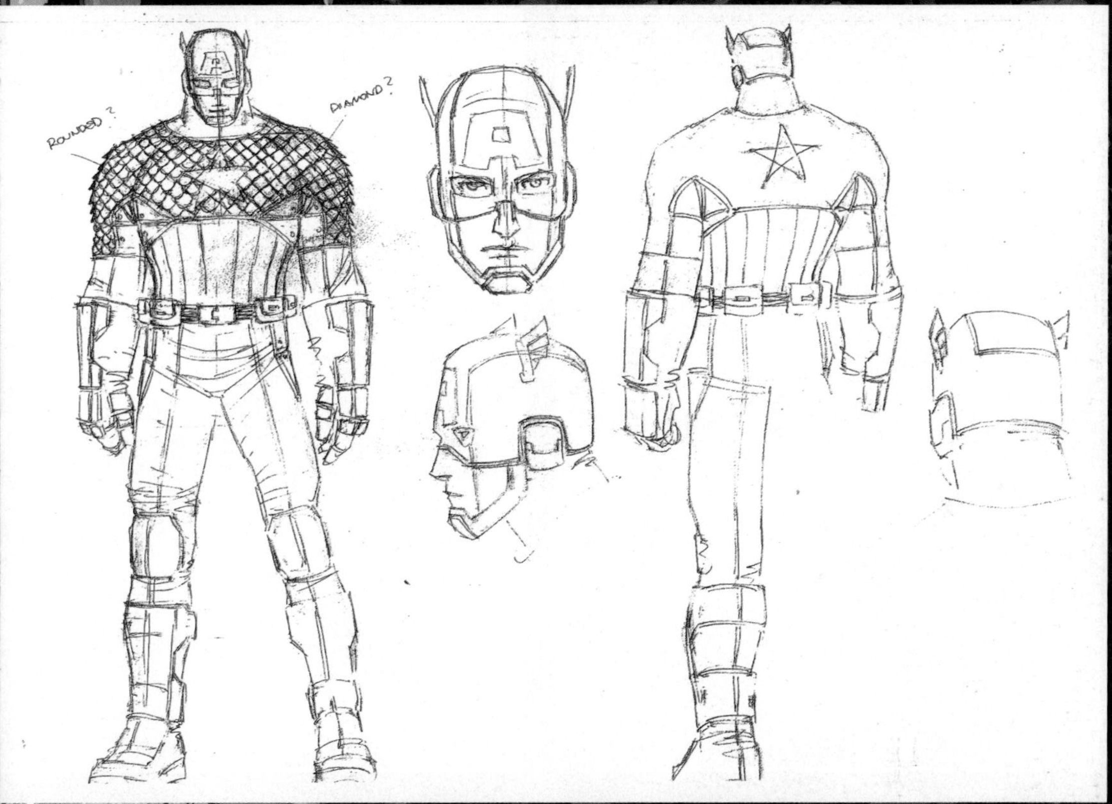
ROUNDED ?
DIAMOND ?

CAPTAIN AMERICA CHARACTER DESIGNS BY JOHN ROMITA JR.

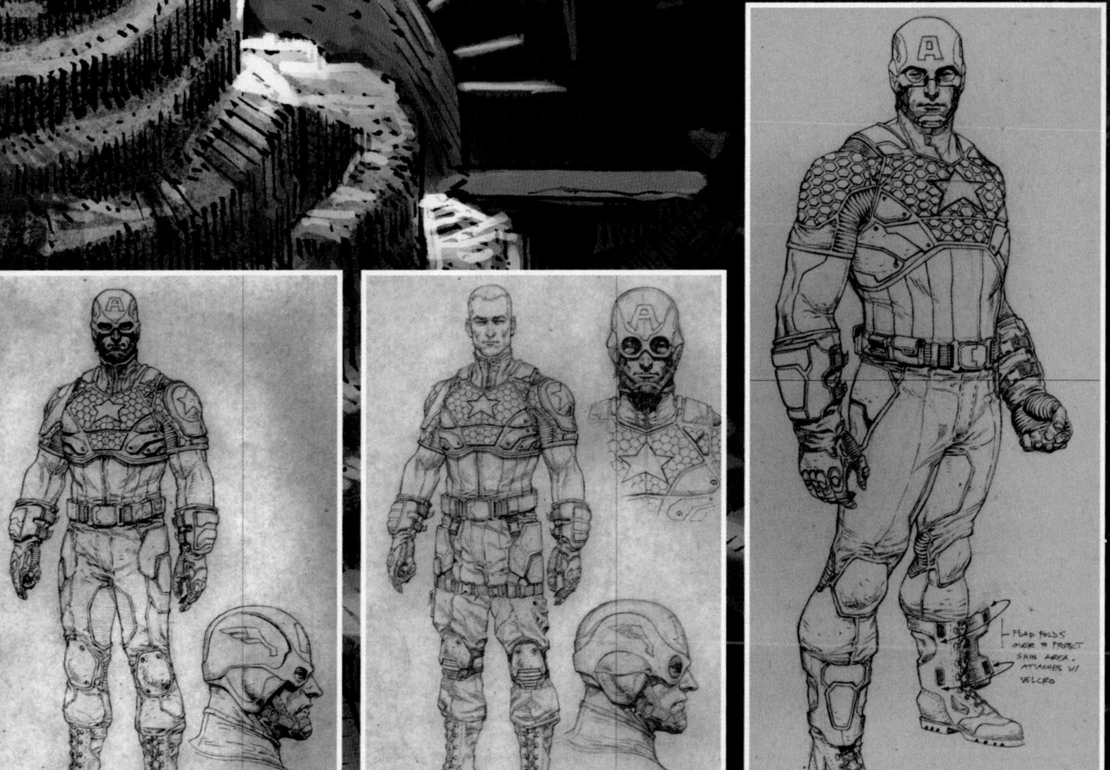
FLAP FOLDS OVER TO PROTECT SHIN AREA. ATTACHES W/ VELCRO

CAPTAIN AMERICA CHARACTER DESIGNS BY JEROME OPEÑA

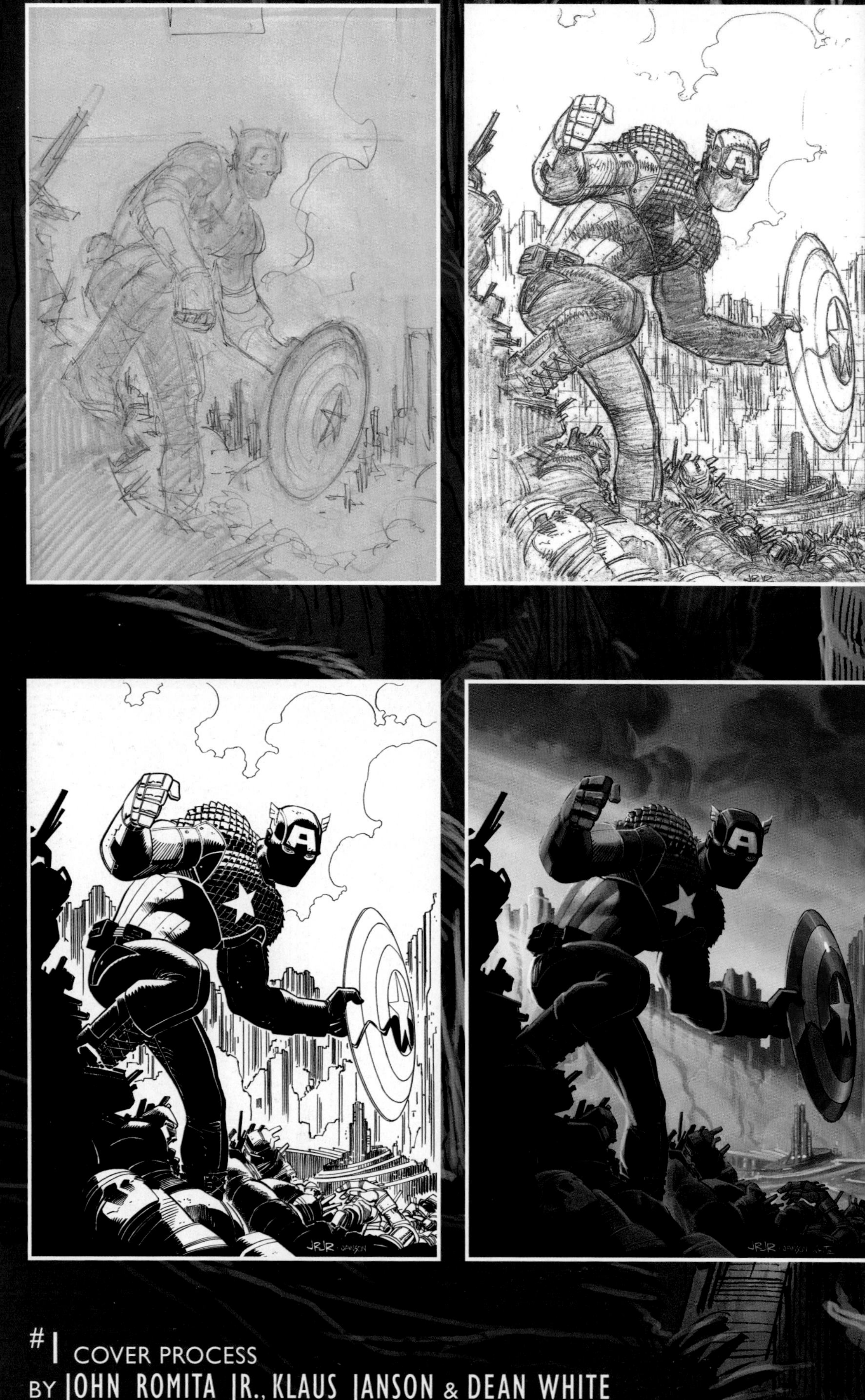

#1 COVER PROCESS
BY JOHN ROMITA JR., KLAUS JANSON & DEAN WHITE

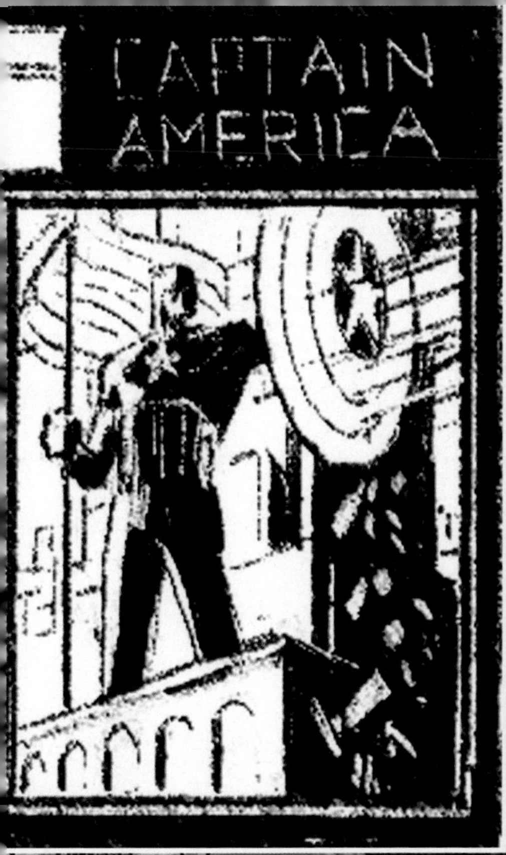
CAPTAIN
AMERICA

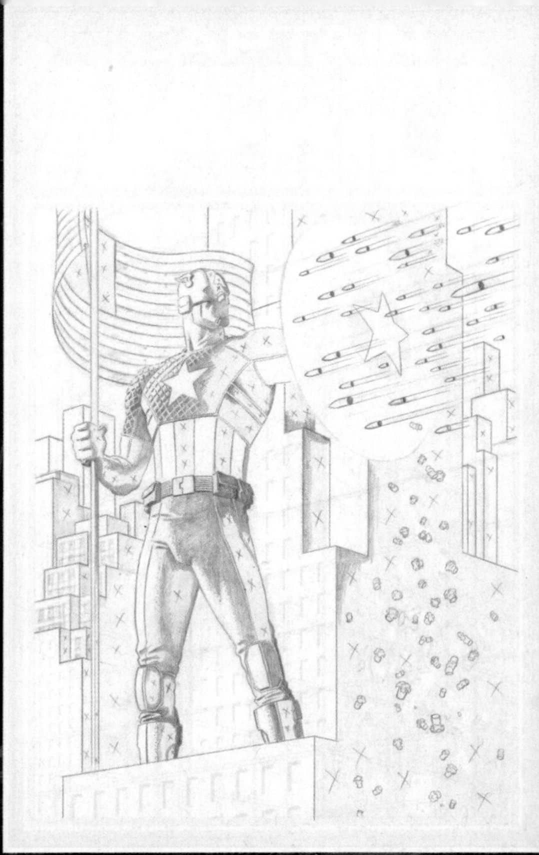

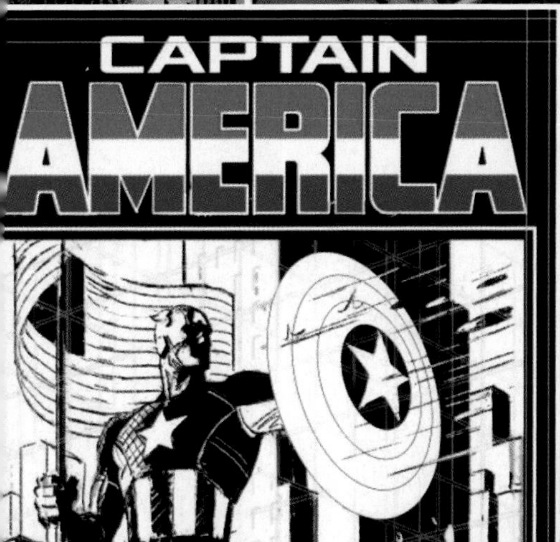
CAPTAIN
AMERICA

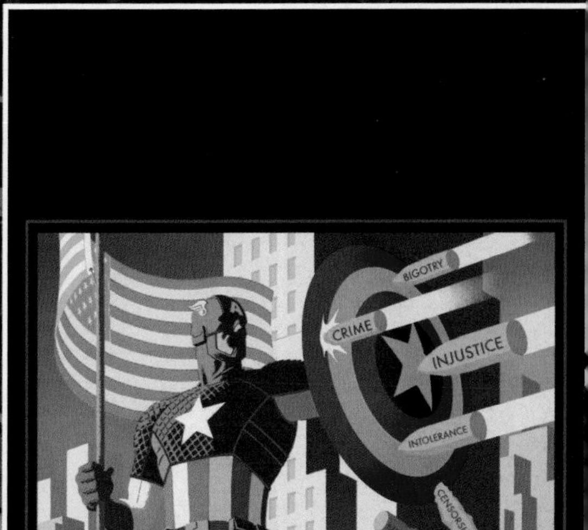
BIGOTRY
CRIME
INJUSTICE
INTOLERANCE
CENSORSHIP
TERRORISM
DESPOTISM
CORRUPTION
OPPRESSION
TYRANNY
GRAFT

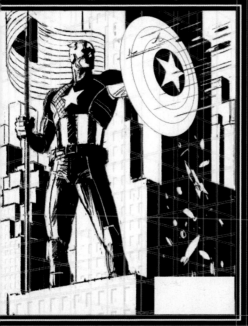

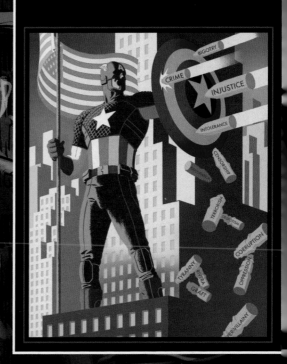

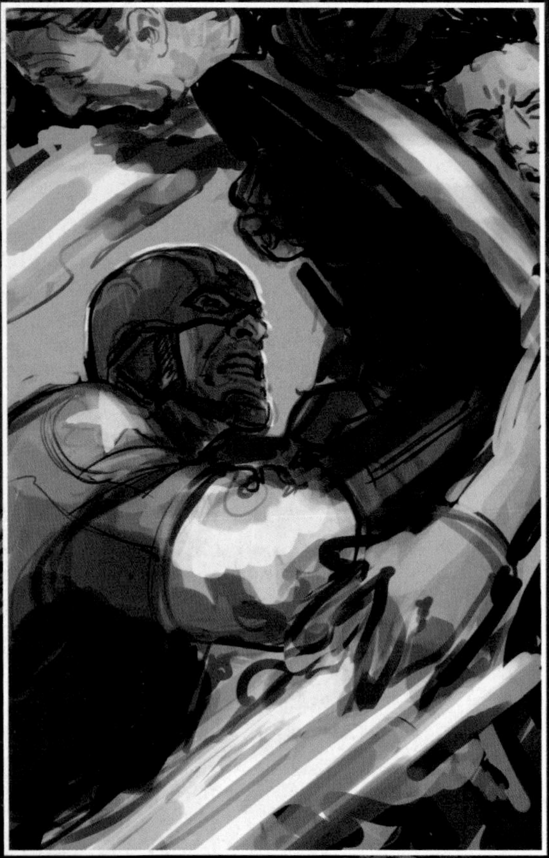

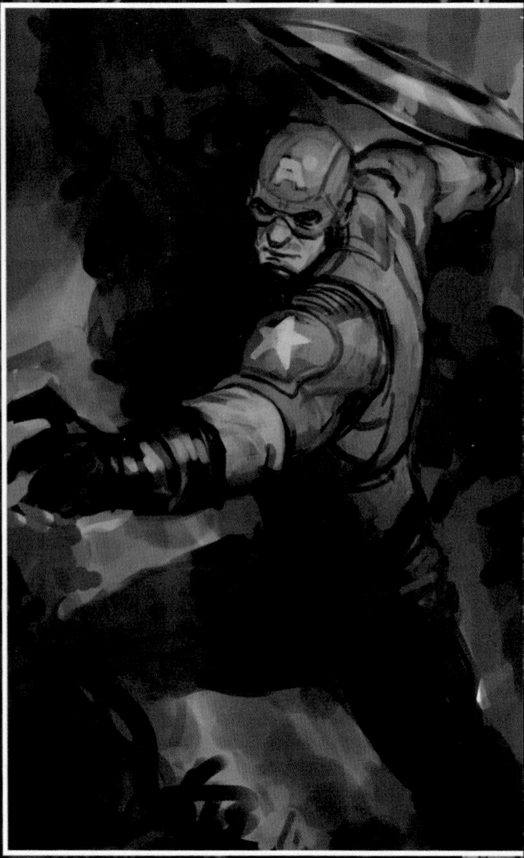

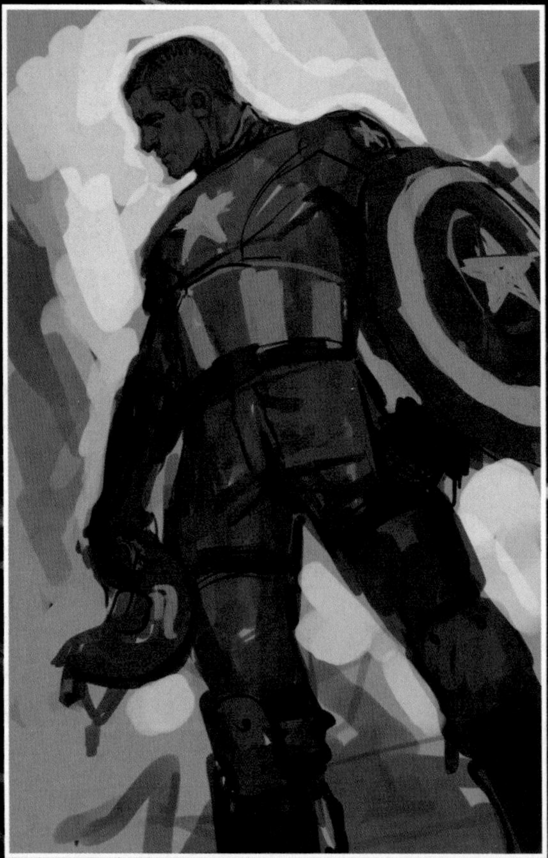

#1 VARIANT CONCEPT SKETCHES BY RYAN MEINERDING

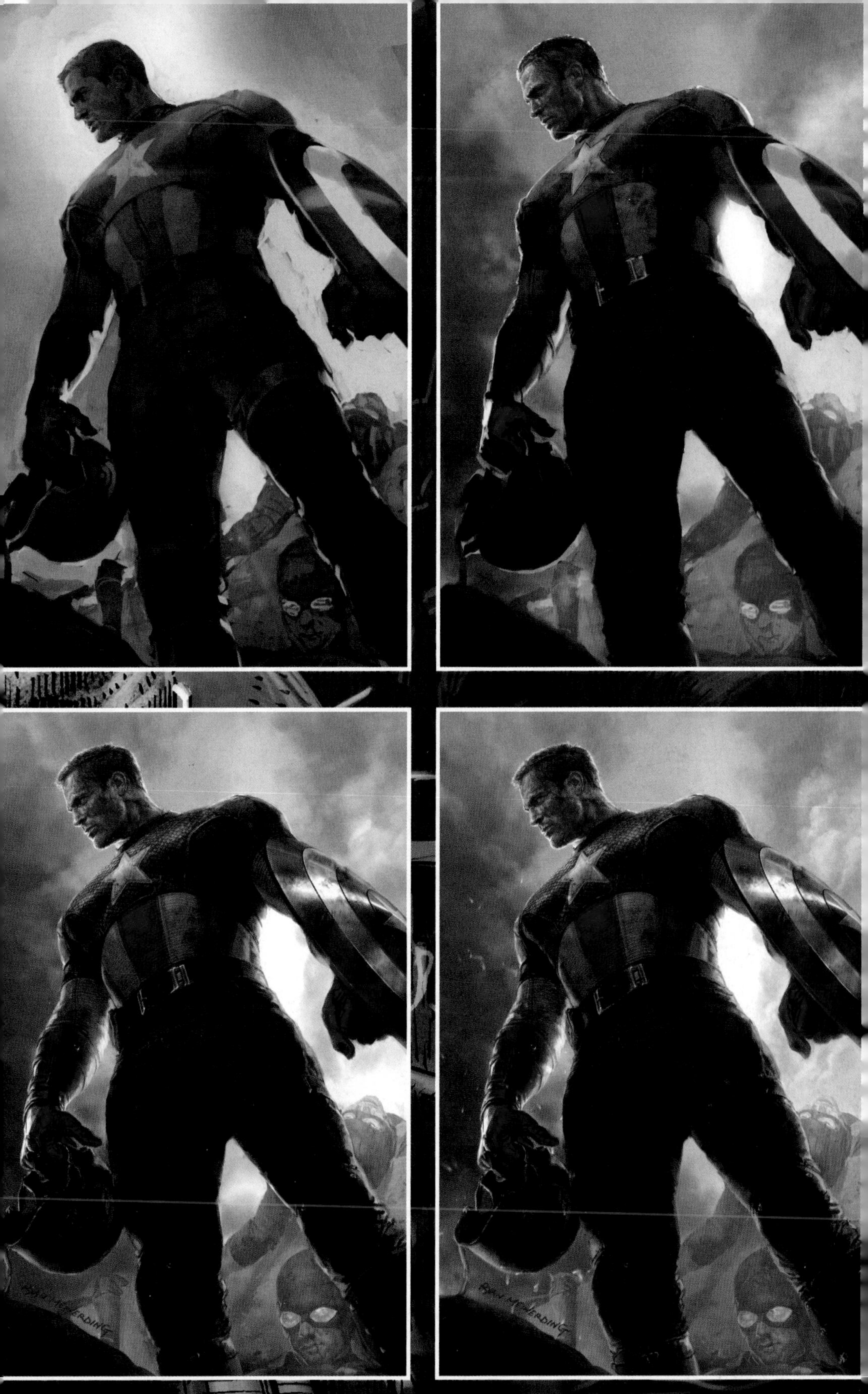
RYAN MEINERDING
RYAN MEINERDING

#1 VARIANT WORK IN PROGRESS BY RYAN MEINERDING

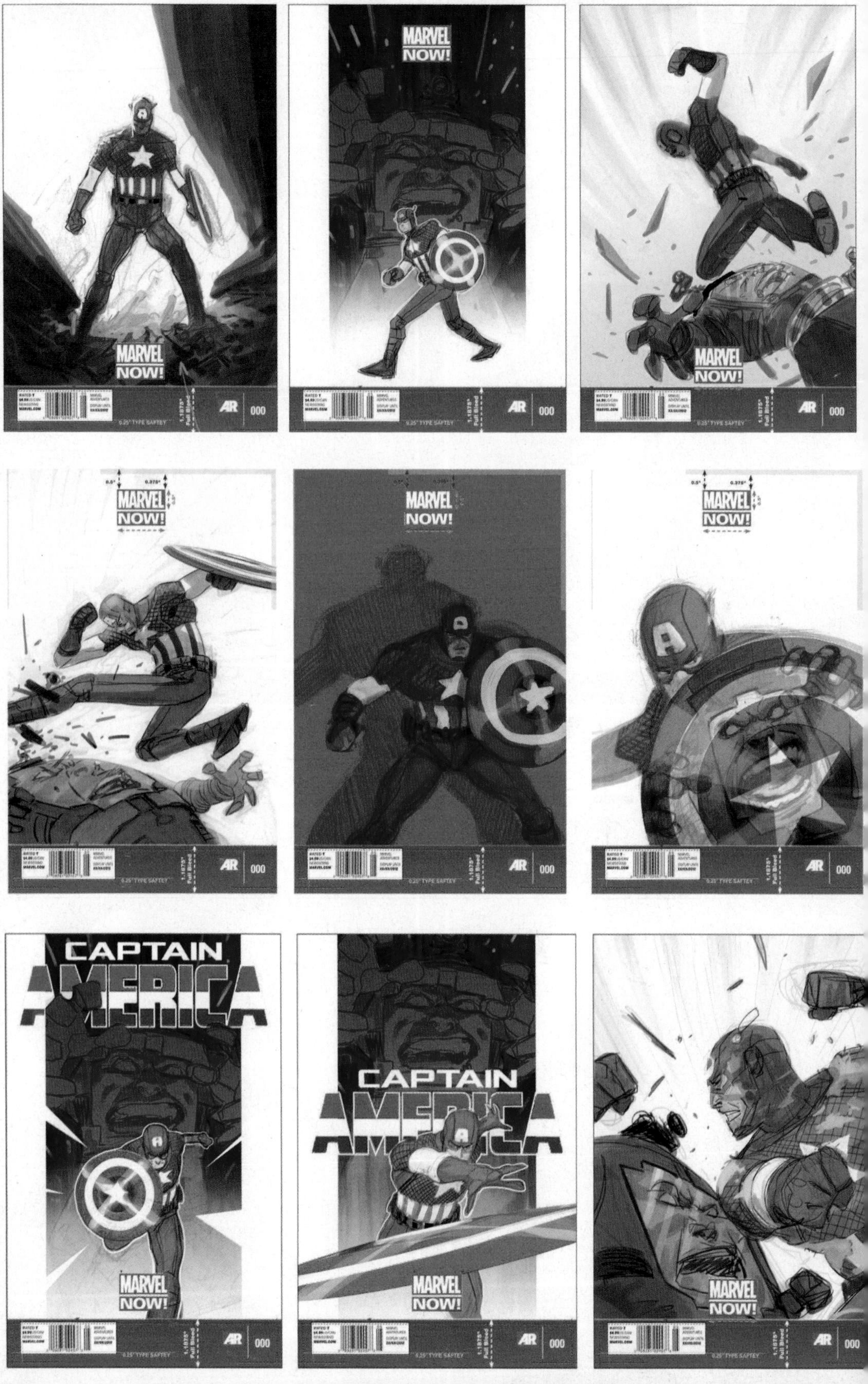
MARVEL NOW!
AR 000
MARVEL NOW!
AR 000
MARVEL NOW!
AR 000
MARVEL NOW!
AR 000
MARVEL NOW!
AR 000
MARVEL NOW!
AR 000
CAPTAIN AMERICA
MARVEL NOW!
AR 000
CAPTAIN AMERICA
MARVEL NOW!
AR 000
MARVEL NOW!
AR 000

#2 VARIANT CONCEPT SKETCHES BY JULIAN TOTINO TEDESCO

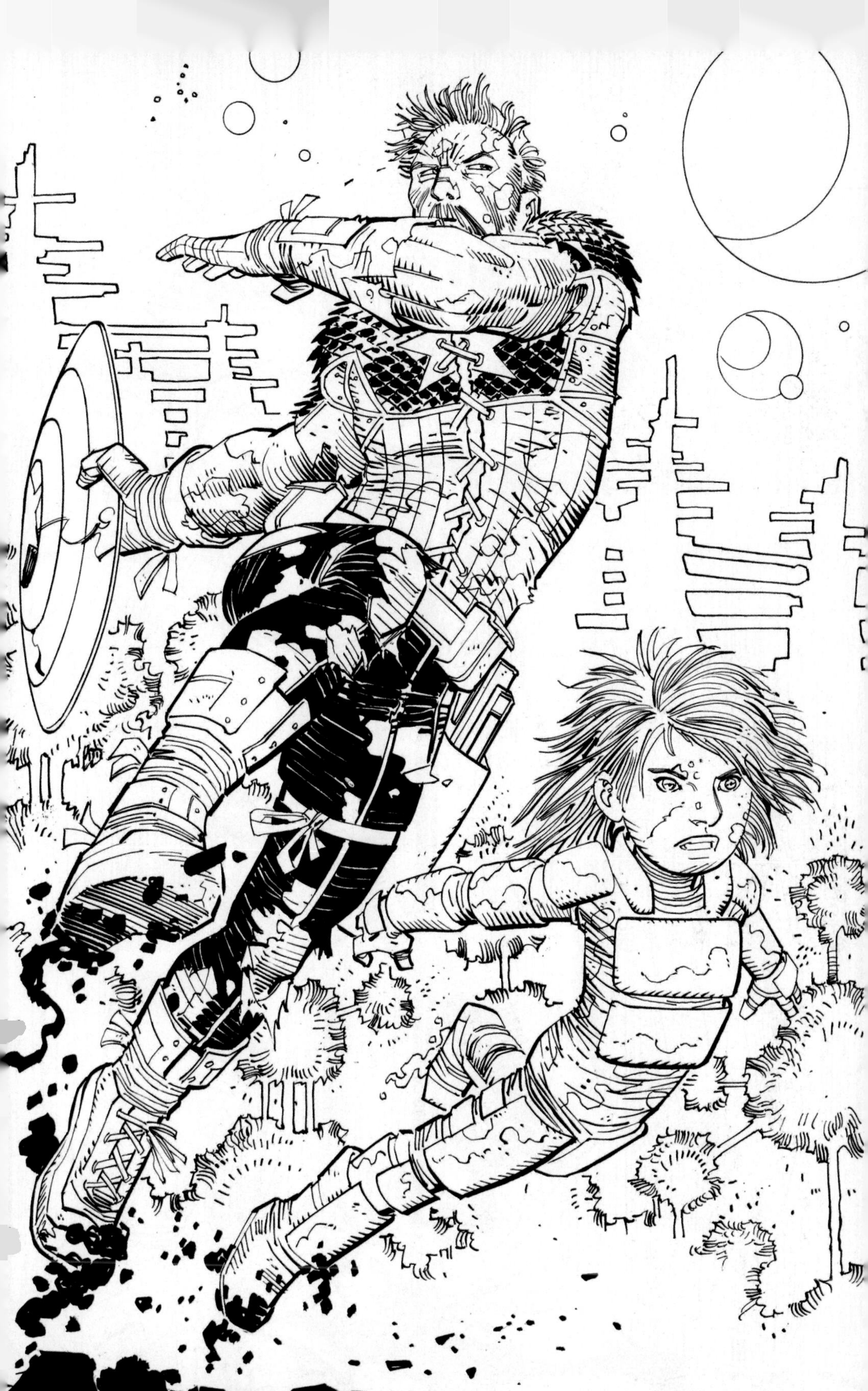

#4 PAGE ... JOHN ROMITA JR. & KLAUS JANSON

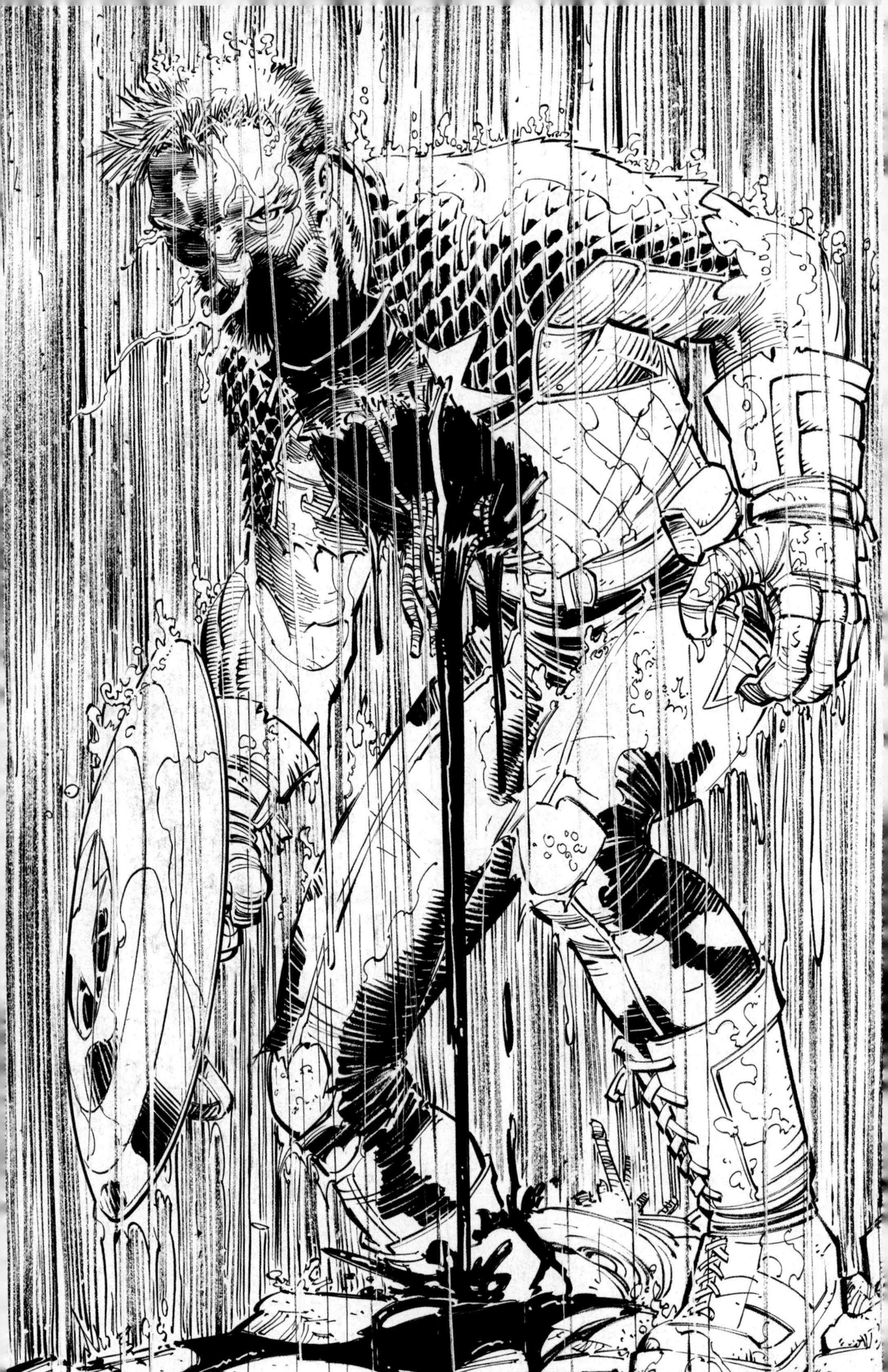

SCOTT HANNA

"THIS IS A TYPICAL HICKMAN BOOK: UNCONVENTIONAL [AND] SMART"– CBR.com

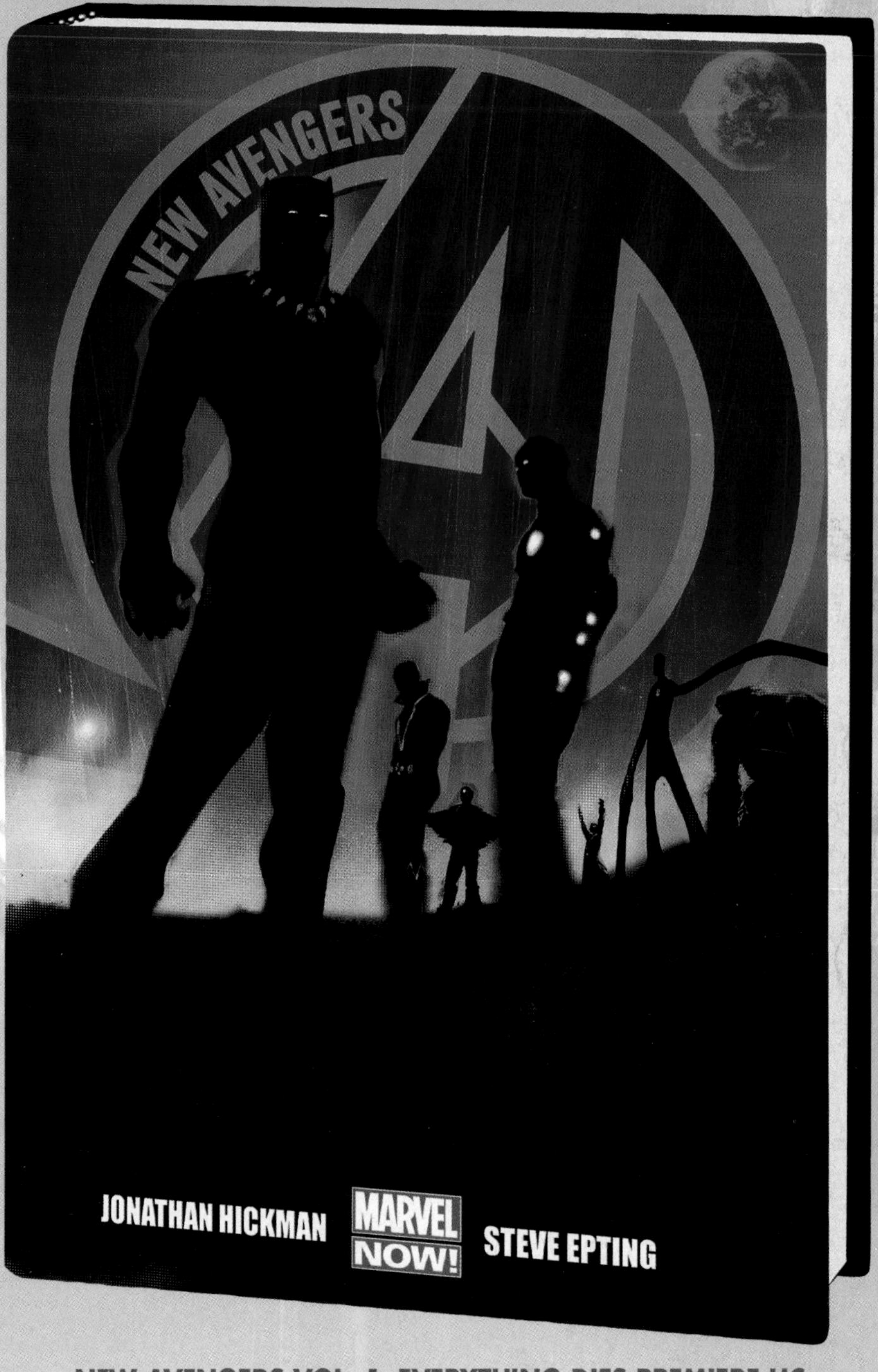
NEW AVENGERS
JONATHAN HICKMAN
MARVEL NOW!
STEVE EPTING

NEW AVENGERS VOL. 1: EVERYTHING DIES PREMIERE HC

978-0-7851-6836-2 • APR130719

"STORY TELLING AT ITS BEST"– Comicvine.com

MARVEL NOW!

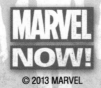

CAPTAIN AMERICA

AR INDEX

Captain America #1

Art evolution .... Pages 4-5, Panel 9

Art evolution .... Page 10, Panel 6

Art evolution .... Page 12, Panel 1

Arnim Zola character bio .... Page 16, Panel 1

Rick Remender introduces the series .... Page 22, Panel 1

Captain America #2

Talking heads with Jake Thomas & Lauren Sankovitch .... Page 11, Panel 1

Art evolution .... Page 19, Panel 1

Captain America #3

John Romita Jr. on the Phrox & beasties .... Page 5, Panel 1

Captain America through time .... Page 17, Panel 3

Captain America #4

John Romita Jr. on Captain America throughout the series .... Page 4, Panel 1

Art evolution .... Page 10, Panel 1

Captain America #5

John Romita Jr. on Dimension Z .... Page 1, Panel 2

Mick Schuber on Captain America and the Super-Soldier Serum .... Page 6, Panel 1